# Visitor to Windwa

## • Dominica • St. Lucia •
## • St. Vincent and the Grenadines •
## • Martinique • Grenada •

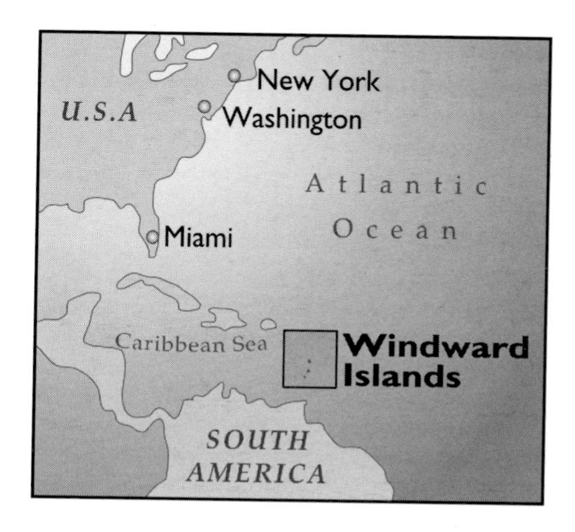


### How to Use This Guide

This MPC Visitor's Guide has been designed in an easy-to-use format. Each chapter covers an island or island group and provides travel itineraries in a natural progression which supply the reader with all the background information necessary to enjoy their visit fully. MPC's distinctive margin symbols, places of interest printed in bold type and a comprehensive index enables the reader to locate information with ease.

Each chapter includes detailed information on eating out and a listing of useful facts for visitors including a comprehensive accommodation section as well as other useful tips to help plan a visit both prior to travel and during a stay.

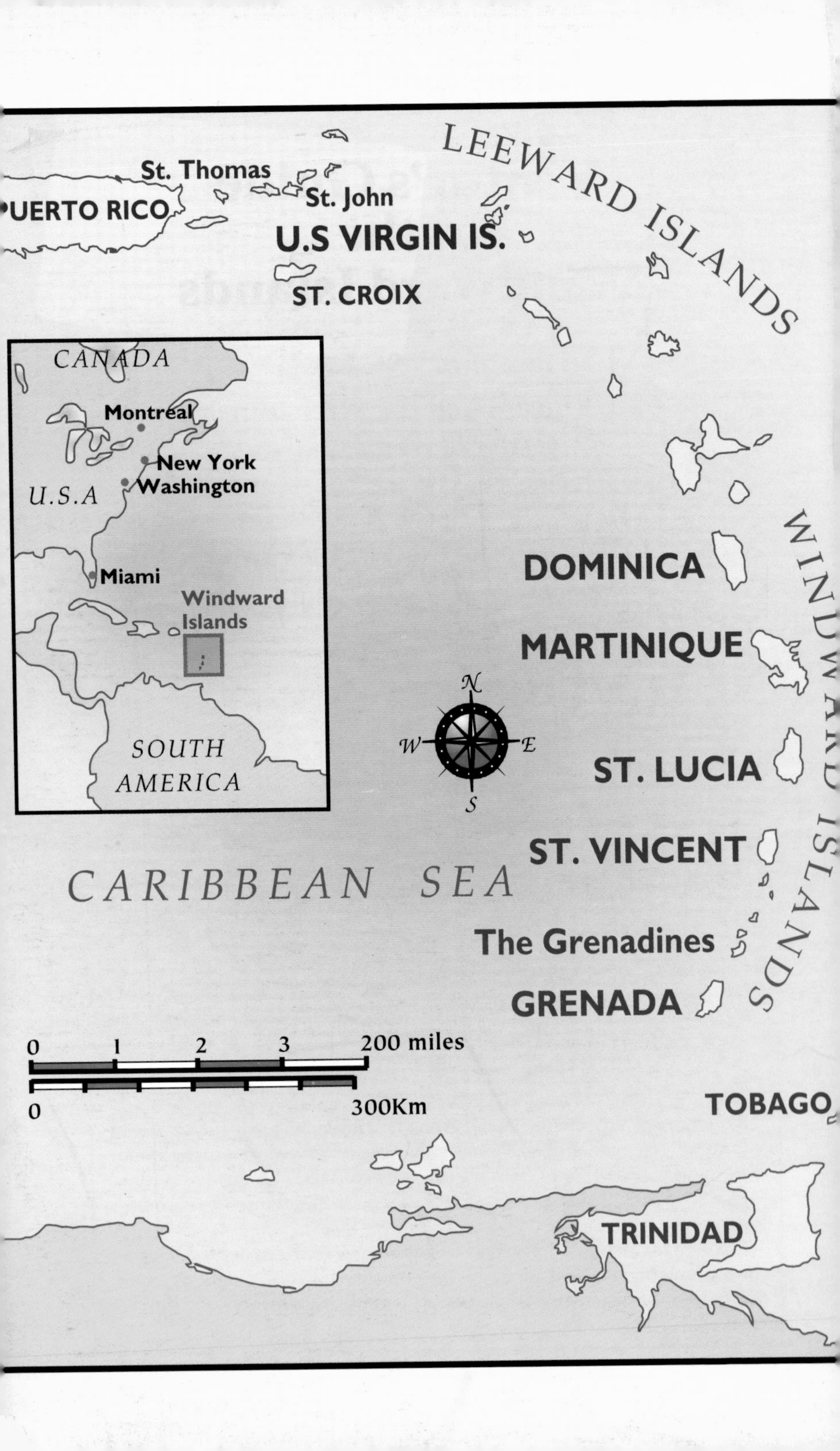

St. Thomas
St. John
UERTO RICO
U.S VIRGIN IS.
ST. CROIX
LEEWARD ISLANDS
CANADA
Montreal
New York
Washington
U.S.A
Miami
Windward Islands
SOUTH AMERICA
DOMINICA
MARTINIQUE
ST. LUCIA
ST. VINCENT
The Grenadines
GRENADA
WINDWARD ISLANDS
CARIBBEAN SEA
N
W
E
S
0
1
2
3
200 miles
0
300Km
TOBAGO
TRINIDAD

# Visitor's Guide to the Windward Islands

**• Dominica • St. Lucia •**
**• St. Vincent and the Grenadines •**
**Martinique • Grenada •**

MPC

Published by:
Moorland Publishing Company Ltd,
Moor Farm Road West, Ashbourne, Derbyshire DE6 1HD England

Published in the USA by:
Hunter Publishing Inc,
300 Raritan Center Parkway,
CN 94, Edison, NJ 08818

ISBN 0-86190-5598



British Library Cataloguing in Publication Data:
A catalogue record for this book is available from the British Library.

Colour origination by: GA Graphics
Printed in Spain by: South China Printing Co. (1988) Ltd.

Front cover: *Enchanting Britannia Bay on Mustique;* Back cover: (*left to right*), *colourful fishing boats; the Tobago Cays in the sparkling Caribbean Sea; the delicate hibiscus can be found throughout the Windward Islands;* (*centre*) *golden sunset over Salt Whistle Bay, Mayreau.*
Page 3: *Yachts moored in the clear waters of the Tobago Cays.*

*Photographs by*: Debbie Gaiger, Lindsey Porter, David Uptmor
*Edited and Designed by*: Debbie Gaiger
*Cartography*: Mark Titterton



## KEY TO SYMBOLS USED IN TEXT MARGIN AND ON MAPS

| | |
|---|---|
| Garden | Church/Ecclesiastical site |
| Castle/Fortification | Building of interest |
| Other Place of Interest | Archaeological site |
| Nature reserve/Animal interest | Museum/Art Gallery |
| Parkland/Forest | Recommended walk |
| Beautiful view/Scenery | Birdlife |
| Beach | Watersports |
| Airport | Fishing/Aquatic interest |

## Table of Contents

The Windward Islands are located in the Lesser Antilles in the eastern Caribbean and feature a wealth of fabulous beaches, coral reefs, world-class diving, excellent watersports and fishing, great food and accommodation, a colourful history, and above all, a genuinely friendly people whose welcome is as warm as the year-round sunshine.

The secluded palm-fringed beaches are everyone's idea of the perfect tropical island dream, with golden sands and sparkling clear turquoise warm waters.

## History of the Islands

The first settlers on the Windward Islands were Amerindian Siboneys, who travelled to the islands from South America in the first century AD. About 600 years later, the Arawaks arrived, having followed the same path. They were peaceful farmers and fishermen, and no match for the Caribs who began to arrive in their war canoes around 1000AD.

The Caribs were feared not only because of their fighting skills, but also because they were believed to be cannibals — although there is no evidence of this. They were excellent hunters and brought many innovations to the islands. They discovered that the pulped cassava root produced a liquid which acted as a preservative and meat boiled in the liquid could be kept for indefinite periods. This practice is the basis today of the famous pepper pot and provided the liquid is brought to the boil each day, the meat retains its freshness, therefore as some of the contents are eaten, new ingredients can be added to the pot.

Christopher Columbus was the first European to 'discover' the Windward Islands during his voyages in the 1490s. This heralded the start of a conflict which spanned centuries as various European nations vied for ownership of the islands. Many early attempts at settlement failed because of Carib attacks, but gradually European footholds were established. Today each island has its own unique and fascinating story to tell.

### Grenada

In 1609 the British attempted to establish a trading post at Megrin, close to La Sagesse, but were driven out by the Caribs. A similar attempt by the French in 1638 also failed. In 1650, the French governor of Martinique, Du Parquet, purchased Grenada from the Caribs and established the settlement of Port Louis with 200 people. The Caribs, realising they had been cheated, attacked the French settlers but were no match for the heavily armed soldiers brought in from Martinique. In 1651, a force of 800 Caribs armed with clubs and bows and arrows, attacked Fort George but the French, armed with cannon, rifles and pistols, massacred them. The surviving Caribs fled, and rather than be taken alive, leapt into the sea to their deaths. Traces of their culture still remain, however, with rock paintings, burial sites, pottery and many words of Amerindian origin.

In 1665 the island was sold to the French West India Company and passed to the French Crown in 1674. In 1762, it was captured by the British without a single shot being fired, and a year later was formally ceded to Britain in the Treaty of Paris. In 1767 the island, declared a free port by the British, saw a rapid expansion in trade, and as sugar cane could only be grown economically with cheap labour, the slave trade flourished.

The French sided with America during the 1775-6 War of Independence, which led to war with Britain. In

1778, a French fleet landed troops on Grenada and captured St. George's in a surprise attack. Grenada remained in French hands until 1783 when the Treaty of Versailles returned it to Britain. As part of the British expansion, huge numbers of slaves were introducted to work the plantations. In 1795, the slaves and 'free coloured' led by Julien Fedon, a French planter supported by Martinique, rebelled . The two-year long rebellion was finally crushed by a large force led by Sir Ralph Abercromby, and many of the ring leaders were publicly hanged in St. George's. Fedon eluded capture and disappeared, but the seeds of emancipation had been sown. However, it was not until 1834 that slavery was finally abolished.

Even after Emancipation, all newly-freed slaves were 'apprenticed' for four years, during which time they had to work without pay for their former owners for three-quarters of their working week. As more slaves gained their freedom, there was a need for new workers, and indentured labour was introduced. Indentured servants worked for three to seven years for board and lodging without pay, in the expectation of receiving a land grant at the end of their service. Many sugar estates, however were forced to close as they could not compete with the Spanish plantations who were still utilizing slave labour. In 1843, nutmegs were introduced into Grenada from Indonesia, and today nutmegs, cocoa and bananas (which have only been grown as an economic crop since the 1950s), are the island's main agricultural exports. Tourism is now a major source of income which is developing rapidly.

Between 1885 and 1958 Grenada was the seat of the Windward Islands government. On 3 March 1967, it became a self-governing state in association with the United Kingdom, and an independent nation on 7 February 1974. On 13 March 1979, while the Prime Minister was visiting the United States, a coup took place and on 29 March, the People's Revolutionary Government was proclaimed ruling party with 35 year-old lawyer Maurice Bishop as the new Prime Minister. Its rule ended in October 1983 during an internal power struggle in which Bishop, ten members of his cabinet, and many civilians were killed. A Revolutionary Military Council assumed control, but at the request of the Governor General Sir Paul Scoon, a US and Caribbean-led force invaded the island, arrested the leaders of the coup and returned the Governor General to power. The peacekeeping force remained until 1985 although constitutional government had been restored, and general elections held the previous December.

## St. Vincent

St. Vincent was named by Christopher Columbus because he first sighted it on 22 January 1498 — St. Vincent's Day. In 1626, the French tried to establish a settlement but they were ousted by the English the following year. There were then several attempts to settle the island by the Dutch, English and French but most failed because of Carib hostility. Among the first successful settlers from across the Atlantic were Africans — slaves who were shipwrecked off Bequia in 1675. They managed to swim ashore in the Grenadines and many made their way to St. Vincent, where they settled and integrated with the native Caribs. The descendants of these Black-Caribs, as they were known, still live on St. Vincent. In the 1720s, the French established a settlement at the request of the native Caribs who believed the Black Caribs were becoming too dominant, and they introduced the

Above: Sparkling river on the lush island of St. Vincent.
Opposite top: Enchanting harbour setting on Grenada.
Opposite: Londonderry Bay, near to Marigot on Dominica.

first African slaves to work their plantations. The Black Caribs, to avoid capture and a return to slavery, moved into the hills.

Although the 1748 Treaty of Aix-la-Chapelle, signed by Britain and France, declared St. Lucia, St. Vincent and Dominica neutral territory, the two nations continued to fight over possession of these islands.

In 1762, during the Seven Years War, the British General Robert Monckton captured St. Vincent and British settlement led to conflict with the Indians and the First Carib War.

In 1779, the French who were allies of the American colonies in their War of Independence, attacked St. Vincent and overran the island with hardly a shot fired. At the time all the British soldiers had been transported to the north of the island to help gather the harvest on the Governor's plantation.

The French stayed until the Treaty of Versailles in 1783, which restored the island to Britain. Further confrontations led to the Second Carib War in 1795. French militants from Martinique and Guadeloupe, along with their newly-freed slaves, backed the Caribs in their rebellion. Fighting continued for several months but resistance was finally slowly and harshly crushed. In 1796, General Abercromby delivered an ultimatum to the Caribs to surrender or themselves be wiped out. Almost 5,000 Caribs surrendered, most of whom were deported to Roatan, one of the Bay Islands off Honduras and Belize,

where there is still a large Carib community today.

Emancipation in 1834 led to a shortage of labour to work on the estates which produced sugar cane, Sea Island cotton, and arrowroot. As a result Indian and Portuguese labourers were imported as indentured labourers.

Sugar beet was planted widely throughout northern Europe in the late nineteenth century which caused the price of sugar cane to crash. St. Vincent endured a long depression, exacerbated by the hurricane which hit the island in 1898, and the volcanic eruption in 1902 which virtually eliminated agricultural production in the north, and claimed over 2,000 lives. Economic recovery was slow although St. Vincent became a leading exporter of bananas and arrowroot — the mainstay of its twentieth century agriculture produce.

On 27 October 1979, St. Vincent and the Grenadines gained full independence. The Prime Minister James Mitchell was elected to his third term of office in 1994.

## St. Lucia

There have been so many calls to arms throughout the centuries over St. Lucia that it earned the name 'Helen of the West Indies'. The island changed hands fourteen times as France and England vied for possession of this Caribbean gem.

It was thought that Columbus named the island during his fourth voyage on 13 December 1502, the feast day of St. Lucia, although it was probably 'discovered' by Europeans around 1500, and is first mentioned as St. Lucia in Spanish Royal Court documents in 1511. It was a base for pirates during the sixteenth century and the hide-out of the legendary Francois de Clerc, known as Jamb de Bois because of his wooden leg.

The Dutch established a base at Vieux Fort around 1600, but early attempts by the English at colonisation in 1605 and 1638 were unsuccessful because of disease and Carib hostility.

In 1651 the French West India Company established their first settlement with a small colony from Martinique, but in 1664 Thomas Warner, son of the Governor of St. Kitts, reclaimed the island for Britain. Over the next 150 years it changed hands many times. In 1746, the French established Soufrière as the first town on the island, and by 1778 twelve French towns had been founded.

Starting in1763, French planters from St. Vincent and Grenada established sugar and cotton plantations but many were destroyed by the hurricane in1780 hurricane. However, they were soon re-established because of slave labour and were quickly brought back into production.

In 1778 St. Lucia passed into British hands again and Gros Islet became an important naval base. The English fleet sailed out of Gros Islet Bay in 1790 to engage the French in the Battle of the Saints, the most decisive naval engagement ever fought in the Caribbean.

The effects of the French Revolution were felt on St. Lucia and a guillotine was set up in Soufrière town square. Freed slaves and French deserters fought a three-year guerilla war with the British until finally being beaten in 1798. In 1814, St. Lucia was ceded to Britain in the Treaty of Paris and became a Crown Colony. In 1834 slavery was totally abolished, and without cheap labour the plantations ceased to be profitable and the decline of the sugar cane industry set in.

Castries, the capital, flourished in the late 1800s as a major coaling station. The first coal-fired steamship berthed in Port Castries in 1863, and within a few years, hundreds of steam ships began to dock every year to take coal on board. Indentured Indians were brought to the island to load the ships. Its importance as a fuelling station strengthened after the opening of the Panama Canal in 1914, but the industry declined in the 1920s when ships switched to oil. Most estates switched to banana and cacao cultivation and the sugar cane industry ended in 1964. Today tourism has overtaken agriculture as the highest foreign exchange earner.

St. Lucia gained full independence on 22 February 1979.

## Martinique

The island was first sighted by Christopher Columbus in 1493, but he did not land until 1502 during his fourth voyage of exploration. In 1635, a Frenchman named Pierre Bélain d'Esnambuc, established a small colony with eighty settlers at Fort Saint Pierre at the mouth of the Roxelane River. In 1636, he handed over control to his nephew Jacques-Dyel du Parquet, who purchased the island from the Compagnie des Isles d'Amérique. Sugar cane was introduced in 1654 and by 1658, there were 5,000 settlers on the island. In 1664, the island was granted to the Compagnie des Indes Occidentales, and in that year the first slave ships from Senegal were unloading their human cargos. In 1674, Martinique was declared a domain of the French crown, and despite several invasion attempts by the British, treaty settlements always returned the island to France.

In 1763, France relinquished all rights to Canada in exchange for the French West Indies.

In 1794, during the French Revolution, slavery was abolished, which posed as such a threat to the plantation owners that they invited the British to run the island as slavery was still legal in the British Empire. The British remained until 1802 when the French assumed control and re-introduced slavery. In 1804, the British landed on Diamond Rock, a 600ft pinnacle of rock at the mouth of Fort-de-France bay and occupied it for eighteen months, operating it as if it were a warship.

Plantation owners were facing increasing dissent from their slaves and there were frequent uprisings until 1848 when over 70,000 slaves were given their freedom. This created major labour problems and indentured labour was imported from India and China. The Indians are still called 'coolies' in Martinique today. During World War I, more than 52,000 Martinicans sailed for Europe to fight for their 'Mother' country. In 1946 Martinique was declared a Departément of France and designated a Region in 1974.

## Dominica

The island was 'discovered' by Columbus on 3 November 1493, and named Dominica (God's Day) because it was a Sunday. About 3,000 Caribs, direct descendants of the earliest settlers still live on Dominica today.

The first European colonists were French and arrived in 1632, about the same time as French colonies were being established on Martinique and Guadeloupe. The French and British fought long and hard over the island and even the Treaty of Aix-la-Chapelle in 1748, which declared it neutral, did not stop the fighting. French planters continued to settle the island until 1759 when the British captured it and Dominica was formally ceded to Britain in 1763. The island fell again to the French in 1778 when an army from Martinique ousted the British. At the same time, Dominica became the refuge for large numbers of slaves who had managed to escape from the surrounding islands. Known as Maroons, they avoided capture by living deep in the dense forests.

In 1783, the British retook the island and for twenty years fought off attacks from the French and the growing number of Maroons. During the French Revolution, plantation owners loyal to the French Crown fled to Dominica and linked up with the Maroons. A guerilla war ensued and was fought with the Maroons until 1814 when they were finally defeated and their leaders publicly executed. After Emancipation on Dominica in 1834, the island continued to be a refuge for slaves escaping from the surrounding French islands.

The Rose's Lime Juice factory was built in 1875 and continued to operate until the 1950s, with Dominica the world's largest producer of lime.

Dominica was declared a separate colony in 1771, but in 1883 was absorbed into the Leeward Islands until 1940, when it became a separate colony as part of the Windward Islands.

Dominica joined the West Indies Federation in 1958, and when this was disbanded in 1962, a number of options were discussed leading in 1967 to Dominica becoming a self-governing member of the West Indies Associated States in free association with the United Kingdom.

During the 1970s there were periods of unrest caused by the Dreads, so-called because they wore their hair in dreadlocks, and waged a violent campaign against authority before finally being eradicated.

On 3 November 1978, the anniversary of the island's discovery, Dominica achieved full independence.

In the June 1995 General Election, the Freedom Party was defeated after fifteen years in office by the United Workers Party, and the new Prime Minister is the Hon. Edison C. James.

## Climate

The Windward islands enjoy a tropical climate with average year-round temperature of 29°C (84°F), but this can rise to 32°C (90°F) and higher during the summer, and fall to 18°C (65°F) and lower overnight in the mountains. Prevailing onshore winds provide welcome breezes and reduce humidity. The sun rises and sets quickly so dawn and dusk do not last long. However, the golden sunsets, as the sun sinks below the horizon far out at sea, are usually fantastic. Rainfall varies from about 40in (100cm) around the coasts, to over 200in (450cm) in the mountainous interior. The rainy season generally lasts from late June to December but tropical showers can occur at any time of year.

All the Windward Islands lie in the hurricane belt, although these violent tropical storms are not common occurrences. Early warning systems give ample notice of the approach of any storm, and visitors should follow the advice given locally.

## The People

The majority of the population of the Windward Islands is descended from African slaves, but there are also descendents of the Indians brought to the islands as indentured labourers to replace the freed slaves, as well as the descendents of British and French settlers, and more recent immigrants from North America and Europe. Dominica also has a large and distinctive group of Caribs, direct descendants of the first settlers. English is the official language on all the islands except Martinique, although a form of *patois* is still widely spoken which visitors find almost impossible to understand.

Above: Children play in the Westerhall Rum Plantation on Grenada.
Below: Bird's eye view of Clifton Harbour on Canouan in the Grenadines.

## Culture

All islanders love to sing, dance and play music, and this all comes together every year in Carnival. Although Carnival was celebrated before Emancipation, it was a subdued affair because slaves and 'free coloureds' were not allowed to participate. Today, it is a time for music, dance, celebration and, of course, calypso, which traces its roots back to West African traditional songs. Grenadian-born Slinger Francisco, known as The Mighty Sparrow, is regarded by most as the 'Father of Modern Calypso'. The essence of calypso is topicality, highlighting or satirising political and social issues with clever lyrics and catchy melodies. There is traditional music such as biguine and mazurka, romantic music, and the captivating rhythms of zouk, reggae and salsa.

Most islands have fine dance and folk groups, who perform regularly at hotels. Traditional dances include the bongo, performed when someone has died to help their soul travel safely to heaven, and the colourful Bele, the West Indian version of the Lancers and Quadrille, with the addition of traditional African steps.

The islands have a long tradition of producing fine craftsmen, including potters, weavers and artists.

## Flora and Fauna

The lush vegetation and wildlife are part of the Windward Island's unique charm and there is a year-round growing season. Virtually all the land that could be cultivated was utilised by the plantations, and great efforts are now being made to protect and conserve the remaining forest reserves.

Most of the islands have a volcanic landscape and several different types of palms can be found everywhere. The highest altitudes are covered with dwarf woodlands, but in the rainforests, trees can tower over 100ft (30m) into the canopy. At slightly lower altitudes there is montane thicket with trees of enormous girth and few ground shrubs, although there is a thick carpet of ferns, grasses and small orchids, as well as creepers. Because of the humidity there is also plenty of moss.

The islands truly are a tropical paradise and virtually everywhere is greenery and lush growth. There are giant ferns and bamboos, banana plantations, coconut groves, hanging breadfruit, mango, nutmeg, cocoa and pawpaw, along with the most incredible array of spectacular flowering plants ranging from giant African tulip trees festooned with scarlet blossom to tiny orchids. Bougainvillea flowers everywhere and there are scores of varieties of hibiscus, frangipani and poinsettia. The flamboyant tree is also known as the tourist tree because it bursts into scarlet bloom during the summer.

Along the coast there are stunning beaches, mangrove swamps and marsh woodlands. Beach morning glory with its array of pink flowers is found on many beaches, and is important because its roots help prevent sand drift. Other beach plants include seagrape and the manchineel, which is dangerous. This apple-like fruit is poisonous, and sap from the tree causes very painful blisters. Sap is released if a leaf or branch is broken, particularly after the rain. Any contact with the tree should be avoided. This includes eating the fruit, sitting under the tree or on a fallen branch. Sap should be washed off skin as quickly as possible.

The underwater life abounds with brilliantly-coloured fish and spectacular coral and marine plants. It is not necessary to be an experienced diver to enjoy the underwater spectacle around the islands, visitors will find that snorkelling around shallow rocks will reveal magnificent underwater scenes. However, the best way to enjoy the true essence of the marine life is by scuba diving or taking a trip in one of the many glass-bottomed boats.

There are numerous hard and soft corals and only one that poses a threat to swimmers and divers is fire coral as it can cause a stinging skin rash if touched. Among the more spectacular corals are deadmen's fingers, stag-horn, brain coral and fan coral. There are huge sea anemones and sponges, and myriad tropical fish species include the parrotfish, blue tang surgeonfish, damselfish, angelfish and brightly-coloured wrasse.

Coastal swamps provide a rich habitat for wildlife. Tiny tree crabs and edible land crabs scurry around in the mud trapped in the roots of mangrove trees, just above water level. Herons, egrets, pelicans and often frigatebirds roost in the higher branches. The mangrove cuckoo shares the lower branches with belted kingfishers.

Inland, gardens are a blaze of colour with flowers in bloom throughout the year, growing alongside exotic vege-tables like yam, sweet potato, and dasheen. Bougainvillea grows every-where and seems to be in bloom year-round in a host of different colours, The colour, in fact, does not come from petals but from the plant's bract-like leaves which surround the small petalless flowers. Dominica's National Flower is the scarlet *Bwa Kwaib*, which is actually a deciduous tree which grows to around 15ft (4m) high. It can flower twice a year and is a member of the legume family.

The flowers attract hummingbirds, like the doctorbird, as well as the carib grackle, a strutting, starling-like bird with a paddle-shaped tail, and friendly bananaquit. Tree lizards can be spotted, along with the larger geckos which hunt at night.

The roadsides and hedgerows in the countryside are adorned with vinelike caralita, calabash with its gourd-like fruits, tamarind and the distinctive castor bean, whose seeds when crushed yield castor oil. Areas of scrubland have their own flora and fauna, with plants bursting into colour immediately after the first heavy rains after the dry season. The century plant, with its prickly, sword-like leaves grows for up to twenty years before flowering. The yellow flower stalk grows at a tremendous rate for several days and can reach 20ft (6m) in height, but having bloomed once the whole plant dies. Other typical scrubland vegetation includes aloe, acacia, prickly pear and several species of cactus. Fiddlewood provides hard timber for furniture, and sea island cotton used to provide the very finest cotton. Scrub vegetation also plays host to birds such as the mockingbird, ground dove, kingbird and grassquit, and it is the ideal habitat for lizards.

The rainforests provide the most prolific vegetation amidst the towering mahogany trees and their fascinating black and red seeds, often used for necklaces. There are magni-ficent swathes of giant ferns, towering bamboo groves, enormous air plants, and a host of flowering or variegated plants such as heliconia, philodendron and wild fuchsia. There are balsa wood trees, the world's lightest wood, the flowering vine marcgravia, and the prolific mountain cabbage palm. One can also easily catch glimpses of hummingbirds and parrots in the verdant foliage and floral cover.

The wildlife on the islands is diverse although there are few large animals. On Grenada, there is the mona monkey, a small, long-tailed primate

Above: Crab plovers take flight in the Tobago Cays.
Below: Glorious flamboyant trees can be found through the Windward Islands.

from West Africa introduced by slaves. Most of the islands have armadillo, iguana, agouti and two species of opossum, including the manicou, which lives in trees, forages over huge areas at night, and is not averse to searching through trash cans for delicacies. There are also many species of bats.

There are piping frogs in the woodlands and highlands, and giant toads which croak loudly all night long. On Dominica, the large edible crapaud frog is known as the 'mountain chicken' because it tastes so good, and the island is also home to the rare 'fantastic' gecko, which rarely grows more than one and a half inches (3cm) long. All islands have geckos and lizards and some have snakes, such as the tree boa on Dominica. Mongooses, which grow up to 2ft (0.5m) in length including tail, were said to have been first introduced into Jamaica from Burma, to kill snakes and rats gnawing at the sugar cane.

Lumbering sea turtles come ashore at night between May and September to lay their eggs in the sand. There are butterflies and less attractive insects such as mosquitoes, ants and sand flies.

There is a remarkable rich and colourful native bird life with over 150 native species including mangrove cuckoos, hummingbirds, tanagers, ibis, mockingbirds, herons, egrets and many others. There are also many more migrants which pass through the islands between their breeding grounds in North America and over-wintering grounds in the Caribbean or South America.

Offshore the magnificent frigate-bird is easily recognisable by its long black 7ft (2m) wing span, forked tail and seemingly effortless ability to glide on the winds. There are brown boobies, named by sailors from the Spanish word for 'fool' because they were so easy to catch. Pelicans which look so ungainly on land, but are so agile in the air, are common, as are laughing gulls and royal terns. Several species of sandpiper can usually be seen scurrying around at the water's edge.

The St. Lucian parrot is the island's endangered national bird, and there is also the rare St. Lucia oriole and St. Lucia black finch. There is the St. Vincent parrot of which there are thought to be less than 500 in the wild.

There are two species of parrot, both of which are endangered species which are only found on Dominica — the Imperial parrot or sisserou, Dominica's national bird with a mauve breast and green wings, and the smaller red-necked parrot, also known as the Jaco. The tiny blue-headed humming bird is only found on the island and neighbouring Martinique. Other interesting birds are the rusty-tailed flycatcher, scaly-breasted thrasher, black-billed thrush, Lesser Antillean bullfinch and Lesser Antillean tanager which are only found in the Lesser Antilles.

It is believed that less than 100 Grenada dove exist in the wild, and despite measures to protect it, it is in danger of extinction because of hunting and habitat destruction. Other endangered and protected species include the Grenada hookbilled kite and the Euler's flycatcher.

Keen bird-watchers should pack a small pair of binoculars. Mini-binoculars are ideal for island bird watching because the light is usually good enough to give a clear image despite the small object lens.

Binoculars are also useful for whale spotting — in particular humpback whales who winter in the warm waters.

Many of the plants, fruits, vegetables and spices will be new to the first time visitor, the following brief descriptions are offered:

**Bananas** are an important export and grow everywhere, hence their nickname 'green gold'. There are three varieties. The banana normally bought in supermarkets which originated in Malaya and was introduced into the Caribbean in the early sixteenth century by the Spanish. The large banana, or plantain, originally came from southern India, and is used mostly in cooking. It is often fried and served with fish and meat. The third variety is the red banana, not grown commercially, but which can be seen around the island. A banana produces a crop approximately every nine months. Although they grow tall, bananas are not trees but herbacious plants which die back each year. Once the plant has produced fruit, a shoot from the ground is cultivated to take its place, and the old plant dies.

The **Bay** tree is a native of the Windward Islands, a member of the Laurel family and can grow to a height of 30ft (9m). The leaves are gently crushed for their oil which is used in the perfume industry. The oil is also used to produce a special rum which is said to have antiseptic qualities, while the leaves are used in cooking.

**Breadfruit** was introduced to the Caribbean by Captain Bligh in 1793. He brought 1,200 breadfruit saplings from Tahiti aboard the *Providence*, and these were first planted in Jamaica and St. Vincent, and then quickly spread throughout the islands. It is believed that it was Bligh's attempts to bring in young breadfruit trees that led to the mutiny on the *Bounty* four years earlier. Bligh was given the command of the 215 ton *Bounty* in 1787 and ordered to take the breadfruit trees from Tahiti to the West Indies where they were to be used to provide cheap food for the slaves. The ship had collected its cargo and had reached Tonga when the crew under the command of Fletcher Christian mutinied. The crew claimed that Bligh's regime was too tyranical, and he and eighteen members of the crew who remained loyal to him, were cast adrift in an open boat. The cargo of breadfruit was promptly dumped overboard. Bligh, in a remarkable feat of seamanship, navigated the boat for 3,600 miles (5,796km) until reaching landfall on Timor in the East Indies. It has been claimed that it was the breadfruit tree cargo which sparked the mutiny, as each morning the hundreds of trees in their heavy containers had to be carried on deck, and then carried down into the hold at nightfall. The trees also used up most of the ship's water supply.

The breadfruit is a cheap carbohydrate-rich food, and best eaten fried, baked or roasted over charcoal. The large green fruits can weigh 10 to 12lb (4 to 5kg), and it is said that no one goes hungry when the breadfruit is in season.

**Calabash** trees are native to the Caribbean and have huge gourd-like fruits which are very versatile when dried and cleaned. They can be used as water containers and bowls, bailers for boats, and as lanterns. Juice from the pulp is boiled into a concentrated syrup and used to treat coughs and colds, and the fruit is believed to have many other medicinal uses.

**Cinnamon** comes from the bark of evergreen trees, also related to the laurel. The bark is rolled into 'sticks' and dried. It is then ground or sold in small pieces and used as a spice to add a sweet, aromatic flavour to many dishes. Oil from the bark is used to flavour sweets, soaps, toothpastes and liqueurs, while oil from the leaves is used in perfumes.

**Cocoa** is another important crop, and its Latin name *theobroma* means 'food of the gods'. A cocoa tree can produce several thousand flowers a year, but only a fraction of these will develop into seed-bearing pods. It is the heavy orange pods that hang from the cocoa tree which contain the beans which contain the seeds that produce cocoa and chocolate. The beans, containing a sweet, white sap that protects the seeds, are split open and kept in trays to ferment. This process takes up to eight days and the seeds must be kept at a regular temperature to ensure the correct flavour and aroma develops. The seeds are then dried. In the old days people used to walk barefoot over the beans to polish them to enhance their appearance. Today, the beans are crushed to extract cocoa butter, and the residue powder is cocoa. Real chocolate is produced by mixing cocoa powder, cocoa butter and sugar. Cocoa balls or rolls, like fat chocolate fingers, can be purchased in the markets and can be made into a delicious drink. Simply dissolve the ball in a pan of boiling water, allow to simmer and then add salt, sugar and milk or cream, for a rich chocolate drink. Each ball will make about four mugs of chocolate.

**Coconut** palms are everywhere and should be treated with caution. Anyone who has heard the 'whoosh' of a falling coconut, and leapt to safety, knows how frightening the sound can be. Very few people actually get injured by falling coconuts which is unbelievable in view of the tens of thousands of palms all over the islands. Visitors may wish to keep in mind however that it is not a good idea to picnic in a coconut grove.

Coconut trees are incredibly hardy and are able to grow in sand, even when regularly washed by salty sea water. They can also survive long periods without rain. Their huge leaves, up to 20ft (6m) long in mature trees, drop down during dry spells so a smaller surface area is exposed to the sun, reducing evaporation. Coconut palms can grow up to 80ft (24m) tall, and produce up to 100 seeds a year. The seeds are the second largest in the plant kingdom, and fall when ripe.

The seed and protective coverings can weigh 30lb (13kg) or more. The seed and casing is waterproof, drought proof and able to float. This explains why coconut palms which originated in the Pacific and Indian oceans are now found throughout the Caribbean — the seeds literally floated across the seas.

The coconut palm is extremely versatile. The leaves can be used as thatch for roofing, or cut into strips and woven into mats and baskets, while the husks yield coir, a fibre resistant to salt water and ideal for ropes, brushes and brooms. Green coconuts contain a delicious thirst-quenching 'milk', and the coconut 'meat' can be either eaten raw or baked in ovens for two days before being sent to processing plants where the oil is extracted. Coconut oil is used in cooking, soaps, synthetic rubber and even in hydraulic brake fluid. Groups of men and women can often be seen around the islands splitting coconuts in half with machetes preparing them for the ovens. The halved coconut shells neatly laid out on the corrugated tin roofs of some homes are being dried before being sold to the copra processing plants.

**Dasheen** is one of the crops known as 'ground provisions' throughout the islands, the others being potatoes, yams, eddo and tannia. The last two are close relatives of dasheen, and all are members of the aroid family — some of the world's oldest cultivated crops. Dasheen with its 'elephant ear' leaves, and eddo grow from a corm, which when boiled thoroughly can be used like potato, while the young leaves of both are used to make callaloo, a spinach-like soup. Both dasheen and eddo are thought to have originated from China or Japan, but tannia is native to the Caribbean and its roots can be boiled, baked or fried.

**Guava** is common throughout the islands, and this aromatic, pulpy fruit is a favourite food of birds who then distribute its seeds. The fruit-bearing shrub can be seen on roadsides and in many gardens. It is used to make a wide range of products ranging from jelly to 'cheese' — a paste produced by mixing the fruit with sugar. The fruit which vary in size from a golf ball to a tennis ball, is a rich source of vitamin A and contains considerably more vitamin C than citrus fruit.

**Mango** can be delicious, if somewhat messy to eat. It originates from India but is now grown throughout the Caribbean. Young mangoes can be stringy and unappetising, but ripe fruit from mature trees which tower over 50ft (15m) or more, are usually delicious, and can be eaten either raw or cooked. The juice is a great reviver in the morning, and the fruit is often used to make jams and other preserves. The wood of the mango tree is often used by boatbuilders.

**Nutmeg** trees are found throughout all the islands, but Grenada is one of the world's top producers. The nutmeg comes from the Banda Islands in Indonesia and for centuries its source was kept secret because it was such a valuable commodity to the merchants selling it. The first tree is believed to have been planted in the West Indies on Grenada's Belvedere Estate in 1843. In 1851, disease swept through the Far Eastern nutmeg plantations. The price rocketed and Grenadian farmers immediately seized the opportunity and planted nutmeg trees in earnest, although it was thirty years later in 1881 before the first were exported.

The tree thrives in hilly, wet areas and the fruit is the size of a small tomato. The outer husk or pericarp, splits open while still on the tree, and is used to make the popular nutmeg jelly which is delicious when spread on toast, desserts or meat. Inside, the seed is protected by a bright red casing which when dried and crushed, produces the spice mace. Finally, the dark outer shell of the seed is broken open to reveal the nutmeg which is dried and ground into a powder, or sold whole to be grated for flavouring dishes. In Victorian times it was fashionable to carry a nutmeg or wear it in a pendant to ward off illness, and the islanders still use grated nutmeg to help fight colds.

**Passion fruit** is not widely grown but it can usually be bought at the markets. The pulpy fruit contains hundreds of tiny seeds, and many people prefer to press the fruit and drink the juice. It is also commonly used in fruit salads, sherbets and ice creams.

**Pawpaw** trees are found throughout the islands and are commonly grown in gardens. The trees are prolific fruit producers but grow so quickly that the fruit soon becomes difficult to gather. The large, juicy melon-like fruits are eaten fresh, pulped for juice, or used locally to make jams, preserves and ice cream. They are rich sources of vitamins A and C. The leaves and fruit contain an enzyme which tenderises meat, and tough joints cooked wrapped in pawpaw leaves, or covered in slices of fruit usually taste like better cuts. The same enzyme, papain, is also used in chewing gum, cosmetics, the tanning industry and in making wool shrink resistant. A tea made from the unripe fruit is said to be good for lowering high blood pressure.

**Pigeon peas** are widely cultivated and can be found in many back gardens. The plants are very hardy and drought resistant, and are prolific yields of peas which can be eaten fresh, or dried and used in soups and stews.

**Pimento**, or allspice, was intro-

Above: Nutmeg are grown throughout the entire Windward Islands.

duced from Jamaica. The dried berries are said to have the combined flavours of cinnamon, clove and nutmeg, which is how it gets its name. The dried fruit is used for pickling, for curing meat and flavouring wines, and it is usually an ingredient in curry powder. An oil pressed from the berry and leaf is used in perfumes and pharmaceutical products.

**Pineapples** were certainly grown in the Caribbean by the time Columbus arrived, and were probably originally brought from South America by the Amerindians. The fruit is slightly smaller than the Pacific pineapple, but the flavour is more intense.

**Sugar cane** is grown commercially for producing rum on many of the islands, although some now import molasses. The cane grows up to 12ft (4m) in height, and after cutting, have to be crushed to extract the sugary juice. Most estates had their own sugar mill powered by water-wheels or windmills. The remains of many of these mills can still be seen throughout the islands, and much of the original machinery, mostly made in Britain, is still in place. After extraction, the juice is boiled until the sugar crystalises. The remaining mixture is molasses which is used to produce rum.

**Sugar apple** is a member of the annona fruit family, and grows wild and in gardens throughout the islands. The small sugar apple fruit can be peeled off in strips when ripe, and is like eating thick apple sauce. They are eaten fresh or used to make sherbet or drinks.

**Soursop** is a member of the same family, and its spiny fruits can be seen in hedgerows and gardens. It is eaten fresh or used for preserves, drinks and ice cream.

**Turmeric** is often sold as saffron — but there is a big difference. Saffron comes from the dried stigmas of the crocus and is extremely expensive, while turmeric comes from the dried root and underground stems of a plant which is a relative of ginger. The bright yellow spice is used to flavour foods, and as a colouring.

The **vanilla** plant is a climbing member of the orchid family which produces long, dangling pods containing beans. The vanilla is extracted by distilling the beans and is used as a food flavouring and in the pharmaceutical industry.

## Food and Drink

Dining out in the Caribbean offers the opportunity to experiment with a variety of unusual spices, vegetables and fruits, with creole and island cuisine, and, of course, with rum punches and other exotic cocktails.

Many hotels have a tendency to offer buffet dinners or barbecues which can often be interesting and tasty affairs. Eating out is generally very relaxed and few restaurants have a strict dress code, although most people prefer to dress a little smarter at dinner after a day on the beach or out sightseeing.

Lunches are best eaten at beach cafés, which usually offer excellent barbecued fresh fish and conch — often appearing on menus as lambi (not to be confused with lamb). Lobster and crab are also widely available in season. Dishes are served mostly with local vegetables such as fried plantain, cassava and yam. Fresh fruit such as pineapple, mango, golden apple or papaya make an ideal and light dessert.

There is an enormous choice when it comes to dinner. Appetizers include traditional Caribbean dishes such as Christophene and coconut soup, or callaloo soup made from the leaves of dasheen, a spinach-like vegetable. There is also a strong French tradition in such dishes as *soupe germou* made from pumpkin and garlic, and *pouile dudon,* a chicken stew flavoured with coconut and molasses. Fish and clam chowders are also popular starters. Some interesting dishes include heart of palm salad; excellent fresh shrimps or scallops; smoked kingfish wrapped in crepes or crab backs; succulent land crab meat sauteed in breadcrumbs and seasoning, served restuffed in the shell. It is much sweeter than the meat of sea crabs.

The fish is generally excellent, and one should not be alarmed to see dolphin on the menu. This is not the protected species made famous by *Flipper*, but a delicious close-textured, flat-faced fish called dorado. There is also snapper, tuna, swordfish, baby squid and mussels. Try a seafood jambalaya where chunks of lobster, shrimp and ham are served on a bed of braised seasoned rice; shrimp creole with fresh shrimp sauteed in garlic butter and parsley and served with tomatoes; or fish creole with fresh fish steaks prepared in a spicy onion, garlic and tomato sauce and served with rice and fried plaintain. Other island specialities include sauteed scallops with ginger, curried fish steaks lightly fried with a spicy sauce and served with sliced bananas, cucumber, fresh coconut and rice.

It is a pity to travel to the Caribbean and eat burgers and steaks, although these are available. There are so many more exciting meat dishes available which include succulent curried chicken served in a coconut shell; curried goat; gingered chicken with mango and spices; or Caribbean souse with cuts of lean pork marinated in shredded cucumber, onions, garlic, lime juice and pepper sauce.

A bottle of pepper sauce is found on most tables. It usually contains a blend of several types of hot pepper, spices and vinegar, and should be treated with caution. Try a little on the side before splashing it all over a meal, as these sauces range from hot to unbearable.

Vegetarians will enjoy the excellent and varied salads, stuffed breadfruit, callaloo bake, stuffed squash and pawpaw, baked sweet potato and yam casserole.

For dessert, try fresh fruit salad, or one of the exotically-flavoured ice creams. There are also mouthwatering banana fritters and banana flambe, coconut cheesecake and tropical fruit sorbets.

Most menus and dishes are self-explanatory, but bear in mind that when green fig appears on a menu, it usually means green banana, which is peeled and boiled as a vegetable.

There is often a dish called pepper pot on the buffet table. It is usually a hot, spicy meat and vegetable stew to which small flour dumplings and shrimp may be added. There are wonderful breads to be sampled in the Caribbean such as banana or pumpkin bread, and delicious cakes like coconut-loaf cake, guava-jelly cookies and rum cake.

Roti which is an East Indian creation is available almost everywhere and is delicious. It is a paper-thin dough wrapped around a spicy, hot curry mixture containing beef, chicken, vegetables or fish. The chicken roti often contains bones which some people like to chew on.

While many of the restaurants offer excellent service, time does not always have the same urgency as it does back home, and why should it? So relax, enjoy a drink, the company and the ambience and do not worry if things take a little longer — the wait is generally worth it

## Drink

Rum is *the* Caribbean drink. There are almost as many rums in the West Indies as their are malt whiskies in Scotland (Britain), and there is an incredible variety in strength, colour and quality. The finest rums are best enjoyed served on the rocks (with ice only), but in order to capture some of the Caribbean spirit, try a couple of rum punches.

To make a Plantation Rum Punch, thoroughly mix three ounces of rum, with one ounce of lime juice and one teaspoon of honey. Pour over crushed ice and add a pinch of freshly-grated nutmeg.

Most hotels and bars also offer a wide range of cocktails both alcoholic — usually very strong — and non-alcoholic. Beer, drunk cold from the bottle is the most popular drink. Wine, where available, is often expensive because of taxes and the choice is very limited.

Tap water is safe to drink as are ice cubes made from it. Mineral and bottled water is widely available, as are soft drinks.

# Dominica

# DOMINICA

The Commonwealth of Dominica (pronounced Dom-ee-nee-ca) is the most unspoilt of the Windward Islands and its natural, often wild beauty, is one of its greatest charms. The island should not be confused with the Spanish-speaking Dominican Republic which lies 500 miles (800km) to the west in the Greater Antilles.

Dominica lies between French Guadeloupe to the north and French Martinique to the south. It is 29 miles (47km) long, 16 miles (26km) wide, and covers 290 sq miles (752 sq km), making it the largest of the Windward Islands. Roseau in the south-east is the capital and chief port.

The island is volcanic with sulphur vents and bubbling hot springs. There are dense forest-clad mountains in the north and south. The mountains are separated by a central plain formed by the Layou River which flows to the west and Belle Fille River which flows to the east. The highest peaks are Morne Diablotin 4,747ft (1,447m) in the north and Morne Trois Pitons 4,550ft (1,387m) in the southern mountains.

## Getting There

**By air**: Access by air is usually via connecting flights from Antigua, Barbados, Guadeloupe, Martinique, Puerto Rico, St. Maarten and St. Lucia. There is a Dominica Information Desk in the arrival terminal of V C Bird International Airport in Antigua to assist passengers travelling to Dominica. American Airlines, Air Canada, Air France, Air Martinique, BWIA, British Airways, Continental and Lufthansa fly to these gateways. Connecting services are provided by Air Guadeloupe, Carib Express, Cardinal Airlines, LIAT and WINAIR.

LIAT flies between Dominica and many other Caribbean islands. Carib Express operates short take-off and landing jets between Dominica (Melville Hall) and Barbados, Grenada, St. Lucia (Vigie), St. Vincent, Tobago and Port of Spain.

Cardinal Airlines is the only Dominican-run airline and runs a daily service to St. Maarten, Antigua, Barbados and Guadeloupe. The aircraft are also available for charter.

The main airport is Melville Hall on the north-eastern coast, about 36 miles (60km), or a one hour drive from the capital of Roseau. There is a smaller airport at Canefield which is about 4 miles (6km) north of Roseau.

On airline tickets Melville Hall is denoted by the letters DOM, and Canefield by DCF. Check your ticket to make sure you know which one to return to at the end of your stay.

**By Sea**: There are entry facilities at Portsmouth and Roseau, which has a deep-water facility at Woodbridge Bay. Scheduled ferry services operate between Dominica, Martinique and Guadeloupe operated by Caribbean Express and Madikera. Reservations for seats should be made during the high season. Cruise ships regularly visit Dominica docking at either Roseau or Portsmouth.

## Getting Around

There are 470 miles (757km) of roads on the island, of which around 300 miles (482km) are paved, but nevertheless mediocre condition. The roads are poorly maintained away from the main roads.

Taxis and minibuses for hire are recognised by registration numbers starting with the letter 'H'.

**Taxis**: There are taxis at both airports and in Roseau during the day. Fewer taxis operate after 6pm and it is advisable to book in advance for an

evening trip. There are set fares for most taxi journeys, but agree a price and the currency it is being quoted in, before setting off. Typical fares are:
Canefield Airport to Roseau EC$20, to Portsmouth EC$110, to Soufrière EC$60.
Melville Hall Airport to Roseau EC$45, to Portsmouth EC$30. Taxis hired for tours and sightseeing usually charge around EC$45 an hour for up to four passengers.
**Minibuses**: These are for cheapest form of transport on the island. Visitors can catch buses for Trafalgar and the Roseau Valley from Valley Road near the police headquarters. Buses for Soufrière and the south leave from the old market; for the west and north from near the new market close to West Bridge; and for the east from Queen Mary Street.
Typical fares are Roseau to: Salisbury EC$3.50, Portsmouth EC$7.50 and Canefield EC$1.50.
**By Air**: LIAT and Air Guadeloupe operate special day tours.
**By Boat**: Fishing boats can be hired for sea sightseeing and fishing trips, and diving centres also organise tours.

## ROSEAU

Roseau is a busy, colourful little town which is a hive of activity and noisy traffic during the day, and quiet at night. It is an eclectic mix of old and new, faded and smart. The waterfront area has been considerably renovated and makes a delightful place to stroll during the day or evening. The oldest part of town, around Old Market Square, has several colonial-style old buildings which fortunately survived Hurricane David in 1979. The newer section of town, just south of the Roseau River, has offices and shops and numerous bazaars whose wares often spill onto the sidewalks.

Roseau is the only large town on Dominica and gets its name from the French word for 'reed', which grew profusely in the mouth of the river.

The best way of seeing Roseau is on foot. There are fine old buildings, including interesting churches. Many of the oldest buildings are made of stone and wood and have elaborate gingerbread fretwork, wrought-iron balconies and louvred shutters known as jalousies. One of the finest buildings is La Robe Creole Restaurant in Fort Street — a classic stone building of West Indian architecture with its arched doors and windows. Another is the Fort Young Hotel which used to be the town's main fortification.

The old warehouses and many of the homes are built on stone foundations with a wooden upper floor, complete with louvres and balconies overhanging the pavements.

The waterfront area, **Bay Front,** was officially opened on 9 August 1993. The Roseau Seawall and Bayfront Development Project involved a new sea wall 60ft (18m) beyond the Bayfront, designed to reduce the impact of stormy seas in future hurricanes. It has also greatly enhanced the waterfront area, as land in front of the sea wall has been reclaimed and landscaped with footpaths, ornate street lighting and benches. The new jetty has improved facilities for visiting yachts and other small craft, and the new cruise ship berth opened in June 1995. The old Post Office is being renovated to house the Division of Tourism. It will also include public toilets and reception area for cruise passengers and tourists to the town.

The market is where everything seems to happen during the day. The sight of the local people in their brightly-coloured costumes, the assortment of fruit and vegetables protected by an array of kaleidoscopic golf umbrellas, all adds to the

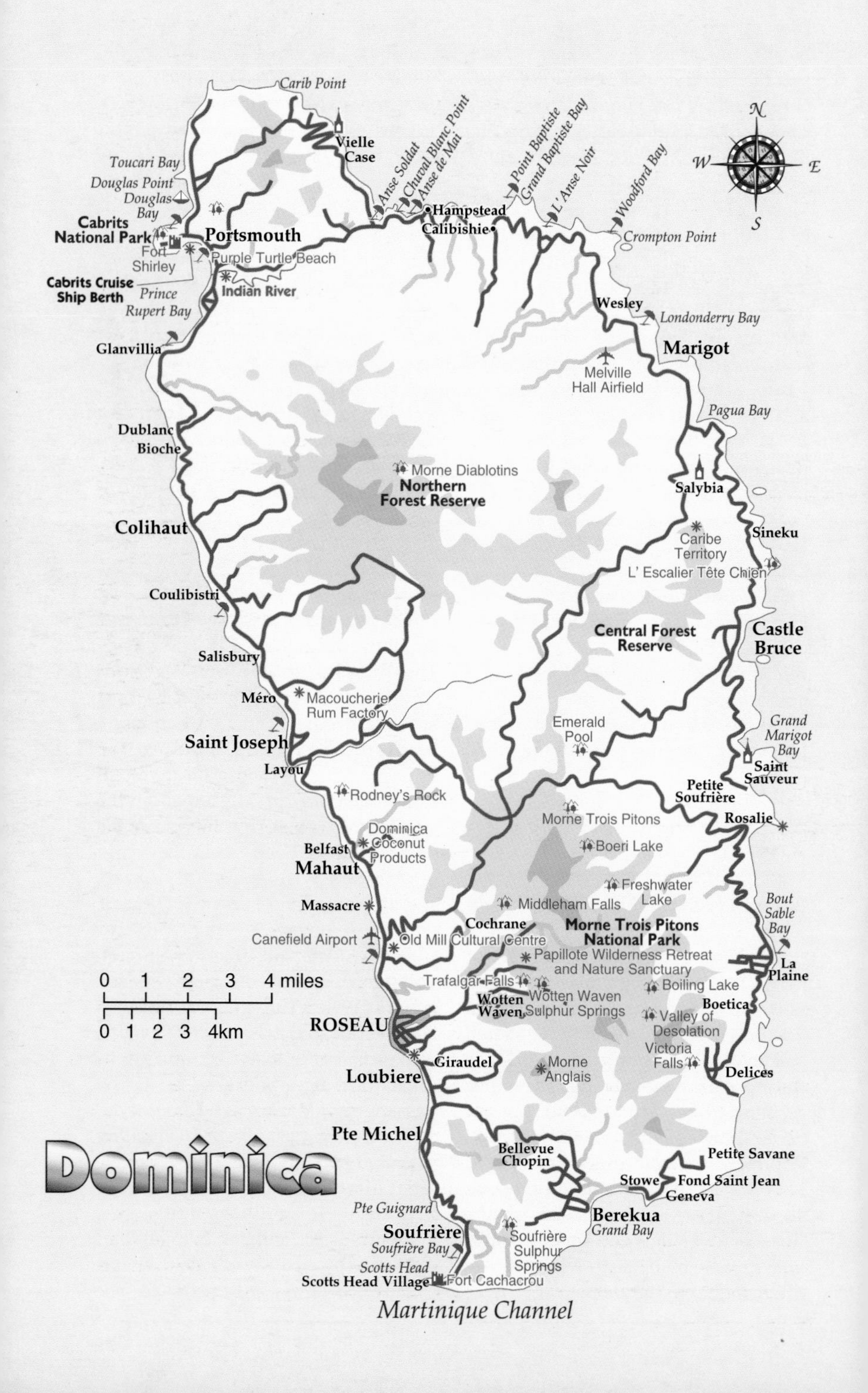

Carib Point
Vielle Case
Anse Soldat
Chaval Blanc Point
Anse de Mai
Point Baptiste
Grand Baptiste Bay
L'Anse Noir
Woodford Bay
N
W
E
S
Toucari Bay
Douglas Point
Douglas Bay
Cabrits National Park
Fort Shirley
Hampstead
Calibishie
Portsmouth
Crompton Point
Purple Turtle Beach
Cabrits Cruise Ship Berth
Prince Rupert Bay
Indian River
Wesley
Londonderry Bay
Glanvillia
Marigot
Melville Hall Airfield
Pagua Bay
Dublanc
Bioche
Morne Diablotins
Northern Forest Reserve
Salybia
Colihaut
Sineku
Caribe Territory
L' Escalier Tête Chien
Coulibistri
Castle Bruce
Central Forest Reserve
Salisbury
Méro
Macoucherie Rum Factory
Emerald Pool
Grand Marigot Bay
Saint Joseph
Layou
Saint Sauveur
Petite Soufrière
Rodney's Rock
Morne Trois Pitons
Rosalie
Dominica Coconut Products
Belfast
Mahaut
Boeri Lake
Freshwater Lake
Massacre
Middleham Falls
Bout Sable Bay
Cochrane
Morne Trois Pitons National Park
Canefield Airport
Old Mill Cultural Centre
Papillote Wilderness Retreat and Nature Sanctuary
La Plaine
0 1 2 3 4 miles
0 1 2 3 4km
Trafalgar Falls
Boiling Lake
Wotten Waven
Wotten Waven Sulphur Springs
Boetica
ROSEAU
Valley of Desolation
Victoria Falls
Giraudel
Morne Anglais
Delices
Loubiere
Pte Michel
Bellevue Chopin
Petite Savane
Dominica
Stowe
Fond Saint Jean
Geneva
Pte Guignard
Berekua
Grand Bay
Soufrière
Soufrière Bay
Soufrière Sulphur Springs
Scotts Head
Scotts Head Village
Fort Cachacrou
Martinique Channel

Above:The colourful market in Roseau is an interesting place to find an assortment of fruit and vegetables and other local produce on sale.

excitement of a visit. The old market, which was also the slave market and scene of public executions, is close to Fort Young. In 1895, a Dominican philanthropist left £500 for a covered building to be erected in the square and this now houses handicrafts stalls and a small café. It has recently been revamped as Dawbiney Market Plaza.

On Bay Front there is the **old Post Office**, originally the Market House built in 1810, the new Court House and Registry. The nearby **Peebles Park** has a bandstand, and benches where one can sit and relax.

The **Cable & Wireless** offices are in Old Street, a couple of streets inland from the Post Office, and Barclays Bank is a little further down the street.

The northern half of the town is laid out in grid style drawn up in the 1760s after the British took over the island, and now has a one-way system to control traffic over the river. **Government Headquarters** are at the top of Kennedy Street, and the Fire and Police Headquarters are at the corner of Bath Road and King George V Street. There is a health centre on Hillsborough Street. Novelist Jean Rhys was born in Cork Street in what is now Vena's Guest House.

The area south of the Old Market, which was the heart of the first settlement, is a maze of small, narrow streets. Between Virgin and Turkey lanes the **Methodist Church** sits alongside the near Gothic-Romanesque Roman Catholic **Cathedral of Our Lady of the Assumption**, consecrated in 1841. Although the majority of the islanders were and still are Catholic, the colony was officially Anglican and refused to help finance the cathedral's construction. The congregation therefore worked at night gathering stones from along the Roseau River for the building. Although consecrated in 1841 it was not until 1916 that the building was finished with the completion of the west steeple. The pulpit is reputed to have been donated by prisoners on Devil's Island.

The **St. George's Anglican Church**, built in Regency style in 1820 and enlarged in the early part of the twentieth century, was destroyed by Hurricane David, and hit again during rebuilding. Across the road, amidst fine grounds is the refurbished white **State House** with the **House of Assembly** just south on Victoria Street. Until independence, State House was the official residence of the Governor, and is now used for state receptions and similar functions.

**Fort Young** was built between 1700 and 1783 to protect the sea approaches when Roseau became the capital. It was heavily fortified with extremely thick walls, and these now keep the interior cool when it is blisteringly hot outside. It opened as a hotel in 1964. The flagstones in the shaded courtyard are original and cannon are still dotted around the hotel and grounds. Opposite, on the beach side of the road are the **library** and radio station. The **Cenotaph** is in Victoria Street, and further along are the ruins of the Georgian **Old Court House** built in 1811, but burnt during unrest in 1979.

The **Botanical Gardens** are on the outskirts of Roseau at the foot of the Morne Bruce Hill, worth walking up for the views from the summit close to the large crucifix and shrine erected in 1924. One can drive or walk up by taking Jacks Walk from the Botanical gardens.

There are two entrances to the gardens, the Main Gate or North Gate, is off Valley Road, and the Roseau Gate is off Bath Road. The gardens cover 40 acres (16 hectares), and have around 85 inches (212cm) of rain each year which explains the lush vegetation and prolific growth of so many tropical flower species.

The gardens, on the site of a former sugar cane plantation, were originally planted in 1890. There was an ornamental garden and one used for testing plants for commercial importance. Although today they are only a shadow of their original glory, the gardens have survived remarkably in view of tropical storms. They were badly hit by Hurricane David in 1979 which lashed the grounds for eight hours. The force of the hurricane uprooted a huge baobab tree causing it to crush a bus. There is a leaflet — *Guide to Selected Trees and Shrubs* — which indicates where different trees and shrubs are located.

The aviary in the gardens is a breeding station for the island's two endangered parrots, the Jaco and the Sisserou.

Close to the gardens in Elmshall Road is the Alliance Francaise of Dominica with a library and small theatre. It is open weekdays between 9am and 12noon and 2pm and 7pm. ☎ 448-6008.

The suburb of **Potters Ville** and **Goodwill** are across the Roseau River and just inland of both is Limefields. The Princess Margaret Hospital is in Goodwill, and the island's teacher training college is at Limefields.

## Eating Out in Roseau

**Blue Max Cafe and Deli** $
16 Hanover Street
☎ 449-8907
A café offering snacks, deli style sandwiches and excellent coffee.

**Callaloo Restaurant** $-$$
66 King George V Street
☎ 448-3386
A great Caribbean restaurant, specialising in traditional island dishes such as callaloo soup, crapaud, lobster and crayfish. Ingredients are fresh every day, so the menu reflects what is available. Open Monday to Saturday 7.30am-10pm.

**Cartwheel Cafe** $
Bay Street
☎ 448-5353
On the Bay Front and offering snacks and lunches.

**Continental Inn** $-$$
37 Queen Mary Street
☎ 448-2214
A small and friendly restaurant serving creole cuisine.

**Creole Kitchen** $-$$
Woodstone Mall
Cork Street
☎ 448-6052
Good creole cooking at very affordable prices.

**Evergreen Hotel** $-$$
Castle Comfort
☎ 448-3288
The Crystal Terrace restaurant is set in a spectacular tropical garden overlooking the Caribbean Sea and specialises in local cuisine.

**Fort Young Hotel** $$-$$$
Victoria Street
☎ 448-5000
A very good restaurant offering à la carte creole and international dishes in the historic setting of the ruins of Fort Young. Buffet dinners are offered regularly and provide the chance to taste island specialities. There is also a reasonable wine list.

**The Garraway Hotel** $$-$$$
Bay Front
☎ 449-8800
The restaurant with its fine views offers a wide choice of food from quick snacks to full meals featuring traditional creole and international dishes.

**Green Parrot** $
10 Bay Front
☎ 448-8944
Offers snacks and light meals.

**Guiyave Restaurant and Bar** $-$$
15 Cork Street
☎ 448-2930
Dine in style on the balcony of this old town house. The restaurant is rightly popular and serves good, local dishes.

**Kent Anthony Guest House** $
3 Great Marlborough Street
☎ 448-2730
The restaurant is open to the public and offers local cuisine at very affordable prices.

**La Robe Creole** $-$$
Fort Street
☎ 448-2896
On the Bay Front opposite Peebles Park, air-conditioned and offering a snack menu as well as excellent à la carte creole dishes. Friendly and attentive service by staff dressed in traditional island costume, thus the restaurant's name.

**La Tropicale** $-$$
15 King George V Street
☎ 448-3772

**Mange Dominique** $-$$$
Cork Street
☎ 448-7100

**Margheritia's Pizzeria** $
10 Old Street
☎ 448-6003
More than just a pizzeria with excellent cheesecake, pastries and ice cream.

**Mousehole** $
Fort Street
☎ 448-2896
Tasty snacks in the basement of La Robe Creole Restaurant

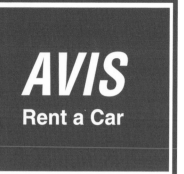

**Orchard Restaurant** $-$$
Corner of King George V and Great George Streets
☎ 448-3051
A great place for a snack or traditional creole meal with lambi, goat, chicken or fish. There are also vegetarian dishes usually available. Try the roti and black pudding. Open Monday to Friday 8am-10pm, and Saturday 8am-4pm.

**Paiho Restaurant** $-$$
10 Church Street
☎ 448-8999
The island's first Chinese restaurant which specialises in Hunan-style country cooking. Take away is available.

**Pearl's Cuisine** $
19 Castle Street
☎ 448-8707
Excellent local cuisine, especially fresh fish, shrimp and chicken. Open from breakfast to dinner. Take out available. There is a good value set three-course lunch and dinner

**Pina Colada Bar** $
30 Bath Road
☎ 448-6921
Offers snacks, light meals and drinks and evening entertainment.

**Pizza Palace** $
River Bank
☎ 448-4598
Fast food outlet offering pizzas, other snacks and soft drinks.

**Raffoul Snackette** $
13 King George V Street
☎ 448-4145
Great for a quick snack of pattie and fruit juice at lunchtime or during the day.

**Trends** $-$$
Hillsborough Street
Snacks, light meals and drinks, and evening entertainment.

**World of Food** $-$$
Queen Mary Street
☎ 448-3286
A popular restaurant for lunch and dinner where you can dine in the courtyard shaded by the large mango tree.

## Eating Out Around Roseau

**Castaways Beach Restaurant** $$-$$$
Castaways Hotel
Mero
☎ 449-6244
Fine dining in the Almond Terrace Restaurant which serves tasty creole dishes.

**Gachette's Seaside Restaurant** $$
Scott's Head
☎ 448-4551
Some of the best fish on the island which is fresh daily and locally caught.

**Good Times Restaurant** $-$$
Checkhall
☎ 449-1660
Snacks and drinks available and a fun place in the evenings.

**Lauro Club** $$
Salisbury
☎ 449-6602
The restaurant, perched on the cliffs, is noted for its local cuisine, especially fish and shrimp.

**Layou River Hotel** $$
Layou
☎ 449-6081
The restaurant specialises in local creole and authentic Chinese cooking.

**Ocean Terrace** $$
Anchorage Hotel
Castle Comfort
☎ 448-2638
The restaurant offers a choice of local creole specialities and international dishes.

**Papillote Wilderness Retreat**
Trafalgar Falls Road
☎ 448-2287
This recently renovated restaurant is set in tropical gardens beside a natural hot mineral pool. It serves local creole dishes, health-food oriented dishes and a variety of Caribbean and international foods.

**Reigate Hall Hotel** $-$$
Reigate
☎ 448-4031
Enjoy traditional creole and international cuisine in the hotel's unique restaurant.

**River Side Cuisine** $-$$
Loubiere
☎ 448-6447
Local dishes.

**Seamoons Club** $-$$
Massacre
☎ 449-1061
Snacks and local dishes

**Shipwreck** $-$$
Donkey Beach
Canefield
☎ 449-1059
Snacks and local dishes and specialising in fish.

**Tony's Corner** $-$$
Mero
Snacks and local dishes available.

## The South

The tour heads south from Roseau along the coast through the suburbs of Charlotteville and Castle Comfort and its few hotels, towards Loubiere, where the road divides.

The inland road is steep and climbs over the mountain before descending to the sea at historic **Bereuka** on **Grand Bay.** In the mountains at **Bellevue Chopin** you can take a walking detour north to **Morne Anglais**, the home of some of the island's largest plantations. It is still predominantly agricultural, producing citrus fruits — especially grapefruit.

The great sweep of Grand Bay was protected by forts on the headlands at Carib Point and Pointe Tanama, and remains of fortifications can still be seen on the cliffs.

Grand Bay, with its steep streets, has an interesting church decorated with local scenes painted over the doors and fearsome-looking gargoyles. The crucifix in the cemetery is the oldest on the island, and was carved around 1720 from a solid piece of stone. The bell tower was relocated in the hills in order for its peals to be heard over a wider area.

From Berekua take the road west to visit the **sulphur springs** above the village of **Soufrière**, but these are best visited from the village itself.

Our road continues around the coast to **Fond Saint Jean** and **Petite Savane**. There are the remains of old sugar mills at **Geneva** and **Stowe**, and at **Bagatelle** close to Fond Saint Jean. The area around Petite Savane, a village with strong French traditions, is a centre for bay oil production and there are a number of small distilleries giving off its sweet, heady aroma. There is a small cricket pitch perched on the edge of the cliff.

Because of the steep mountains which plunge straight into the sea, the road ends at Petite Savane, but there is a path inland which runs parallel to the coast and down to the sea at Pointe Mulatre.

## South from Loubiere

Continue south at Loubiere rather than drive inland, and follow the coast road beneath the towering cliffs of Solomon, the scene of fierce fighting between the British and French in 1778, past **Pointe Michel** and **Pointe Guignard**. The road runs inland for a short way round **Morne la Sorcier**, where Caribs allegedly threw their unfaithful wives to their deaths, and then back to the coast and Soufrière. This entire stretch of coastline was heavily fortified and the ruins of Fort Cachacrou on Scotts Head are great to explore.

**Soufrière** is a friendly little village, and one of the island's first settlements. The French named it after the sulphur which emits from the ground a little way up the valley. The church, noted for its murals of village life, is beside the beach surrounded by boats and palm trees.

Soufrière was also the site of the famous Rose's Lime Juice factory. Limes grown around the island were hauled or shipped to the factory for pressing and processing and at one time, exports of lime juice accounted for half of the island's income. One can visit the ruins of the lime press and the old sugar cane mills. Today the area is noted for the production of aloe.

Soufrière is also noted for its jump-ups, or street party festivals called Korne Korn La.

Drive or walk along the unmade road through the Soufrière River Valley to the sulphur springs and hot water pools. The original baths were built for French soldiers. Along the river there are stands of towering bamboo, and the villagers take advantage of the hot water for bathing and washing their clothes. The water temperature ranges from hot to extremely hot, so exercise caution before jumping in!

**Scotts Head** on the south-western tip of the island was dominated by **Fort Cachacrou**, now in ruins, named after the Carib word 'cashachou' which means 'that which is being eaten by the sea'. Scott was one of the British officers who helped capture the island from the French in 1761. In 1778 during the American War of Independence, the French General de Bouillé landed his invasion force close to the fort which was quickly captured, and he then went on to capture the whole island.

The fort has wonderful views of Martinique to the south, and northwards along the western coast to Roseau and beyond, and one can see the different shades of blue where the Atlantic Ocean and Caribbean Sea meet.

The area between Scotts Head and Soufrière is a protected marine reserve, and has been divided into zones to accommodate fishing, swimming, snorkelling and scuba diving. The reserve is ideal for both novice and experienced divers and snorkellers. It is also ideal for artists, photographers, enjoying a picnic and sunbathing.

**Soufrière Bay** is famed for the phenomenon known as a white squall, caused by winds which occasionally come powering down the steep, leeward mountain sides. As the winds hit the water, they cause a swell which then races out to sea until it is dissipated; but woe betide any yachts or small boats in its path.

Having visited Scotts Head, the only way back to Roseau is to retrace the route north along the same coast road.

## The Interior from Roseau

It is best to hire a guide to lead a walk on any of the trails. It is not only more interesting, but also more sensible up in the rainforest along the rough terrain.

There are no trans-island routes in the southern third of the island, but there are a number of roads which provide access into the interior and the spectacular **Morne Trois Pitons National Park**, which is best explored on foot. Always wear sturdy, non-slip footwear and carry rain wear and a warm sweater, because it can be cool if the sun is hidden and the winds pick up.

The park was the first nature reserve in the Caribbean and contains many of Dominica's most spectacular natural attractions.

The easiest trip is to **Trafalgar Falls** and is accessed by taking the road that is the extension of King George V Street, which crosses the Roseau River and continues through Bath Estate for just under 5 miles (8km) to the trailhead. At Ford Cani take the left fork for the Falls and Laudat, and after about

Above: The area from Scott's Head to Soufrière is a protected marine reserve.
Below: The Trafalgar Falls cascade through a narrow gorge into pools below.

one mile (1.5km) take the right hand fork to the falls. It is a well-marked trail, although there is a little scrambling through the rocks beyond the viewpoint, and the rocks can be slippery in places. There are two falls which cascade down through a gorge into pools below that are dotted with huge black rocks and surrounded by lush ferns and orchids. The larger of the falls on the left is 'Father', and the smaller one 'Mother'. The flow of both is less than it used to be because the falls have been diverted to provide hyrdro-electric power. Take swim-wear as halfway up 'Father' there is a hot pool where one can relax. Do not climb up the middle of the falls where the water is extremely hot. The red oxide staining indicates the flow of the hot water.

Close to the falls is the **Papillote Wilderness Retreat and Nature Sanctuary**, which includes a small, secluded hotel and good restaurant, set in tropical gardens, with hot mineral pools, waterfalls, fountains and paths through heavily-scented flowers. The owners have won eco-awards for their sensitive development of the property. The retreat was first developed in 1969 on the verdant mountain slope beneath Morne Macaque. As time passed, footpaths and terraces were developed consistent with the contours of the land.

The **Wotten Waven Sulphur Springs** are across the valley from the falls. There are pools of mineral-rich hot water and bubbling which are reputed to have therapeutic properties —a legacy of the island's volcanic past. Always test the temperature of the water carefully before entering a pool. The sulphur laden air is also considered to be healthy.

Morne Trois Pitons National Park covers 17,000 acres (6,800 hectares) of rainforest, and contains the Titou Gorge, the Boeri and Freshwater crater lakes, Bubbling Lake and the Middleham Falls located to the north-west of Laudat. All these natural attractions can be reached by trails. Take the same road out of Roseau and head for the Trafalgar Falls but take the left hand turning for Laudat at the fork in the road.

Visitors heading for Freshwater Lake can drive in a four-wheel drive vehicle a couple of miles beyond Laudat to the trail.

The 9 acre (4 hectare) **Freshwater Lake**, the largest in Dominica, is 2,500ft (762m) above sea-level, and the road to it runs round the southern edge of Morne Macaque. The lake, the source of the Roseau River, has been tapped to augment the island's hydro-electric power supplies. The area is home to much of the island's fauna and the lake is believed to contain a huge serpent with a jewel embedded in its head.

There are picnic sites around the lake and interpretive signs. A number of hiking trails start in the area. It is about a three-and-a-half hours walk to Boiling Lake and nearly two hours to Grand Fond. There is a short steep climb from Freshwater Lake south-east to a viewpoint overlooking the village of Grand Fond and the Atlantic coast beyond.

It is another three-quarters-of-an-hour from Freshwater Lake along the trail through elfin woodlands and past several hot and cold springs to the 4 acre (2 hectare) freshwater **Boeri Lake** in the crater of an extinct volcano 2,800ft (854m) above sea level. There are good views of Morne Trois Pitons, Dominica's second highest mountain, directly ahead. Be careful when walking near the water's edge as the stones are very smooth and slippery.

The **Middleham Trail** lead to the tumbling 300ft (91m) **Middleham Falls** and **Tou Santi**, the stinking hole. They can be reached from either Providence on the Laudat Road, or the village of Cochrane, just off the Transinsular Road, accessed via Canefield and then taking the inland feeder road. From Sylvania, the trail runs through a former coffee plantation now reclaimed by the forest although some of the old buildings can still be seen. The path is easy to follow with steps over the steeper sections. Some streams have to be crossed or jumped. The falls plunge for 200ft (30m) and then tumble in a series of cascades and pools for a further 100ft (30m), before joining with nearby streams to form the Boeri River. The stinking hole is a lava tube which emits sulphur gas. From Providence it is about one hour to the falls, but allow almost double from Cochrane. The Cochrane route also provides access to other trails in the northern half of the Morne Trois Pitons National Park.

There is a hiking trail from Laudat which leads to the summit of **Morne Trois Pitons**, named because of its three peaks, the tallest of which is 4,550ft (1,387m).

The **Valley of Desolation** is worth visiting because of its totally volcanic landscape. The valley gets its name because virtually nothing can grow in its sulphur laden atmosphere. It is an area of giant rocks, hot springs and bubbling multi-coloured mud pools, with the smell of sulphur obvious long before you reach the valley. There are more than fifty vents in the valley, and the water and rocks in the streams are coloured by the different minerals that are washed into them from the volcanic soil. It is a 5 mile (8km) hike along a trail from the village of Laudat. The last volcanic activity was in 1880 .

The hike into the valley and Boiling Lake is quite strenuous up and down hills, down into Breakfast River Valley and then up and over Shark's Tooth Peak at 3,002ft (915m), the highest point on the trail. Allow at least four hours each way.

**Titou Gorge** is at the beginning of the walk into the Valley of Desolation. Getting to it is more of a swim than a hike through the various large rock pools along the floor of the 50ft (15m) high gorge where hot and cold streams meet. The gorge was carved by lava not water. The trail starts from Laudat and is well worth the effort. It passes through lush forest as you climb the slopes of Morne Nicholls, which has stands of *wezinye montayn*, the island's only native conifer.

**Boiling Lake**, up to 200ft (61m) across, is the second largest of its kind in the world, and gets its name from the gases bubbling up through a fumarole — a flooded vent in the crater in which it has formed. The flow of gases is so powerful that the water level can be raised up to 3ft (1m) by the bubbling and steam rising from the water. Occasionally the gases stop and the water disappears as if going down a giant plughole, suddenly to re-emerge geyser-like when the lake fills up again. Be careful to stay on the trail as the earth's crust is very thin in places and off the path it is possible to break through the crust and fall into boiling mud. The nearby **Morne Nicholls** (2,965ft/904m) and **Morne Watt** (4,017ft/1,225m) are named after the two men who in March, 1875, made their way to the Boiling Lake and subsequently wrote about their exploits.

The right hand fork at Fond Cani splits with the left fork providing an alternative access to the Wotten Waven Sulphur Springs. The right hand fork leads to Morne Prosper.

From the village of **Giraudel** just over 2 miles (3km) inland from Roseau, there is a trail close to the summit of **Morne Anglai** at 3,683ft (1,123m). The trail, which will take two hours to ascend ends in elfin woodland. The last part can be very difficult because of landslides, and caution is advised.

## The Western Coast

The spectacular drive north from Roseau along the coast to Portsmouth follows a road which in many places had to be carved from the mountain sides which slope steeply into the sea.

The road out of Roseau passes Woodbridge Bay with the cruiser terminal and deep-water facility and heads for **Canefield** where one can visit the **Old Mill Cultural Centre** which is open daily. It is in the grounds of an old plantation with an old water wheel, modern equipment and a fascinating little museum with pre-Columbian exhibits. There is also a gallery displaying the work of local artists and sculptors. There is a wood-carving school in the grounds, and the old sugar cane fields have been converted into the airport and the industrial estate.

The road passes **Canefield Airport** leading towards **Massacre**, named after an incident in 1674. Governor Warner of St. Kitts had one son by a Carib woman, and a second, Philip, by his English wife. When the Governor died, Carib Warner no longer had anyone to protect him, so he fled to Dominica to become a powerful Carib Chief. In 1674, Philip was chosen by the Governor of the Leeward Islands to lead a military force to Dominica to quell the Caribs. According to legend, the two half-brothers met for a feast, but Philip treacherously stabbed his brother to death which signalled his troops to start killing the other Caribs.

On the right there is a pretty Catholic chapel perched on the hill looking out over the village and the sea beyond.

The road continues through the small fishing village of **Mahaut**, and through **Belfast** where the Dominica Coconut Products' factory is based. This factory was recently acquired by a US consortium and has been one of the island's many success stories — turning copra into oil for soaps, cosmetics and detergents. It processes the island's entire crop and produces international brands such as Imperial Leather and Palmolive for the Caribbean. Belfast is also home of the D-Special Rum Distillery.

The road continues northwards past the large rock outcrop known as **Rodney's Rock**, named after the British Admiral, and up the coast under the shadow of Morne Diablotin. One story suggests the mountain was named after the large black-necked petrol, known locally as the diablotin, which nested on the slopes. The bird nested on the ground meaning its eggs were easy to take, and by the nineteenth century it had disappeared from the island.

On the stretch between Mahaut and Layou, slow down and look at the coconut groves on the left between the beach and the road. At times it is possible to see hundreds of land crabs burrowing in the sand. It is known locally as 'Crab City'.

**Layou** is a small fishing village with a pretty, black sand beach. Layou River is the longest on Dominica and has some beautiful pools just inland from the estuary. There are also longer walks up the Layou River Valley as far as Belles on the Transinsular route where visitors can arrange to be collected. Jacko Steps, about one mile (1.6km) west of the village of Belles in the Layou Gorge rise 300 feet (100m) to a former Maroon camp. The steps were cut into the volcanic rock and the distance between each is deliberately large to slow down attackers. Visitors can still walk the steps which are kept clear by the local schoolchildren.

The land north of the Layou River bridge is the **Hillsborough Estate**, once famous for tobacco production and now growing coconuts, coffee and

cocoa. The remains of the old factory can be seen and the estate house still looks out over the valley.

The Castaways Hotel is on Mero Beach beyond the village of Saint Joseph. The road runs close to the Macoucherie Distillery, and through the small coastal villages of Salisbury, Coulibistri, Colihaut and Dublanc, where there is a feed road providing access inland to Morne Diablotin and the Northern Forest Reserve area with its many walks.

## A Trip to Morne Diablotin

The **Northern Forest Reserve** includes Morne Diablotin 4,747ft (1,447m), with the Syndicate area just to the north-west, which is important as the home of the endangered sisserou and jaco parrots. Morne Diablotin, the second highest peak in the Lesser Antilles, was an active volcano millions of years ago, and its frequent eruptions spawned the many other peaks in the north of the island.

Visitors who have the opportunity to view Morne Diablotin from the sea will see how all the ridges and valleys fan out from the mountain. The steep slopes are covered in dense forest, but there is a trail to the summit. Allow between two or three hours to reach the top depending on your fitness and stamina. The trail starts from the Syndicate Estate and is reached from a feeder road inland from the main road, just north of the village of Dublanc on the west coast.

The path leads through towering forest, swampy ground, elfin woodland and finally over rocky ground covered with lichens and mosses.

The Maroons, the slaves who managed to escape in the eighteenth century, used the mountain as a hide-out and they often escaped capture by disappearing into the seemingly impenetrable forest.

Dr John Imray and two friends are credited with the first ascent of the mountain in 1868. Accompanied by nine porters and locals armed with machetes to clear a path, they took two days and two nights to reach the summit, camping out along the way. Nowadays, the return trip can be made in six or seven hours, but allow extra time for picnic and frequent rest stops. A guide is strongly recommended.

The **Syndicate Nature Trail** is through a 240 acre (96 hectare) section of the forest developed by the Dominican Government in 1989. The area is popularly known as the 'parrot preserve' and the thirty-minute trail which opened in 1994 runs through superb tropical rainforest. Many trees are labelled and it is possible spot the Sisserou parrot; Dominica's national bird, and smaller Jaco or red-necked parrot. The blue-headed humming-bird, also found only on Dominica, can sometimes be seen along the path, as well as red-necked pigeons and broad-winged hawks swooping down over the trees.

There are no large mammals on the island, but large rodents called agoutis frequent the forest, and lizards and plentiful, although usually so well camouflaged that one only sees them when move. Return to the coast and head north through Windward Estates and Glanvillia, to the Indian River.

## A Trip Up The Indian River

A trip up the Indian River is an experience one is unlikely to forget. Take a row boat rather than a motor boat which scares a lot of the wildlife. Expect to pay around EC$15 to 20 a person depending on the number of passengers per boat, and remember to take a camera.

The river is named after the Caribs who lived and fished along its banks.

Ships that anchored in Prince Rupert Bay would send crews in rowing boats up river to trade with the Caribs.

Shortly after setting off up river, one passes the large banana barges that are towed by tugs out to the ships anchored in the bay. When the banana boat is in, all the small boats lend a hand to move the crop as quickly as possible.

Make a right turn into the 58 acres (23 hectares) of swamp that run alongside the river. The waters here have mullet, pike and crayfish and teem with crabs. The boatmen who operate as guides, take a pride in their work and are very knowledgeable, usually providing a non-stop commentary about the history of the river, the area and its wildlife. The journey gently meanders for about half-a-mile (1km) up the river which is lined with mangrove and bwa mang trees, whose buttresses-like roots conceal edible crabs.

The water is over 10ft (3m) deep in places and usually very clear, although it does get cloudy after rain. A short way up the river is the wrecked railway bridge destroyed by Hurricane David. The railway, the only one built on Dominica, was constructed in the early twentieth century and ran for a short stretch down the west coast. The journey ends as the river narrows and further progress is blocked by a series of mini rapids. There is, however, a stopover at the ramshackle bar on the river bank among the trees, which serves a variety of rum and local drinks including powerful coconut punches.

It is advisable to wear lightweight clothes, and not many of them. The weather may be perfect at the beginning of the journey up river but within minutes the skies may change and the heavens may open with a tropical downpour. Fortunately, it rarely rains for long, and the sun soon dries everyone off.

A trip along the Indian River is a must, not just because it is delightfully relaxing, but because it provides the experience of a mangrove river and swamp, along with all its wildlife.

**Portsmouth** is Dominica's second largest town and was originally planned to be the capital because of its natural harbour in Rodney Bay. However, the nearby marshes were infested with malaria-carrying mosquitoes, so the settlers relocated to Roseau.

Rodney Bay is a popular anchorage for visiting yachts and there are immigration and customs facilities at the police station in Bay Street. The new **Cruise Ship Berth and Visitor Centre** stands at the foot of Fort Shirley and were opened in 1990 on the site of the old military jetty and dockyard. It is the only cruise ship port in the Caribbean where passengers can disembark straight into a national park.

The bay is also a centre for many trading ships that ply between the Caribbean islands. Within a short distance of the jetty there is a bank, petrol station and tourist information office. The market is close to the sea in Bay Street and sells locally-grown fruit and vegetables. The Roman Catholic Church is inland and further uphill, the small Portsmouth Hospital.

The palm tree-lined **Purple Turtle beach** is one of the finest on the island, and popular with visitors and islanders living in Roseau. Visitors can buy bread and cakes, drinks and other groceries at the local stores in town.

Portsmouth makes an ideal place for a leisurely holiday. There are good walks in the area, both along the coast and inland, and fishing boats may be hired for trips out to sea. Accommodation is mainly in small guesthouses and the local bars and restaurants offer snacks and local specialities

The best sandy beaches are to the north of townn close to the Purple Turtle Beach Club, and this is also the closest refreshment stop for visitors to the National Park..

## Eating out in and around Portsmouth

**The Cabin Restaurant** $-$$
☎ 445-5695
Snacks and local dishes

**Coconut Beach Restaurant** $$-$$$
☎ 445-5393
A near perfect place to enjoy dinner beside the Caribbean. Good food, especially local creole dishes, friendly service and a great atmosphere

**Douglas Snackette and Restaurant** $-$$
☎ 445-5253
Good value snacks, juices and local dishes

**La Flambeau** $$-$$$
Picard Beach Cottage Resort
☎ 445-5131
The restaurant overlooks the sea and offers fine dining with local creole and international cuisine.

**Mango Bar & Restaurant** $-$$
☎ 445-3099
Open daily for breakfast and lunch, and Sunday to Thursday for dinner. Try a traditional creole breakfast, and speciality dishes like baked chicken, fish, lobster and sea eggs

**Purple Turtle Beach Club** $-$$
☎ 445-5296
Snacks and local dishes, especially fish.

**Sango's Sea Lodge** $-$$
Picard Estate
Portsmouth
☎ 445-5211
Local creole dishes and specialising in fish.

## Cabrits National Park

The park covers 1,313 acres (525 hectares), including 1,053 acres (421 hectares) of marine area. There is an enormous amount to see and do, so visits should not be rushed. The site contains the ruins of the eighteenth century Fort Shirley, the volcanic peaks of East and West Cabrit, tropical forest, the largest swamp on the island, sandy beaches, and spectacular coral reefs just offshore to the north.

Wear sensible footwear to explore the park as there are some fairly steep walks, and after rain, the ground may be slippery. Remember to take swimwear in order to take a cooling swim in the sea.

For anyone planning to spend a full day in the park, carry plenty of drink and food for lunch, and remember a camera and binoculars. Diving enthusiasts should bring their gear to explore the coral reefs in Douglas Bay.

The park is named after the Portuguese word 'cabrit', which means goat. It was common for sailors to leave goats to run wild at various places along routes they sailed frequently, so there would be a constant supply of fresh meat.

The first visitors to Rodney Bay were Amerindians who arrived in their dug-out canoes from South America. After Christopher Columbus 'discovered' Dominica in 1493, the sheltered waters in the lee of the headland were often used by passing ships. Crews would come ashore for water and to trade with the Caribs for food after their Atlantic crossing. Rodney Bay was particularly popular as an anchorage for Dutch trading ships and Spanish treasure ships. Because of the rich pickings to be had from these vessels, the waters were also patrolled by English privateers such as Drake and Hawkins, as well as French corsairs.

Above: Fort Shirley in Cabrits National Park was once a major military stronghold.

Admiral Horatio Nelson often anchored here as a young officer serving in the Caribbean fleet. Prince Rupert of the Rhine landed in 1652 and explored the hinterland, after which the bay was subsequently named after him. Whalers from Massachusetts used it as their base, and Ann Davison, the British yachtswoman, became the first woman to sail the Atlantic single-handed, when she landed in Rodney Bay in 1953 after her sixty-five day voyage in 23ft (7m) *Felicity Ann.*

A small British military force was stationed on Cabrits in 1771 and Royal Engineers started work on Fort Shirley in the hollow between the two volcanic domes. It was named after General Thomas Shirley, later Governor of Dominica. Both the English and French continued building work until 1826 during which time more than fifty different military buildings were constructed. The fort had seven gun batteries, seven huge cisterns for gathering and storing drinking water, powder magazines, ordnance stores, barracks and officers' quarters to house the 500-600 men stationed there, and room for another 500 men in the event of an emergency, as well as the commandant's house. The massive ramparts were built from volcanic stone. The fort was finally abandoned in 1854 and quickly fell into disrepair. Many of the buildings were damaged as stone was removed for construction in Portsmouth and elsewhere, and the ruins quickly became overgrown as the forest took over.

The recommended way to visit the park is to begin at the **Fort Shirley Museum**. Then follow the paths which lead from the entrance to the commandant's house, the centre battery at the top of the Inner Cabrit, the Douglas Bay battery, and finally, the fortifications and buildings that make up the Outer Cabrit perched on Prince Rupert Bluff.

The grounds are home to abundant wildlife including large lizards and iguanas. The freshwater swamps are a bird-watcher's paradise, especially during the migration season. The coral reefs in **Douglas Bay** are also protected as part of the National Park, and the palm and almond tree fringed beach along the bay makes a great place for a picnic. There is a fascinating underwater trail for snorkellers, which is marked out by white buoys in the middle of the bay. The coral grows on top of volcanic rock outcrops, and the bay floor is covered with sea grass, home to shoals of brightly-coloured tropical fish. For the more adventurous diver, there are rock and coral formations to be explored at the foot of the cliffs at the northern end of the bay. Local fishing can be hired for the short trip to the cliffs.

From Portsmouth the road runs north to Douglas Bay and Toucari Bay just beyond. Estates along the coast here were awakened to the sound of cannon fire on the morning of 12 April 1782 to witness the Battle of the Saints fought just offshore.

The road then runs north through Morne Soleil, Cottage and Clifton to Capucin and the Capucin Cape on the north east tip of the island. The waters off the coast can be very rough and there are a number of shipwrecks off the cape. The route back to Portsmouth is along the same road.

Just north of Portsmouth there is a feeder road which runs up into the foothills around Morne aux Diables, and from here one can visit the **Tanatane Waterfall** and the mountain.

The main road from Portsmouth cuts inland through palm forests for about 6 miles (9.6km), through what is known as 'coconut country', to the north-eastern coast and some of the island's finest beaches.

## The East Coast

The interior road from Roseau to **Melville Hall Airport** was originally started in 1909 as the Imperial Road. It finally emerged on the east coast in 1956, having been renamed the Transinsular Road.

From Roseau, drive north to Canefield and then turn inland for the spectacular drive through the magnificent tropical rainforest. Whilst it is not a fast road, there are quite a lot of sharp bends, so take care. Invariably motorists use their horns a lot to warn each other of their approach. In the mountains it rains frequently and heavy downpours can start as quickly as they end. However, they make the roads very slippery, and mud and other debris may be washed on to the road.

The **Middleham Trail** lead south from the road into the Roseau Valley to the impressive Middleham Falls and then on to the village of Laudat. It is possible to arrange for a taxi to meet you in the village to save the long walk back along the same route.

The road runs through Roger and Pont Cassé where there is a police post. Morne Trois Pitons is only two miles or so to the south east but often difficult to see because of the dense vegetation. At Point Cassé the road splits into three, the left fork curves back into the Layou Valley and runs on to the west coast; the middle fork — the main road — runs through the Central Forest Reserve and Carib Territory to the east coast at Pagua Bay; and the right fork runs virtually parallel to this, reaching the east coast just south of Castle Bruce near Anse Quanery.

Visitors wishing to explore the east coast between La Plaine and Delices must take this road, as it is not possible to drive all the way south from Castle Bruce.

## Emerald Pool and the East Coast between Rosalie and Delices

Take the right hand Castle Bruce fork for **Emerald Pool**, a grotto with its own tiny waterfall and pool, surrounded by tropical plants, flowers and ferns. The pool is a gentle ten-minute walk from the road through woodland, about three miles north-east from Pont Cassé. There is a short section of trail paved with rock slabs laid by the Caribs who used them as a main route. This area is rich in birdlife, especially hummingbirds, mountain warbler, and occasionally the rare Jaco parrot can be seen around the pool.

The Emerald Bush Bar and Restaurant at Emerald Pool is the only place to eat in the area, and is located close to the highway along a sign-posted private road.

A short distance beyond the pool, the main road forks again near the Tarrish Pit quarry, with the left fork going to Castle Bruce. Take the right fork south through banana plantations and citrus groves to the coast at **Rosalie** at the mouth of the Rosalie River. One can still see the aqueduct which used to carry the river water to the sugar mill. The ruins of a church are one of the few traces of the village that once flourished. From Rosalie there is a feeder road inland to Grand Fond, which follows the old pathway which was used to cross the island.

The road continues south through Rivière Ciriques and Morne Jaune down to **La Plaine**, named by the French because the area was reasonably flat compared with the mountainous terrain elsewhere. There were many large French plantations in the area. Just before entering La Plaine one passes **Bout Sable Bay**. The black sand beach is fringed with swaying palm trees, with towering cliffs to the north and heavy surf offshore. It is a delightful place for a picnic and paddle, but it is not safe to swim here.

Inland at the head of the valley is the **Sari Sari Waterfall**. There is a memorial at Case O'Gowerie to villagers who died during protests against the imposition of a land tax in 1893. They were shot by a force of Marines and police who landed at La Plaine from the warship *HMS Mohawk*.

The road continues south crossing the Boetica Gorge to Delices, La Roche and the Victoria Falls, which can be glimpsed up the valley. The road ends close to Pointe Mulatre Bay and the estuary of the White River which runs from Boiling Lake. The mineral-laden waters are reputed to have therapeutic properties so a swim is a good idea, if only to cool down. On the other side of the river there is an old French graveyard and several ruins of the once flourishing sugar and coffee plantation. Walkers can continue south to link up with the road at Petite Savane.

## Visiting the rest of the East Coast

The main trans-island road runs north from Pont Cassé through the northern part of the Morne Trois Pitons national park into the Central Forest Reserve. Huge swathes of dasheen adorn the mountain sides, while vines snake up into the massive trees, and the elegant tree ferns spread their huge fronds out like delicate parasols.

At **Belles** there is a trail — an old Maroon path — which cuts down to the west coast along the Layou Valley. It is about an eight mile hike but it is possible to swim part of the way.

The road then crosses **Carib Territory** to the coast.

The Carib Territory covers 3,700 acres (925 hectares) with an extensive shoreline and agricultural land behind. The land was given back to the descendants of the island's original inhabitants in 1903. Today the Caribs engage mostly in fishing and agriculture. They still carve their traditional dug-out canoes by hand which are still used for fishing. They also practice their ancient skills of pottery and basket weaving. The weavers are so expert that they can make baskets that are watertight.

**Concord** and the Floral Gardens Hotel are off the main road about three miles inland. The guesthouse stands at the foot of the tropical rainforest, and has won awards for its 'creative environment', and Island Restaurant serves local creole cuisine. There is also a Carib craft shop, and the opportunity for river bathing and hikes.

A new 'model' Carib village is being built in the territory. It will feature a community hut in which traditional arts and crafts will be demonstrated.

Once at the coast, one can either head north to explore the eastern coast as far north as Point Jaco on the north eastern tip of the island, or head south to explore the coast down to as far as Petit Soufrière where the road ends.

## North to Point Jaco

The road between Pagua Bay and Point Jaco offers some of the most spectacular and unspoiled beaches on the island. The first section of coast to Crompton Point bears the full force of the Atlantic rollers. This is an area of cliffs with many attractive small coves and beaches, but these are not suitable for swimming.

The villages of **Marigot** and **Wesley**, with its high school, both on Londonderry Bay, were founded in the late nineteenth century when a British chocolate company purchased many of the old estates to produce its own cocoa. The islanders did not want to become estate workers again, so labour was recruited from neighbouring English-speaking islands. As a result, the people are Methodist rather than Roman Catholic, which is how Wesley gets its name, after the founder of Methodism.

**Melville Hall**, the island's main airport, is between Marigot and Wesley and the main runway runs inland from Londonderry Beach, parallel with the Melville River. It opened in 1981. The area around Melville Hall is very attractive with coconut groves, palm trees and the Atlantic Ocean rolling onto the black sands of Londonderry beach. Most of the coconut groves around the airport are owned by the Larvell family.

There is a dramatic change in the coastline past **Crompton Point**. The last bay south of the point is appropriately named **Rough Bay**, but after rounding the point, the seas become calm and this stretch of coastline has some fabulous sheltered beaches — Woodford Bay, Turtle Beach (l'Anse Tortue), l'Anse Noir, Pointe Baptiste, Calibishie, Hampstead, Anse de Mai and Anse Soldat.

The colour of sand varies from beach to beach, from the fine black sand which gives its name to L'Anse Noir, to the coarser white sands of Woodford Bay and Pointe Baptiste which are really millions of tiny fragments of ground coral.

The approach from the main road to many of the beaches is either by foot or along old estate roads which are usually accessible in good weather by car. All beaches in Dominica are public but access to some involves crossing private land, so keep to the track.

**Pointe Baptiste** is one of the most idyllic spots on the island. The main house, a typical West Indian timbered home with shaded balcony, is now a guest house atop the red cliffs with

Opposite: Sparkling waters of the Caribbean Sea near to Hampstead.

magnificent views out to sea, while guest cottages are dotted around it. Beneath the cliffs is a lovely secluded beach. The main house has played host over the years to many famous people including Noel Coward, Somerset Maugham and Princess Margaret.

Next is **Calibishie**, a charming village with pretty houses, well-kept gardens, and a sheltered, palm-fringed, sandy beach. There is a mile-long reef just offshore which creates a shallow lagoon for safe swimming. Visitors can enjoy a drink at the Almond Tree Restaurant beside the beach in the heart of the village. Just off Calibishie are two rocks close together which jut out of the sea. They used to be joined in a natural arch and were known locally as the Gateway to Hell.

In **Hampstead** men and women sit beside the road cracking open coconuts which are later baked in ovens for about two days before being sent for pressing at the Dominica Coconut Products factory in Belfast.

The small fishing village of **Anse de Mai** is named after a French officer who was in charge of a massacre of the Caribs here in 1635. From **Chuval Blanc Point** the coastline runs north-west, with steep cliffs and fast-running streams tumbling into the sea down waterfalls and through gorges. There are small villages perched on top of the windswept cliffs and the road should be driven with care because of hairpin bends and blind corners. The views are incredible, but pull off the road to enjoy them.

At **Vielle Case**, visit the stone Catholic Church with its red roof, flat-topped tower and fascinating murals. On the beach visitors can watch the fishermen launch their boats through the fierce surf of Autrou Bay. The village of **Pennville** was first settled by the French, as was Vielle Case, and both still have strong French traditions. The road ends at Pennville, but there is a track north to Point Jaco, and a nature trail which cuts across the tip of the island to Capucin. From the village you can also visit the Bwa Nef Waterfall.

## South to Petit Soufrière

The Roman Catholic St. Marie church in the Carib village of **Saylbia**, sometimes called Salibia, is worth visiting. The altar is in the shape of a dug-out canoe and is an incredible work of art. Walk down the hill to the mouth of the Crayfish River where the water cascades over the rocks into the sea.

At **Sineku** just south of the village is *L'Escalier Tête Chien*, which means 'the snake's staircase'. It is a solidified lava flow which resembles a giant writhing serpent running down the hill and out into the sea. It figures prominently in Carib folklore and legends. There are a number of craft shops along this stretch of coast road.

At **Castle Bruce** the road inland leads back past the Emerald Pool and connects with the main trans-island route. The road runs through the Belle Fille valley and then onto a long straight stretch through the former Castle Bruce sugar cane estate, which is now split up into small farms.

One can usually see Carib canoes beneath the palms along Anse Quanary, also known as St. David Bay. The sea is not safe for swimming because of the strong currents here.

The drive to Petit Soufrière affords tremendous views along the coast. At **Saint Sauveur** on Grand Marigot Bay, there is a charming small church and a few small bay oil distilleries.

The small village of **Petit Soufrière** is the end of the road and its name is a mystery because there is no evidence of any volcanic activity in the area. The houses are built on the steep wind-beaten slopes. There is a walking trail leading south towards Rosalie.

# DOMINICA FACT FILE

## ARRIVAL, ENTRY REQUIREMENTS AND CUSTOMS

An immigration form has to be filled in and presented on arrival.
British citizens and visitors from European Community and Commonwealth countries need a valid passport for entry, but a visa is not required. Visas are only required by citizens of all other foreign countries. Visitors from the United States and Canada staying less than six months can enter on an ID card but must have valid return tickets. French citizens with a Carte Identité are allowed to visit for up to two weeks.

## ACCOMMODATION

Prices unless stated, do not usually include the eight per cent government tax and ten per cent service charge.
In the information provided, the abbreviated terms stand for the following:-

CP: *Continental Plan*
(bed and breakfast)
MAP: *Modified American Plan*
(breakfast and dinner included)
EP: *European Plan*
(bed only, no meals)
AP: *American Plan*
(all meals included)

$ Inexpensive accommodation
$$ Moderate
$$$ Luxury

**Ambassador Hotel** $ EP, CP, MAP
PO Box 413
Roseau
☎ 449-1501
The hotel is two minutes from Canefield Airport, and has ten rooms, a restaurant, bar and conference facilities.

**Anchorage Hotel** $-$$ EP,CP, MAP
Castle Comfort
PO Box 34
Roseau
☎ 448-2638
It has thirty-two rooms, restaurant, bar, pool, squash, conference facilities and special honeymoon packages. It has a full service PADI diving centre on the premises, and its own 41ft (12m) custom diveboat. Organised excursions including whale watching trips can be arranged.

**Casa Ropa Hotel** $ EP
Portsmouth
☎ 445-5492
It has eight rooms and restaurant but self-catering facilities are also available.

**Castaways Beach Hotel** $$ EP
Mero
PO Box 5
Roseau
☎ 449-6244
The island's only beach hotel surrounded by tropical gardens, offering 26 beachfront rooms. creole and international dishes are served in the terraced Almond Tree Restaurant. Sailing, water skiing and tennis are available, and the hotel is a certified PADI diving centre. Tuition is available as well as night dives and wall dives.

**Castle Comfort Lodge** $$ MAP
Castle Comfort
PO Box 63
Roseau
☎ 448-2188
It has ten rooms and a restaurant. The hotel offers good diving and honeymoon packages.

**Coconut Beach Hotel** $-$$ CP, MAP
Picard
PO Box 37
Roseau
☎ 445-5393
It has twenty-two rooms, a bar and restaurant specialising in local creole cuisine, and offers tours, car rentals, diving and honeymoon packages.

**Evergreen Hotel** $$ CP
Castle Comfort
PO Box 309
Roseau
☎ 448-3288
Situated one mile (2km) south of Roseau the hotel has sixteen double rooms. It has a restaurant specialising in local cuisine, bar and pool set in verdant tropical gardens. Diving and island day tours can be arranged.

**Fort Young Hotel** $$-$$$ EP, MAP
Roseau
☎ 448-5000
A luxury but affordable hotel in delightful historic buildings in Roseau, close to the water and the old town. It has thirty-three well appointed air-conditioned rooms, excellent restaurant, bar, pool, conference facilities, direct dial telephones, and honeymoon and diving packages.

**The Garraway Hotel** $$ EP
Bayfront
Roseau
☎ 448-3247
A modern hotel with thirty-two well appointed rooms on the waterfront and close to all Roseau's amenities. Facilities include a fine restaurant, bar, shops, conference facilities. Tours and hikes can be arranged.

**Lauro Club** $$ EP, CP, MAP
Salisbury
☎ 449-6602
It has sixteen units with ocean and mountain views, noted restaurant and self catering facilities, pool and diving packages with East Carib Dive.

**Layou River Hotel** $ EP, CP, MAP
Clarke Hall
Roseau
☎ 449-6081
Nestled on the banks of the Layou River, the hotel makes an ideal base for touring and hiking in the area both along the west coast and inland along the river valley towards Emerald Pool and Carib Territory. It has thirty-five rooms, an award-winning terrace restaurant offering local specialities, bar, pool and conference facilities and offers honeymoon packages.

**Mamie's On the Beach** $ EP
Portsmouth
☎ 445-4295
A delightful small hotel with eight rooms right on the beach, with charming gardens, and good restaurant.

**Papillote Wilderness Retreat** $ EP
Trafalgar Falls Road
☎ 448-2287
It has ten rooms, a restaurant and a self catering cottage by a waterfall.

**Picard Beach Cottage Resort** $$ EP
Picard
☎ 445-5131
It has sixteen rooms, a restaurant and also offers self catering facilities, pool, conference facilities, diving and honeymoon packages.

**Portsmouth Beach Hotel** $ EP
Picard
☎ 445-5142
It is located on one of Dominica's finest, unspoiled golden sand beaches. It has ninety-six rooms, a beach restaurant and bar, pool, and offers honeymoon packages. It also has a dive centre and offers a wide range of watersports.

**Reigate Hall Hotel** $$ EP
Reigate
☎ 448-4031
A very attractive small hotel with sixteen rooms and rustic charm. There is a pool, sauna, bar, and diving and honeymoon packages are available.

**Reigate Waterfront Hotel** $-$$ EP MAP
Castle Comfort
☎ 448-3130
It has twenty-four rooms, restaurant and pool, and offers diving and honeymoon packages.

**Sutton Place** $$
Roseau
☎ 448-4313
In the heart of Roseau's business centre, and has five cosy rooms and three suites with fully-equipped kitchenettes. The restaurant offers creole cuisine and guests can enjoy spectacular sunsets from the rooftop garden.

Enjoy a memorable stay in the intimate surroundings of the Evergreen Hotel, ideally located on the west coast of Dominica, just one mile from the capital of Roseau. Relax and sip exotic cocktails while basking in the glow of the setting sun. Our charming air-conditioned double rooms are all comforably furnished and our beach-front restaurant offers a mouthwatering selection of french creole cuisine.

PO BOX 309, CASTLE COMFORT,
COMMONWEALTH OF DOMINICA,
WEST INDIES
TELEPHONE: (809) 448-3288
FAX: (809) 448-6800

# he Garraway Hotel

Welcome to the Garraway Hotel where our helpful and professional staff will ensure that every stay is unforgettable.
Our luxurious and spacious rooms are air-conditioned and comfortably furnished to international standards.
Whether travelling on business or pleasure, look no further than the Garraway for the ultimate experience.
The oceanfront à la carte restaurant and seaside bar serve a selection of sumptuous Caribbean cuisine along with fine international fare.

PLACE HERITAGE
ONE BAY FRONT
ROSEAU
COMMONWEALTH OF
DOMINICA,
WEST INDIES
TEL: (809) 449-8800
FAX: (809) 449-8807

## Airlines/Airports

**Air Guadeloupe**
☎ 448-2181

**BWIA International**
In the USA 1-800-JET-BWIA

**Cardinal Airlines**
☎ 449-0322

**Carib Express**
☎ 1 800 744 3333 from the Windward Islands,
☎ 809-431-9200 from other locations

**Caribbean Air Services**
☎ 449-1748

**LIAT**
☎ 448-2421

**WINAIR**
☎ 448-2181

## Banks

Banks are open Monday to Thursday 8am–3pm, and from 8am–5pm on Fridays.

**Banque Francaise Commerciale**
Queen Mary Street
Roseau
☎ 448-4040

**Barclays Bank**
Old Street
Roseau
☎ 448-2571

*also at*
Portsmouth
☎ 445-5271

**National Commercial Bank of Dominica**
64 Hillsborough Street
Roseau
☎ 448-4401

*also at*
Portsmouth
☎ 445-5430

**Royal Bank of Canada**
Bay Front
Roseau
☎ 448-2771

**Scotiabank** (Bank of Nova Scotia)
28 Hillsborough Street
Roseau
☎ 448-5800

## Camping

There are no camping facilities on the island and sleeping out, especially on the beach, is not allowed.

## Car Rental

Hire car rates range start from around US$250 a week depending on the type of vehicle and the rental company. Average daily rates start around US$35 and this does not include insurance which costs an additional US$15-20 a day.
A temporary Dominican driving licence is required, and can be obtained on production of a current driving licence on arrival at the airport on any day of the week, the car hire office, or weekdays from the Traffic Department in the High Street, Roseau. The licence costs EC$20 for one month or EC$ 45 for three months. Drivers must be aged between twenty-five and sixty-five, and have at least two years driving experience.
Seat belts are not compulsory but it is advisable to wear them at all times. The speed limit is 30mph (48kph) or lower in town, and there is no reason to go very much faster out of town because you will not fully appreciate the scenery.

**Hire companies include**:

**Anslem's Car Rental**
3 Great Marlborough Street
Roseau
☎ 448-2730

**Avis**
4 High Street
Roseau
☎ 448-2481

**Bonus Rentals**
Fond Cole
Roseau
☎ 448-2650

**Budget Rent-a-Car**
Canefield Industrial Estate
Canefield
☎ 449-2080

**Ken's Taxi Service**
62 Hillsborough Street
Roseau
☎ 448-4850

**S T L Rent-a-Car**
Goodwill Road
Roseau
☎ 448-2340

**Sag Rent-a-Car**
Canefield
☎ 449-1093

**Valley Rent-a-Car**
Goodwill Road
Roseau
☎ 448-32330

*also at*
Portsmouth
☎ 445-5252

**Wide Range Car Rentals**
Bath Road
Roseau
☎448-2198

## Churches

The following denominations are represented: Roman Catholic, Baptists, Anglican, Methodist, Seventh Day Adventist, Christian Union Mission, Pentecostal, Baha'i Faith.

## Departure Tax

There is a departure tax of EC$20 (US$8) for all passengers aged 12 or over leaving the island after a stay of more than 24 hours, and a EC$5 (US$2) security charge. The tax can be paid in either EC or US dollars

## Emergency Telephone Numbers

For police, fire and ambulance dial 999.

## Entertainment

Most of the hotels have some evening entertainment but this largely consists of live music over dinner. The Anchorage has a poolside barbecue on Thursday evenings, the Evergreen Hotel has live music and dinner on Friday evenings, and the Fort Young Hotel has live music over dinner on Wednesday and Sunday with live music in the open air bar area on Saturday nights. The Garraway Hotel has live music in the bar on Friday nights. The Lauro Club Hotel has live music featuring traditional island song and dance on Wednesday, and the Reigate Waterfront features live entertainment as part of its Wednesday night barbecue.
There are weekend discos at Aqua Cade in Canefield, and The Warehouse in Checkhall, while other night-time entertainment spots in Roseau include Trends, the Pina Colada Bar, Etienne's Garden Club at Clarke Hall, Good Times at Checkhall, and the Night Box.

## Ferries

There are regular scheduled ferries from both Martinique and Guadeloupe to Dominica. These are provided by Caribbean Express, ☎ 448-2181, and Madikera, ☎ 448-6977.

## Festivals/Public Holidays *

| | |
|---|---|
| **1 January** | New Year's Day * |
| **February** | Carnival |
| **April** | Good Friday *<br>Easter Monday * |
| **1 May** | Labour Day* |
| **June** | Whit Monday * |

**June and July**
Fishing villages separate the Feast of St. Peter and St. Paul. Villages celebrate on different days so that people can attend them all. During the ceremony, the fishermen, their boats and nets are blessed by the local clergy.

| | |
|---|---|
| **August** | August Bank Holiday |
| **1 November** | All Saint's Day |
| **3 November** | Independence Day * |
| **4 November** | Community Services Day |
| **25 December** | Christmas Day * |
| **26 December** | Boxing Day * |

## Hospitals

The main hospitals are the Dominica Infirmary on Queen Mary Street, Roseau, and Princess Margaret Hospital, Goodwill, Roseau.
There is also a hospital in Portsmouth.

## Media

Dominica has four radio stations: DBS (AM 595Khz, FM 88.1MHz), VO1 (AM 860Khz, FM 96.1MHz), VOL (AM 1060Khz, FM 102.9 and 90.6Mhz), and Radio GNBA Mango (FM 93.5Mhz).
There are two pay cable television stations: Marpin TV has nine channels, and Video 1 two. Nationally broadcast US channels are also usually available.

## Pharmacies

### Roseau

**City Drug Store**
Cork and Old Streets
☎ 448-3198

**Dominica Dispensary**
9a Church Street
☎ 448-2938

**Jolly's Pharmacy**
37 Great George Street
☎ 448-3388

**Kays Pharmacy**
29 Cork Street
☎ 448-2051

**New Charles Pharmacy**
Angle Fields & Cross Lane
Roseau
☎ 448-3198

## Police

The police headquarters is on the corner of King George V Street and Bath Road, Roseau.

## Post Office

The General Post Office is on Bay Street Roseau, and is open 8am-4pm Monday to Friday. There are sub-post offices in Portsmouth and some large villages.

## Shopping

Shops are usually open between 8.30am and 1pm and 2pm to 4pm Monday to Friday, and between 8am to around 12 noon or 1pm on Saturday. Increasingly shops are remaining open at lunchtime. Best buys are the Carib craft items such as woven straw goods like mats, hats and baskets, pottery, handpainted candles, leather craft, wood carvings and paintings by local artists. There are also batiks, handmade cigars, locally produced coconut oil-based soaps, and a host of spices, spice-based products, preserves and syrups, and of course, island distilled rum, and Dominica Bay Rum, an invigorating body freshener.

## Sightseeing and Tours

Sightseeing and island tours by land or sea can be organised through hotels, tour representatives or one of the many specialist tour companies on the island. These include:

**Alex Forest Tours**
☎ 448-2831

**Anisons Tours**
Woodstone Shopping Mall
Cork Street
Roseau
☎ 448-6460

**Antours**
Woodstone Shopping Mall
Roseau
☎448-6460
Offers day hikes and island tours.

**Astaphan Tours**
☎ 448-3221

**Didier's Tours**
Greens Lane
Goodwill
Roseau
☎448-3706
Offers half day and day tours, hikes, birdwatching, photo safaris, scuba diving.

**Dominica Tours**
Anchorage Hotel
Castle Comfort
Roseau
☎448-2638
Offers scuba, diving and water sports, whale watching, island tours and hiking,

**Emerald Safaris**
☎448-4545

**Ken's Hinterland Adventure Tours**
Roseau
☎ 448-4850
Day tours and longer for sightseeing, hiking, photo safaris and birdwatching.

**Linton's Tours**
Elmshall
Roseau
☎448-2558
Sightseeing tours by hour, half day and day, hikes with guides.

**Mally's Tour & Taxi Service**
64 Cork Street
Roseau
☎ 448-3114
Sightseeing day tours including drinks and lunch and tours by the hour to view sights of interest, plus hikes, bird watching, photo safaris and personalised itineraries.

**Mussons Travel**
Old Street
Roseau
☎448-2550

**Nature Island Tours**
Roseau
☎ 448-3397
Offers photo safaris and hikes.

**Paradise Tours**
Steber Street
Pottersville
Roseau
☎ 448-5999
Island tours and tours to specific attractions.

**Pierro Nature Safari**
King George V Street
Roseau
☎ 448-2292
Offers island tours, trail hiking and photo safaris.

**Rainbow River Tours**
Roseau
☎ 448-8650
Day trips around the island, weekend packages, overnight hikes

**Sun Link Tours**
Dorset House
Roseau
☎ 448-2552
Offers a wide range of sea and land excursions

**Whitchurch Travel Agency**
Old Street
Roseau
☎ 448-2181
Offers day tours

**Wilderness Adventure Tours**
Bath Road
Roseau
☎ 448-2198
Offers naturalist and photo safari tours, wild and tame garden tours, and hikes

## Sport

### Fitness Gyms/Health Centres

**Carlian Aerobic and Dance Centre**
Old Street
Roseau
☎ 448-6602

**Mac's Health Club**
Old Street
Roseau
☎ 448-8050

### Hiking

There are some spectacular walks on Dominica ranging from the easy to the long and strenuous. If you are planning to walk to remote interior locations it is advisable to hire a guide for the trip. Guides can be arranged at very reasonable cost, and they will ensure that you get the most out of your trip — and find your way back.

### Scuba Diving

The waters off Dominica offer some of the best diving in the world. The waters are warm and clear, the reefs are easily accessible and they teem with marine life. The best diving areas are around the Cabrits National Park and Douglas Bay on the north-west coast, and around Scotts Head on the south western tip of the island. The following offer diving training, tours and watersports:

**Anchorage Dive Centre**
Castle Comfort, Picard and Portsmouth
☎448-2638

**Dive Castaways**
Mero
☎449-6244

**Dive Dominica**
Castle Comfort
☎448-2188

**East Carib Dive**
Salisbury
☎449-6602

**Nature Island Dive**
Soufrière
☎449-8181

**Windward Island Divers**
Portsmouth
☎ 445-5104

### Squash

**Anchorage Hotel**
Castle Comfort
☎ 448-2638

### Tennis

There are courts at
**Castaways Beach Hotel**
Mero
☎ 449-6244

**Reigate Hall Hotel**
Roseau
☎448-4031

### Water Sports

This is available at all resorts and most large hotels. Sea kayaking has just been introduced, and is offered by

Nature Island Dive and Ken's Hinterland Tours ☎ 448-4850.

## Taxes

There is a Government tax of five per cent on all hotel rooms, and a Government Sales Tax of three per cent. A ten per cent service charge may also be added to restaurant bills. Menus and tariffs sometimes include these charges so check to ensure they have not been added twice.

## Tourist Offices

There are tourist information centres in Roseau at the Old Market, in Portsmouth near the cruise docks, and at both airports. There is also a tourist information desk in the arrivals terminal at Antigua's international airport for passengers flying on to Dominica.

The tourist office is part of the
**National Development Corporation**
PO Box 293
Roseau
Dominica
☎448-2351

**Belgium**
OECS Embassy
Rue des Aquatiques 100
1040 Brussels
☎ 322-733-4328

**Canada**
OECS Mission
Suite 1050
112 Kent St. Ottawa
Ontario K1P 5P2
☎ 613-236-8952

**United Kingdom**
Caribbean Tourism Organisation
Suite 3/15, Vigilant House
120 Wilton Road
London SW1V 1JZ
☎ 0171-233-8382

**United States of America**
Caribbean Tourism Organisation
20 East 46 Street
New York
NY 1001-2452
☎ 212-682-0435

## Weddings

Requirements for getting married on Dominica are:

• Visitors must have been resident on the island for two working days before applying for a marriage licence. This application can be made through a local solicitor to the Attorney General.

• produce a certificate of non-marriage from a priest, lawyer or registrar on official note paper, attesting that neither party is married.

• produce final divorce documents if applicable.

• produce passport and birth certificates.

Many hotels also offer wedding packages and will make all the arrangements for you. The application must be filed at least four working days before the date of the wedding. Most denominations of church weddings can be arranged in advance, and registrars usually charge a fee plus travel costs. Valentine's Day is a very popular day for weddings, and registrars are usually very busy rushing around conducting marriage after marriage.

## Whale Watching

Tours are organised by
Anchorage Dive Centre
Castle Comfort
☎ 448-2638

# Grenada

# GRENADA

Grenada is a three-island state consisting of Grenada, Carriacou and Petit Martinique, covering an area of 344 sq miles (892 sq km). Grenada is 21 miles (34km) north to south, 12 miles (19km) from east to west, oblong in shape, and covers 120 sq miles (311 sq km). It has six parishes and five main towns. The capital, St. George's, is on the south-west coast and is also the island's main port, as well as one of the main yachting and boat charter centres in the eastern Caribbean. From Grenada there are a number of small islands — Bonaparte Rocks, Large Island, Rose Rock, Frigate Island, Saline Island and White Island — which lead to the Grenadines. Carriacou, is the largest island of the southern Grenadines, and lies about 23 miles (37km) north-west, covering an area of 13 sq miles 32 sq km). Petit Martinique is a small volcanic cone, covering only 486 acres (194 hectares), and lies just off the north-east coast of Carriacou.

Grenada was formed during a series of volcanic eruptions about twenty-five million years ago. It has many extinct craters and a central ridge of forested mountains running like a spine from north to south. Mount St. Catherine is the highest point at 2,756ft (840m), and when not shrouded in cloud, dominates the northern half of the island.

## Getting there

**By Air**: There are international flights into Point Salines International Airport, which is five miles (8km) from St. George's. These include Aereotuy, Air Europe, Airlines of Carriacou, American Airlines, BWIA, British Airways, Caledonian Airways, Canada 3000, Helenair and LIAT.

Carib Express, launched in 1995, operates the only jet service between the islands, flying 146s which require relatively short runways for take-off and landing. It flies between Barbados, Grenada, Dominica (Melville Hall), St. Lucia (Vigie), St. Vincent, as well as Tobago and Port of Spain.

American Airlines flies from the United States to Grenada via its Caribbean hub in Puerto Rico. BWIA International provides direct services from New York, Toronto, Miami, and London via Trinidad and other Caribbean Islands. Other North American carriers, including Air Canada, have flights to Barbados and Antigua which connect with LIAT and BWIA flights to and from Grenada. British Airways and British Caledonian provide direct services from London.

Charter services are provided by Aereotuy from Venezuela, Helenair from Grenada to nearby islands, Airlines of Carriacou to Carriacou and the Grenadines, and Canada 3000.

**By Sea**: A growing number of cruise lines now visit Grenada.

## Getting around

Taxis and minibuses available for hire have registration numbers beginning with the letter 'H'.

There are plenty of taxis and drivers are knowledgeable and make good guides. There are fixed fares on main routes i.e. EC$30 from St. George's to the airport, and EC$7 for journeys of one mile (2km) or less. Longer journeys generally cost EC$4 per mile (1.6km) for the first 10 miles (16km), and EC$3 for each subsequent mile (1.6km). There is a EC$10 surcharge after 6pm. It is advisable to always agree a fare first.

Minibuses are available for most destinations at either Market Square or the Esplanade. There are fixed fares from EC$1.25 to EC$5 according to the distance travelled. There are few buses after dark or on Sundays.

It is possible to tour St. George's and its environs in style in a traditional horse and carriage.

Water taxis are available from the Carenage in St. George's to other points on the Carenage, the cruise pier and Grand Anse.

The island is easy to explore with roads running around the entire coastline and others which traverse the island providing access to remote inland areas. Most roads are paved although care should be taken, especially in the countryside, because of potholes and other unpredictable hazards. Many of the roads are narrow and caution is needed when over-taking, particularly as there are often sharp corners, and in places no hard shoulders and steep drops. Landslides are also quite common after very heavy rains.

## St. George's

Many consider Grenada's capital St. George's as the most picturesque town in the Caribbean, as it nestles on the hillsides which slope down to the water's edge. Historic forts still stand sentinel over the city, and colourful houses with their tropical gardens cling precariously to the hillsides. In the heart of the city there are cobbled streets to explore, markets to visit, restaurants to sample and a wealth of history to absorb.

St. George's was settled by the French in 1705 as Port Royale, but the name changed when control subsequently passed to the British. The town was destroyed by fires in 1771 and 1775. As a result, a law was passed banning the construction of any building not constructed of either brick or stone and covered with tiles. This accounts for the fascinating city which stands today — especially the old red-tile roofed warehouses along the waterfront.

St. George's is bisected by a hill which runs inland from Fort George and separates the Carenage and harbour area from the section known as Bay Town, which makes up the western side of the city. The two areas are connected by the Sendall Tunnel which opened in 1895 and was named after Governor Sir Walter Sendall. It is 340ft (104m) long and 12ft (3m) high, and was considered a major feat of engineering when it was built.

The horseshoe-shaped **Carenage** is the heart of the city and runs round the inner harbour. The tourist office is in a new waterfront building, and is a good place to start a walking tour. Many of the streets are steep, narrow and cobbled, and full of fascinating shops and kiosks. There are red telephone kiosks and pillar boxes, and old cannons have been stood on end in the road to act as bollards.

One quickly adapts to the noise and the atmosphere — Grenadians toot their horns whenever they see some-one they know, and as most people know each other, drivers spend most of their time tooting to say hello, or tooting back in reply.

When passing one of the many lines of immaculately-dressed school-children standing hand-in-hand and smiling from ear-to-ear, wave and smile back.

The Carenage gets its name because ships were once hauled up on to the beach and laid on their sides, or 'careened', in order for repairs to be carried out on the hull.

St. George's owes its expansion to its deep, natural harbour which is the remnant of a submerged volcanic crater. The sheltered anchorage which is protected on most sides by hills was strategically important, and through the centuries was fought over by the

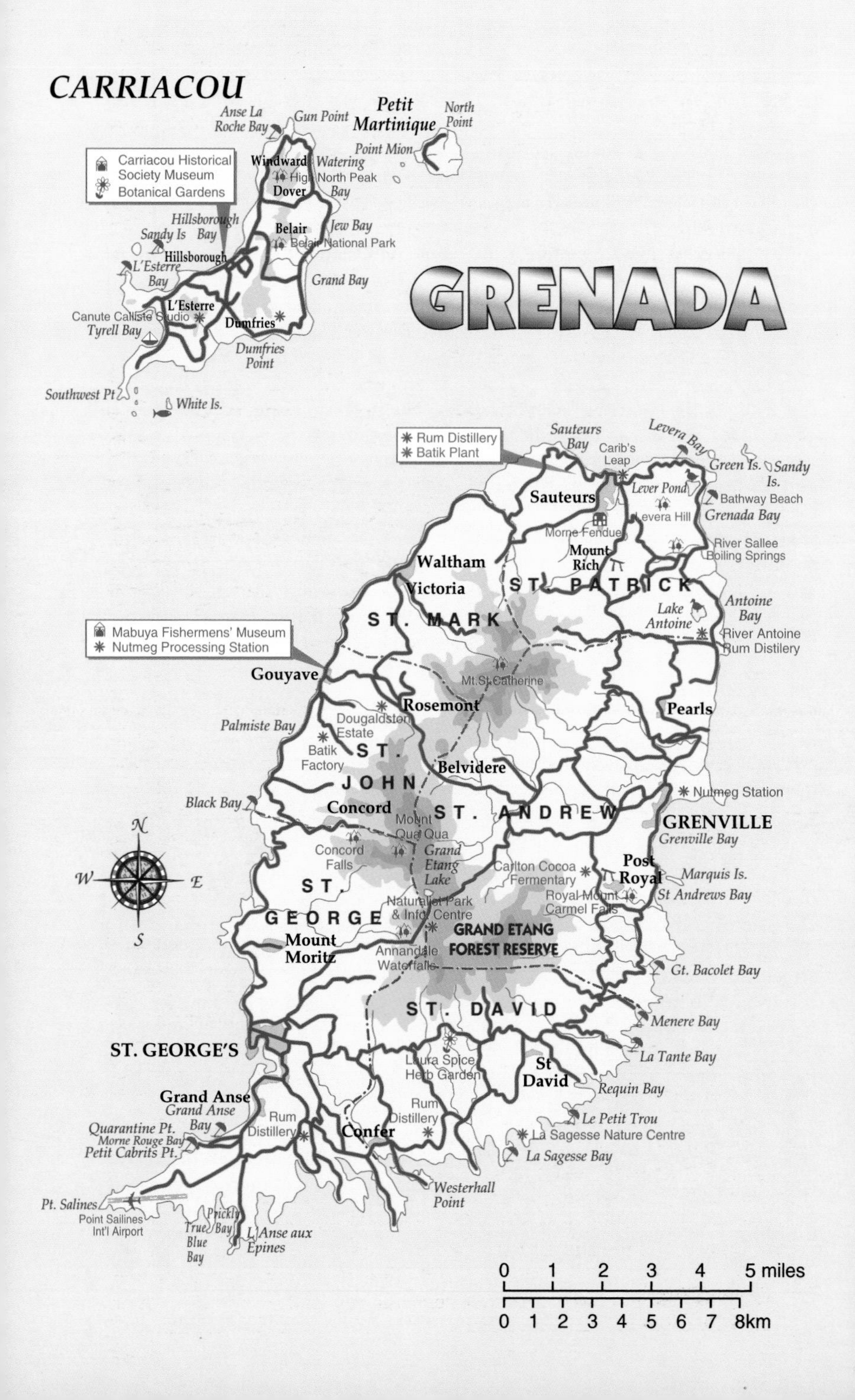
CARRIACOU
Anse La Roche Bay
Gun Point
Petit Martinique
North Point
Point Mion
Carriacou Historical Society Museum
Botanical Gardens
Windward
Watering
High North Peak
Dover
Bay
Hillsborough Bay
Sandy Is
Belair
Jew Bay
Belair National Park
Hillsborough
L'Esterre Bay
Grand Bay
L'Esterre
Canute Calliste Studio
Tyrell Bay
Dumfries
Dumfries Point
Southwest Pt
White Is.
GRENADA
Rum Distillery
Batik Plant
Sauteurs Bay
Carib's Leap
Levera Bay
Green Is.
Sandy Is.
Sauteurs
Lever Pond
Bathway Beach
Levera Hill
Grenada Bay
Morne Fendue
Mount Rich
River Sallee Boiling Springs
Waltham
Victoria
ST. PATRICK
Antoine Bay
Lake Antoine
River Antoine Rum Distilery
ST. MARK
Mabuya Fishermens' Museum
Nutmeg Processing Station
Gouyave
Mt.St.Catherine
Rosemont
Pearls
Palmiste Bay
Dougaldston Estate
Batik Factory
ST. JOHN
Belvidere
Black Bay
Nutmeg Station
Concord
Mount Qua Qua
ST. ANDREW
GRENVILLE
Grenville Bay
N
W
E
S
Concord Falls
Grand Etang Lake
Carlton Cocoa Fermentary
Post Royal
Marquis Is.
St Andrews Bay
ST. GEORGE
Naturalist Park & Info Centre
Royal Mount Carmel Falls
GRAND ETANG FOREST RESERVE
Mount Moritz
Annandale Waterfalls
Gt. Bacolet Bay
ST. DAVID
Menere Bay
ST. GEORGE'S
La Tante Bay
Laura Spice Herb Garden
St David
Requin Bay
Grand Anse
Grand Anse Bay
Rum Distillery
Rum Distillery
Le Petit Trou
Quarantine Pt.
Morne Rouge Bay
Petit Cabrits Pt.
Confer
La Sagesse Nature Centre
La Sagesse Bay
Westerhall Point
Pt. Salines
Point Salines Int'l Airport
Prickly Bay
True Blue Bay
L'Anse aux Epines
0 1 2 3 4 5 miles
0 1 2 3 4 5 6 7 8km

Above: Sunset paints a golden glow over the pretty harbour of St. George's.

British and French. A total of six forts were built by the French and British to protect the city and the sea approaches. Today, three of the forts remain — Fort George, built by the French between 1706 and 1710 to protect the harbour and the surrounding seas, and Fort Matthew and Fort Frederick on Richmond Hill which offer fabulous views over the city, harbour, surrounding countryside and sea beyond.

From the Carenage one can see across the harbour to the cruise ship berth on the left, and Fort George standing majestically on the hill overlooking the harbour entrance on the right. The harbour itself is usually busy with fishing boats and charter ships and at night the view is enchanting when the lights of the city twinkle reflected in the still harbour waters.

The 800ft (244m) pier has berths for two or three ocean-going vessels or cargo vessels up to 500ft (152m) in length, and there is a 250ft (76m) long schooner pier. There is usually at least one fabulous cruise ship in harbour, with others anchored offshore. The entrance to the harbour is protected by buoys and is 600ft (183m) wide and 45ft (14m) deep.

There are a number of restaurants along the Carenage, as well as tourist shops and outdoor stalls selling souvenirs, handicrafts and paintings by local artists. The offices of Grentel are about 900ft (274m) north-west of the tourist information centre and it is possible to telephone internationally from here using local telephone calling cards.

There are water-taxis and larger vessels offering both day time and evening cruises. The Treasure Queen and Rhum Runners are noted for their rum punches and lively music. As a reminder of the island's turbulent history, there is a burnt-out ship's hull protruding from the harbour — a victim of the US intervention in 1983.

A walk along the Carenage leads past the Ristorante Italia and Sand Pebbles Restaurants along the harbour past The Nutmeg Restaurant and Rudolf's Restaurant into Matthew Street with the **National Library** on the corner. The library was established in 1846 and has been housed in this former brick warehouse since 1892. The **Post Office** is further along the Carenage. Turn into Matthew Street to visit the **Antilles Hotel** and the **National Museum** which is located close to the junction with Young Street. The Antilles Hotel is one of the oldest buildings in St. George's and has been a French barracks, British prison, hotel and a warehouse. There are hopes that it one day become a hotel again. The small National Museum, built on the foundations of a former French army barracks and prison in 1704, has a fine collection of exhibits tracing the island's history and culture including with Arawak and Carib artifacts. It is open Monday to Friday 9am-4.30pm, Saturday 10am-4pm. Turn left into Young Street and right into Church Street which runs along the hill dividing the Carenage and Bay Town areas. It gets its name because along its length are the **Roman Catholic Cathedral** with its 1818 tower, the **St. George's Anglican Church** which was rebuilt in 1826 on the site of a building built by French Catholics, and **St. Andrew's Presbyterian Church** and **Knox House**, located before the climb up to Fort George.

The Georgian Anglican Church is noted for its stone and pink stucco, and its interesting plaques and statues. The Presbyterian Church was built with the help of the Freemasons between 1830 and 1831 and is also known as the Scots Kirk. Just beyond St. Andrew's, Church Street crosses over the Sendall Tunnel road which connects the Carenage and Bay Town areas of the city.

**Fort George** is a French bastioned fort which was later controlled by the British and extended. The original French fort was a wooden stockade built in 1650 and had two cannon to protect the settlement of Port Louis. The stone fort was built in 1706 to protect the new town when Port Louis was abandoned and Port Royale established. It is the oldest structure on the island, and although it commanded the sea approaches to the town, it remained vulnerable as it was overlooked by higher ground to the north. During the following years, additional fortifications were constructed in an attempt to rectify this. Today the fort offers spectacular views in all directions, and visitors can explore the tunnels, the interior, and walk along the battlements with its many cannon.

The fort did not see action until late in the eighteenth century, when on 4 July 1779 the French, invaded the island with 10,000 troops and captured the town. The British were taken completely by surprise because the French troops had landed a few miles along the coast and marched inland in order to attack St. George's and the fort from its unprotected flank. The British surrendered, and the French started work on a ring of forts to protect the town from an inland attack. Fort George was the scene of Grenada's assumption of independence on 7 February 1974, and on 13 March 1979, it was the last symbol of authority of the regime overthrown by the New Jewel Movement, who renamed it Fort Rubert. The fort was also the centre of the island's political turmoil, when on 19 October 1983 Maurice Bishop and ten members of his cabinet were executed by a faction of the People's

Revolutionary Government. It is now the headquarters of the Royal Grenada Police Force with barracks and training school, although it is open to the public. The hospital is near the crest of the hill in what used to be the fort's military barracks.

From the vantage point of the fort, there are scenic views of the city and the historic, red-tile roofed, brick eighteenth- and nineteenth-century warehouses. The tiles were brought to the islands as ballast on European trading ships.

Retrace your steps along Church Street past the Scots Kirk, and turn left after about 100ft (30m) and left again into Cross Street which leads to the Esplanade and the Bay Town area dominated by **Market Square**. The square is a blaze of colourful umbrella-shaded stalls bearing fruits, vegetables, spices and herbs of all descriptions, as well as handicrafts such as woven baskets, bamboo brooms, straw hats and bags. There are more stalls inside the tin-roofed market buildings. It is not only a place for buying and selling, but a gathering spot for people from around the island. Visitors can get a refreshing drink of coconut 'milk', drunk straight from a freshly-opened nut, or sample some of the island delicacies like a salt fish sandwich, or slices of fried black pudding. It is also a great place for buying many of the special products made from the island's spices, such as jellies, jams and sauces.

Market Square was opened in 1791 and was the site of the early slave market, and the scene of public executions. The square is still used for political meetings and rallies.

**Esplanade** used to be a quiet residential area overlooking the city, with delightful, tree-shaded walks and beaches. Today, it is a pick-up and drop-off point for the minibuses which ply around the island. There is a medical centre as well as a number of small shops and eateries.

After exploring the market and buying provisions and souvenirs, turn right on Grenville Street and then right again into St. Juille Street which meets Church Street. On the left is the old **Vicariate of the Roman Catholic Cathedral** which is further along on the right. The Vicariate, also referred to as **Norma Sinclair's House** was built between 1914 and 1918 and given to the Presentation Brothers in 1947 for use as a college. The cathedral's tower dates from 1818, although the present church was built in 1884 on the site of the original 1804 building. Follow Church Street south to **York House** which was named after the Duke of York's visit to the island in the eighteenth century. The building was purchased in 1801 and is now the home of the House of Representatives, the Senate and the Supreme Court. York House and the neighbouring Registry, built in 1780, are fine examples of early Georgian architecture. Note the buildings on the right with their sedan porches. The porches were open at both ends so that passengers in sedan chairs could get out in the dry when it was raining.

Continue down Church Street and take Simmons Alley which curves round St. George's Anglican Church, and follow the steps leading to Scott Street. Head north along Scott Street to the police traffic control point at the end, and then cross over into Lucas Street which leads to **Richmond Hill** and **Fort Frederick**.

The bastion fort was completed in 1791 and had the largest guns on the island, capable of firing 32lb (14kgm) shots. Towards the end of the nineteenth century, the fort's huge underground cisterns were utilised by the city to provide a water supply. It was the headquarters of the People's Revolutionary Army during the 1983

Above: The town of St. George's viewed from Fort Frederick.
Below: Cricket is played anywhere there is a space in the Windward Islands.

coup, and saw military action, the scars of which can still be seen. The fortifications have now largely been restored, and the views from the battlements are worth the walk.

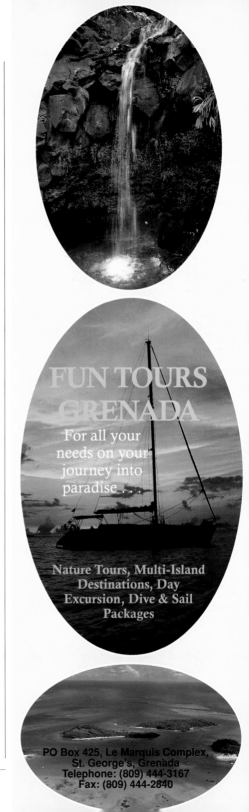

Although not open to the public, **Fort Matthew** can be viewed from Fort Frederick. It is a classic siege fort built by the French in 1779 with huge walls and nine protected gun chambers designed to withstand any attack. There were sixteen further gun positions which faced inland. The fort incorporated barracks, officers and married quarters, two huge cisterns for storing more than 80,000 gallons of water, a cobbler's shop, a parade ground and a kitchen garden. There was also a series of tunnels so that soldiers could move safely between barracks and gun emplacements if under attack. The whole structure was further protected by a deep dry moat.

In 1854 when the British withdrew their forces from the Caribbean, Fort Matthew became the Windward Island's first mental asylum, and it was used as such until in 1983 it was accidentally bombed and finally abandoned in 1987. In 1989 it was adopted by the Grenada National Trust and restoration plans are now well under way. The eighteenth-century kitchen was used until 1987 and has now been cleaned and the plaster removed, revealing the original arched brick ceiling. The central courtyard and some tunnels have also been cleared.

From Fort Frederick visitors can look down over the island's prison, formerly the fort's hospital, with its neat gardens tended by the inmates.

Retrace your route down Lucas Street and take the steps leading down to Green Street. Turn right past the **St. George's Methodist Church** — built in 1820, and the oldest original church building in the city — and turn sharp left into Herbert Blaye Street (formerly

Tyrrel Street and renamed in honour of the former Prime Minister) to visit **Marryshow House** on the corner of Herbert Blaye Street and Park Lane. It was the former home of T A Marryshow, who campaigned for one West Indian nation, and is known as the 'Father of the Federation'. It is now the local centre for the University of the West Indies. The Marryshow Folk Theatre stages a programme of concerts and plays. Further up the hill is **Government House** which was built in 1802 and is set in its own grounds behind large iron gates. Go back along Herbert Blaye Street for about 300ft (91m), before turning left for the short walk back to the Carenage and the tourist office.

Independence Day is 7 February, and the event is celebrated throughout the island, with church services and a parade in Queen's Park. The biggest event of the year, however, is Carnival, held on the second weekend of August. It is a hectic and fun-filled five days of dancing and revelry.

Other places to visit include **St. George's Cemetery** which is situated on the western outskirts of town on Old Fort Road, with its old and interesting graves. The **Botanical Gardens** which opened in 1887 are a five-minute drive east out of St. George's and house displays of many of the island's native plants and flower. **Bay Garden** is in the suburb of St. Paul's where paths lead through several acres of tropical gardens. There is a small admission fee, but it is worth it for the conducted tour which provides a fascinating insight into the island's main crops and spices. St. Paul's, is also home to the award-winning **De La Grenade Industries**, a spice-processing plant which produces jams, jellies, syrups, and liqueurs. It is open to visitors and tours are offered. Just north of the city is **Queen's Park**, the venue for all major sporting events, as well as parades and concerts.

The **Annandale Falls** are a fifteen minute drive north-east of St. George's on the road to Grand Etang, and worth visiting because of their location rather than the size of the cascade. The 30ft (9m) falls, surrounded by dasheen and vines, are in the hills south of **Grand Etang Lake** and surrounded by lush, tropical vegetation. The water flow drops substantially in the dry season, but the pool below the falls is inviting and there is a rest room with changing and washing facilities.

## Eating Out In and around St. George's

| | |
|---|---|
| Inexpensive | $ |
| Moderate | $$ |
| Expensive | $$$ |

**Bobby's Health Stop** $-$$
Gore Street, St. George's & Le Marquis complex
☎ 440-7080
Food for the health conscious

**Chef's Castle** $
Gore and Halifax Street, St. George's.
☎ 440-4778
Fast food

**De Water Hole** $
Opposite Botanical Gardens, St. George's
Local snacks and ice cream

**Deyna's** $-$$
Melville Street, St. George's
☎ 440-6795
West Indian cuisine

**Hole in the Wall** $$
Carenage, St. George's
☎ 440-3158
West Indian

**Judith's** $$
Gore Street, St. George's
☎ 440-5732
West Indian

**Kentucky Fried Chicken** $
Granby Street, St. George's
☎ 440-3821
Fast food

**Kwality Restaurant** $-$$
Corner Cross & Melville Streets, St. George's. ☎ 440-5206
West Indian and East Indian

**Le Bistro** $$-$$$
Ross Point.
☎ 444-0191
French/West Indian

**Little Bakery Coffee House** $-$$
Grand Anse Street, St. George's
☎ 444-3623
West Indian

**Mamma's** $$
Near Grenada Yacht Club
☎ 440-1459
West Indian. Reservations preferred.

**Nutmeg** $-$$
Carenage, St. George's — above the Sea Change Book Shop
☎ 440-2539
West Indian/international

**Portofino Ristorante Italia** $$
Carenage, St. George's
☎ 440-3986
Italian restaurant specialising in delicious pasta dishes. Excellent pizzas.

**Rudolf's** $$-$$$
Carenage, St. George's
☎ 440-2241
Fresh seafood is served in this relaxed restaurant with an English pub atmosphere. European and West Indian dishes also prepared using fresh, local produce.

**Sand Pebbles** $-$$
Carenage, St. George's
☎ 440-2688
West Indian/snacks

**Tropicana** $-$$
Lagoon Road, St. George's
☎ 440-1586
This restaurant overlooking the marina serves both local and Chinese cuisine.

St. George's is in the parish of St. George which covers the south-western corner of the island, and includes the splendid **Grand Anse Bay** — the main resort area with its world renowned, sandy beaches. There are fabulous views from vantage points across the sweeping vistas of sandy, near deserted beaches and warm, inviting seas.

Travelling south out of St. George's one drives past the Grenada Yacht Club towards Grand Anse Bay with a spectacular 2 mile (3km) long white sand beach. A coral reef at the mouth of the bay makes it ideal for safe swimming and snorkelling. Grand Anse has many large hotels, holiday cottages and apartments, as well as a number of restaurants and shopping complexes. The Old Sugar Mill Factory has been converted into a night club.

The road continues south past **Quarantine Point**, (where British troops with smallpox were hospitalised in the nineteenth century), to the south-western tip of the island, Point Salines and the international airport. The stretch of coastline between Petits Cabrits Point and Point Salines has some fabulous beaches, and the waters are excellent for diving. Visit the Portici ruins by the beach. **Point Salines** lighthouse stands on the tip of the headland and is the most westerly point on Grenada. Glover Island to the south was a Norwegian whaling station early in the twentieth century. There are a number of very pretty bays and headlands along this stretch of coastline, and there are some fine houses with magnificent views.

The luxury cruise liner *Bianca C* sank off Point Salines in 1961 and she is the largest of the wrecks scattered off Grenada's shores. The 600ft (183m) long, 18,000 ton cruise ship caught fire on 22 October 1961, and a huge explosion ripped through the engine room. Every boat in the harbour was

# THE HORSESHOE BEACH HOTEL

L'Anse aux Epines
P.O. Box 174
St. George's
Grenada
West Indies

Telephone: (809) 444-4410
Fax: (809) 444 4844

This elegant hotel is set amidst flowering tropical gardens and offers the ultimate in relaxation.
All rooms offer king-size beds, air-conditioning and private patio.
Twelve villas with one bedroom, six suites and four standard rooms make up this paradise overlooking the azure waters of Prickly Bay.
A romantic restaurant offers a nightly feast of West Indian delights and sumptuous international fare.

manned and all 400 passengers and 300 crew were rescued. Two days later the blazing liner was towed out of the harbour in an attempt to beach the ship on a reef close to the southern tip of the island, but the towing cable broke, and she sank almost immediately.

Yachts can dock at jetties in **True Blue Bay** and nearby **Prickly Bay**. There are two marinas at L'Anse aux Epines which offer yacht services and charters.

**Calivigny Point** was the site of the People's Revolutionary Army's main camp and saw a lot of military action when the US troops came ashore. Fort Jeudy used to stand sentinel over Egmont Harbour, although it has long since disappeared, and the area is now occupied by expensive homes.

The **parish of St. David** covers the south-eastern corner of the island and is the only parish on the island without a town of any size, although there are many villages in this predominantly agricultural area which produce sugar cane, cocoa, bananas, nutmeg and other spices.

This area has a beautiful coastline with scores of small bays and inlets, where one can escape from the crowds. The area is one of the few remaining habitats of the rare Grenada dove, and reserves have been established to protect it.

Shortly after crossing into the parish of St. David, on the southern main road, is the entrance of the **Westerhall Estate**, most famous for its rum distillery which has been distilling rum using traditional methods since 1800. The estate's massive old iron water-wheel was used to crush the sugar cane although it no longer operates. Westerhall produces a number of different blends of run ranging from the very smooth Westerhall Plantation Rum to Jack Iron, which is aged in oak barrels, and Westerhall Strong Rum, best sipped on its own to appreciate its full flavour and aroma.

**Westerhall Point** is now a private development with a number of fine homes, many with private beach fronts.

Continuing along the coast, one encounters **La Sagesse Nature Centre**. The centre occupies a house built by the late Lord Brownlow who was equerry to the Duke of Windsor when he abdicated from the British throne in 1936 to marry the American divorcee Mrs Simpson. The house and estate was bought by the Government in 1970. There is a restaurant beside the sandy **La Sagesse beach** and the opportunity for a dip in the shallow waters. There are hikes and nature walks around the woods and mangrove estuary which teems with birdlife. The rest of the estate has been divided into 5 acre (2 hectare) agricultural lots which are worked by experienced farmers as part of a Government-supported model farm experiment.

Off La Sagesse Point lies the wreck of the *SS Orinoco*, which foundered on the rocks on All Saints Day, 1 November 1900. It was the custom at that time on All Saints Day to light a candle on the graves of loved ones. The ship's captain erroneously thought the many lights were the lights of St. George's so turned towards them and hit the rocks.

From Content village, there is a short walk down to the charming **Le Petit Trou** beach. The road then continues uphill to **St. David's** where there is a small police station and a post office. Further along, there is a small road on the right leading to **Requin Bay**, which used to be a flourishing port shipping out cocoa and nutmeg. Most of the materials used in the construction of the small Catholic church on the cliffs were brought in by ships docking here. Inland, near Perdmontemps, visitors can enjoy the **Laura Spice and Herb Garden** (both of which are open daily), featuring displays the island's spices grown in their natural habitat.

## Eating Out In Grand Anse and Morne Rouge

**Bad Ass Cafe** $$
Le Marquis Complex
☎ 444-4020
Mexican

**Beach Side Terrace Restaurant** $$-$$$
Flamboyant Hotel, Grand Anse
☎ 444-4247
A relaxed and charming setting overlooking Grand Anse towards St. George's. Excellent international fare served daily and a Friday night barbecue featuring fresh lobster, fish, steak and chicken.

**Bird's Nest** $-$$
Grand Anse
☎ 444-4264
Chinese/creole

**Camerhogne Park Restaurant** $-$$
Morne Rouge
☎ 444-4587
Grenadian/Continental

**Canboulay** $$
Grand Anse
☎ 444-4401
The restaurant overlooks Grand Anse beach and serves a contemporary menu featuring fresh seafood, chicken, steak and vegetarian cuisine.

**Coconut's Beach** $$-$$$
Grand Anse Beach
☎ 444-4644
A unique dining experience where French/creole cuisine is served in an antique house situated on the beach. Guests may relax and sip an exotic cocktail while watching the golden sun set on the horizon.

**Cot Bam** $-$$
Grand Anse
☎ 444-2050
West Indian and international dishes .

**Coyaba** $$-$$$
Grand Anse Beach
☎ 444-4129
West Indian and international fare.

**Fish & Chick** $-$$
Old Sugar Mill, Grand Anse
☎ 444-4132
Fast food

**Green Flash Restaurant** $$
Siesta Hotel, Grand Anse
☎ 444-4645
International cuisine with a Middle Eastern flair. Alcoholic drinks are not sold here, but guests may bring their own beverages.

**Grenada Renaissance Terrace** $$-$$$
Grenada Renaissance Hotel, Grand Anse
☎ 444-4371
Elegant atmosphere with fabulous views of the Caribbean Sea. Excellent buffets serving international and creole cuisine.

**Hibiscus Hotel** $$
Morne Rouge
☎ 444-4008
Continental/creole

**Jade Garden** $$
Mace Hotel, Morne Rouge
☎ 444-3698
Chinese

**Joe's Steakhouse** $$
Le Marquis Centre, Grand Anse
☎ 444-4020
Local specialities include marinated steaks, spicy chicken and pork dishes, as well as a range of tasty soups and salads.

**La Belle Creole** $$-$$$
Blue Horizons Hotel, Morne Rouge.
☎ 444-4316
Gourmet dining in a friendly atmosphere. The fare includes lobster creole, cream of breadfruit soup and other delicious local cuisine.

**La Dolce Vita** $$
Cinnamon Hill Hotel, Grand Anse
☎ 444-4301
Excellent Italian cuisine including home-made pasta dishes of ravioli, penne and lasagne.

**La Sagesse Nature Centre** $-$$
La Sagesse Beach
☎ 444-6458
A romantic hideaway serving fresh seafood dishes of smoked marlin, fillet of grouper, lobster in garlic butter, grilled tuna and other mouthwatering delights.

**Lift-off** $-$$$
Point Salines Airport
☎ 444-4101
West Indian/international

**Nick's Donut World** $
Grand Anse
☎ 444-2460
Donuts and ice cream

**Parrots Cafe and Bar** $
Grand Anse
☎ 444-5083
Mexican

**Rick's Cafe** $
Grand Anse Shopping Plaza
☎ 444-4597
Fast food

**South Winds** $$-$$$
Grand Anse above South Winds Cottages
☎ 444-4310
West Indian and international cuisine specialising in seafood. Complimentary transportation can be arranged.

**Spice Island Inn** $$-$$$
Grand Anse
☎ 444-4258
West Indian cuisine with seafood as the main house speciality.

**Sur La Mer Restaurant and Aquarius Beach Pavilion** $$-$$$
Gem Holiday Resort
Morne Rouge
☎ 444-4224
Tranquil setting in an exquisite beachside setting. The restaurant enjoys a romantic location right on a white sandy beach and the kitchen services a delicious blend of French and creole seafood dishes. The twice-weekly buffet and barbecue are worth sampling, or simply enjoy a tropical cocktail at Happy Hour watching the magnificent sunsets.

**Tabanca at Journey's End** $-$$
Grand Anse
☎ 444-1300
Dine al fresco on a delicious gourmet meal of fresh local seafood or enjoy speciality cocktails in this friendly cafe.

**Windward Sands Inn** $$-$$$
Grand Anse
☎ 444-4238
International food

## In the South

**Aquarium Beach Club** $$-$$$
Point Salines
☎ 444-1410
Situated on the beach at Port Salinas, this rustic style restaurant serves fine international and seafood and freshly-produced salads. The Sunday lobster barbecue is well worth the visit.

**The Boatyard** $$-$$$
Prickly Bay, L'Anse aux Epines
☎ 444-4662
West Indian and international food is served in a lively atmosphere.

**Bolero** $$
L'Anse aux Epines
☎ 444-1250
A comfortable, friendly restaurant serving a variety of fresh pasta dishes, souvlaki or barbecued dishes.

**Choo Light** $-$$
L'Anse aux Epines
☎ 440-2196
Chinese

**Cicely's** $$-$$$
Calabash Hotel, L'Anse aux Epines
☎ 444-4234
An award-winning restaurant in the grounds of the Calabash Hotel. The fine food makes excellent use of the abundant local produce including fresh seafood served in a variety of delicious sauces.

**Conch Shell** $-$$
Point Salines
☎ 444-4178
West Indian/seafood

**Dr Groom's Cafe & Restaurant** $-$$
Close to Point Salines International Airport.
☎ 444-1979
Good Italian cuisine is served in this lively cafe close to the airport.

**Horse Shoe Beach Restaurant** $-$$
L'Anse aux Epines.
☎ 444-4410
Tasty West Indian and international specialities are served in this fine restaurant with pretty views over the gardens and bay.

**Indigo's** $$
True Blue Inn, True Blue
☎ 444-2000
The restaurant overlooks the tranquil setting of True Blue Bay and is a delightful setting for a fine meal of fresh seafood prepared with fresh local herbs and spices.

**International Restaurant** $$-$$$
Rex Grenadian, Point Salines
☎ 444-3333
A la carte cuisine or an excellent buffet is served in this elegant restaurant. Sample a wide variety of fine local dishes or enjoy freshly-prepared international cuisine served by friendly staff.

**Red Crab** $$-$$$
Near Calabash Hotel, L'Anse aux Epines
☎ 444-4424
Specialising in local seafood and international cuisine, this restaurant serves a varied and delicious menu throughout the year.

**Secret Harbour** $$-$$
Secret Harbour Hotel, L'Anse aux Epines
☎ 444-4439
West Indian and international dishes served in a picturesque setting.

**Villamar Restaurant** $-$$
L'Anse aux Epines
☎ 444-4847
Traditional West Indian dishes including callaloo soup, crab backs and tasty home-made icecream.

Opposite: The pretty church in Grenada's second city of Grenville.

## EAST COAST

The **parish of St. Andrew** has the longest coastline of all the parishes and a rich agricultural interior with many large estates producing cocoa, nutmeg and bananas, as well as other spices, fruits and vegetables, coconuts and flowers. It also boasts the Fleary's Teak Plantation and the Claboney Sulphur hot springs.

There are many roads off the highway to a number of secluded bays and coves including Galby Bay, La Tante Bay and Menere Bay each with fine beaches, Great Bacolet Bay and the sweeping St. Andrews Bay. Often the last part has to be tackled on foot, but there are usually well-worn paths to follow. La Tante beach is a short walk from the village, Menere beach is close to Mabot Village, and Babounot beach can be reached from the Hope Estate.

In **St. Andrews Bay** one can see **Marquis Island**. The village of Marquis is a small fishing community, although it is also noted for its crafts woven from pandanus grass including hats, bags and mats. The Marquis River runs to the bay from an area of hills known as Mount Carmel, where there are two waterfalls. The upper falls, the tallest in Grenada, are a fifteen-minute walk from the main road along a good path. They are properly known as the **Marquis Falls**, but are more often referred to as the **Royal Mount Carmel Waterfalls**. The lower falls are a little farther away and the walk to them along the river is more difficult. These falls are not as high but are much wider. Work on improving access and facilities for both falls is underway.

The remains of eighteenth-century fortifications can be seen at **Post Royal**, the scene of a battle during the rebellion. There are also remains of fortifications on top of **Pilot Hill**, just inland and to the south of Grenville and Battle Hill.

The main town of **Grenville** is affectionately known as Rainbow City by the locals and sits on a wide bay. There are a number of reefs just offshore which have prevented it from developing into a busier port and much of the produce grown locally is taken by road to St. George's for shipping. The French called the town La Baye, and this term is still used to describe the area in and around Grenville. It was once sited south of its present location, but was destroyed during the Fedon Rebellion in 1795 — the first town to be attacked during the island uprising.

The market is situated behind the court house and on Saturdays it is packed with local produce. There are beautiful displays of flowers for sale and locally-woven and plaited goods. The town is known for tasty local dishes.

A fund-raising campaign is underway to raise money to renovate the old Catholic church and convert it into a museum, library and art gallery.

Grenville has the island's largest **nutmeg station** which is open from Monday to Saturday during normal working hours. There is a small fee for admission and a tour conducted by knowledgeable guides who explain how the nutmegs are graded, separated into nutmeg and mace, dried, and sacked for shipment around the world. The old station provides the most incredible and heady aromas. Outside, there are several stalls and shops selling spices and products made from them which make good souvenirs.

The Grenville Carnival is held during the second week of August. It includes the 'Rainbow City Festival of Arts', which features local arts, crafts, entertainments, sporting events, competitions and concerts.

Just north of town is **Pearls**, the site of Grenada's first airport which was used from 1943 until the Point Salines opened in 1984. The runway is still littered with the debris which was scattered over it to prevent take-offs and landings at the time of the US invasion. Two burnt-out planes lie at the end of the runway.

The district has been declared an archaeological site of international importance because it was the site of one of the largest Arawak settlements in the Caribbean. Just inland from the airport is the old Dunfermline Sugar Factory, now a rum distillery. The area around Pearls is also known for its beaches, but the seas can be rough and sometimes treacherous.

At **Carlton Junction** which is open daily Monday to Saturday visitors can see how cocoa is processed. The Cocoa Fermentary buys cocoa from the farmers and prepares it for export. There are government agricultural research stations at **Boulogne** and **Mirabeau** which are both are open to the public and sell a wide range of plants and flowers. Boulogne is primarily a cocoa propagating station and plant nursery, and Mirabeau researches economic plants and vegetable pest control.

## Eating Out on the East Coast

**Bain's** $-$$
Grenville
☎ 442-7337
West Indian/international/seafood

**Ebony** $-$$
Victoria Street
Grenville
☎ 442-7311
West Indian

**Sam's Inn** $$
Grenville
☎ 442-7853
Grenadian specialities

## The North Coast

The northern tip of the island is in the agricultural **parish of St. Patrick**, with old estates and fine homes, many of which have been carefully restored.

The tour follows the main road to Tivoli from where you turn right for the coast, Easter Antoine and the **River Antoine Rum Distillery** — the oldest in the Caribbean. It is open daily for visits and tastings. The 500 acre (200 hectare) **Antoine Estate** with 1.5 miles (2km) of coastline, was purchased by its French owner in 1785 for the equivalent of £200 sterling. It includes what the locals still call Conception Beach, although it is today part of Antoine Bay, which is reputed to be the first strip of Grenadian coastline spotted by Columbus. The estate has now been bought by a consortium of local businessmen, and is being restored. The rum distillery cannot keep pace with demand for its product, which claims to be the strongest rum made on the island.

The road continues north alongside Antoine Bay, with Lake Antoine inland. Three miles (5km) of man-made canals were constructed to carry water from the lake to the working Antoine distillery water wheel. The water is held in a reservoir overnight to build up the pressure and when released it drives the 125-year-old 30ft (9m) diameter water wheel built by Geo. Fletcher & Co at the Masson Works in Derby, England. Up to 3,000 gallons (13,500 litres) of juice are handled every day, mostly from cane produced on the estate. The pulp left after crushing is then used to fire the boilers beneath the copper stills which distil the juice into rum — a system which has not changed since 1785. The estate also grows coconuts, citrus, avocados, bananas and lime.

**Lake Antoine** is the flooded crater

Above: Lake Antoine is the flooded crater of an extinct volcano.
Below: Lake Antoine information board (*left*). Stream close to Lake Antoine (*right*).

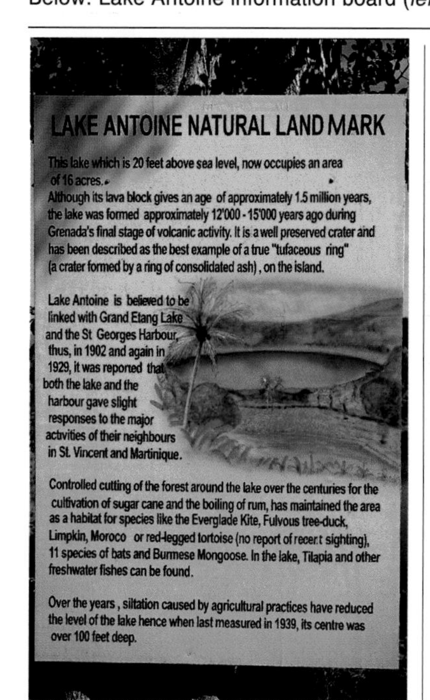

LAKE ANTOINE NATURAL LAND MARK
This lake which is 20 feet above sea level, now occupies an area of 16 acres.
Although its lava block gives an age of approximately 1.5 million years, the lake was formed approximately 12'000 - 15'000 years ago during Grenada's final stage of volcanic activity. It is a well preserved crater and has been described as the best example of a true "tufaceous ring" (a crater formed by a ring of consolidated ash), on the island.
Lake Antoine is believed to be linked with Grand Etang Lake and the St Georges Harbour, thus, in 1902 and again in 1929, it was reported that both the lake and the harbour gave slight responses to the major activities of their neighbours in St. Vincent and Martinique.
Controlled cutting of the forest around the lake over the centuries for the cultivation of sugar cane and the boiling of rum, has maintained the area as a habitat for species like the Everglade Kite, Fulvous tree-duck, Limpkin, Moroco or red-legged tortoise (no report of recent sighting), 11 species of bats and Burmese Mongoose. In the lake, Tilapia and other freshwater fishes can be found.
Over the years, siltation caused by agricultural practices have reduced the level of the lake hence when last measured in 1939, its centre was over 100 feet deep.

Above: The River Antoine Rum Distillery is the oldest in the Caribbean.

of an extinct volcano, and another rewarding bird watching area. Many species nest around the lake.

The road then turns inland for a short distance to the **River Sallee Boiling Springs**. The sulphur springs are believed by the locals to have healing properties, and candles are often lit and placed around the pools.

From here visitors can either cut across country to Sauteurs, via Mount Rose where the remains of an old windmill on a knoll have largely been overgrown by vines, or follow the coast round Grenada Bay to Bedford Point on the north-eastern tip of the island. From here one can look out to **Sugar Loaf Island, Green Island** and **Sandy Island** which lie in an arc running from north-west to south-east just offshore. The islands have a large bird population but are privately-owned and cannot be visited. The road then runs west along the coast past **Levera Pond** on the left with **Levera Hill** 2,781ft (848m) beyond. Levera Beach is an ideal place for picnics and is popular with the locals at weekends and public holidays. Much of the beach and the area inland is now a national park. The information centre has details on the area and guides can be arranged to accompany local walks. About 200 years ago there used to be a jetty into the bay which was used to load produce from local estates onto ships, and a fort was built on **Bedford Point** to protect it. The remains of the fort can still be seen, and there are fabulous views from the headland out to sea.

There is a safe beach at nearby Bathway, with huge rock pools, and a reef which acts as a buffer and reduces the power of the Atlantic rollers. Nearby is the Levera Development, where a number of large modern homes have been built. Also nearby is a small cottage industry producing corn straw dolls and visitors are welcome.

The main town of **Sauteurs** takes its name from an heroic incident in the seventeenth century. The French occupied the island but were still fighting the Caribs for control of it. The Caribs were chased by French soldiers until they were cornered on top of the cliffs overlooking what is now Sauteurs Bay. Rather than be captured, about forty Caribs leapt over the cliffs to their deaths in the rocky waters 100ft (30m) below. The town that grew in the area became known as Bourg des Sauteurs — the Town of the Leapers.

Walk up the hill past the St. Patrick's Catholic School, and through the cemetery to the spot where the Caribs jumped to their deaths. For anyone not afraid of heights, one can carefully look over the edge at **Carib's Leap** and see just how far down it is. Next to the church, which dominates the town, is a small candle factory, and the wax is melted in open fires outside before being carried inside and poured into the moulds. Although there are no official opening times, visitors are welcome during the day from Monday to Saturday, and there is usually someone on hand to show you around. There is also a small batik plant in the town which is worth a visit for its colourful designs for dresses, scarves, cushions and bags.

Even at the beginning of the twentieth century, the only way to reach the capital from Sauteurs was by boat. A jetty used to run into the bay and from it, produce would be loaded onto ships bound for St. George's. The main form of transport at the time was by horse or horse and carriage, and one can still see the tethering rings in the walls of the Anglican Church where the animals were tied while their owners worshipped inside. There are also steps which were built in various places around town to help people get into and out of their carriages. Around this time, a wealthy citizen built a drinking fountain and horse trough so that both riders and animals could get a drink. The fountain is still standing, although it is no longer in use.

In March the town celebrates the Feast of Saint Patrick, now part of the St. Patrick's Day Fiesta, which actually lasts for two weeks. There are displays of arts and crafts, bands, steel bands, calypso, agricultural stands and lots of food. The fiesta attracts visitors from all over the island and is a great occasion.

Just over one mile (2km) south of Sauteur on the Hermitage Road, Amerindian petroglyphs have been found on stones beside St. Patrick's River in the village of **Mount Rich**. The locals have planted flowers near the entrance which is signposted. The carvings show various aspects of the Carib's daily life.

Two old plantation houses have been opened to the public serving lunches and dinners to tourists, but reservations are essential as they are both very popular. **Morne Fendue** is a wonderful stone house built between 1908 and 1912. The mortar used was a mixture of molasses and limestone. It is located within exquisite gardens and one can enjoy an excellent traditional buffet lunch in either the charming old dining room, or outside on the verandah. The house has been in the same family for many generations, and the present owner Betty Mascoll MBE, born in England in 1912, still oversees the cooking.

**Mount Rodney** is another old family home which was built in the 1870s. It has the island's typical fret-worked eaves, and offers tremendous views over the surrounding country-side. The house was recently opened to the public after fifteen years of pain-staking restoration work.

There is a huge subterranean volcano about 7 miles (11km) off the north coast, and the waters over the crater are so turbulent, that boats rock when they pass. This is perhaps why the volcano has the local name of 'Kick 'em Jenny'.

## Eating Out on the North Coast

**Morne Fendue Plantation House** $-$$
☎ 442-9330
West Indian

**Mount Rodney Estate** $-$$
☎ 442-9420
International cuisine served in a delightful restored colonial-style house.

## The West Coast

The **parish of St. Mark** runs down the north-west coast, and most people are engaged in fishing or working on the surrounding estates. It is the smallest of Grenada's parishes and includes Mount St. Catherine, which rises to 2,757ft (840m) and is the island's highest point. From its summit all the island's parishes can be seen, but the climb is steep and only experienced climbers should undertake it with a local guide.

All Grenada's volcanoes are extinct, but hot mineral springs can be found in many parts of the island, one of which is on the slopes of **Mount St. Catherine**, above the Tufton Hall Estate. A forest reserve now covers much of the area occupied by the central hills around Mount St. Catherine.

**Victoria** is the main 'town' of the area, which the French called Grand Pauvre (great poverty) when they were in occupation. Today, the locals often refer to it as 'sunset city', because the sunsets from the beach are so spectacular. It is a large fishing village with a number of old buildings and shacks. The historic and comfortable small, twelve-room Victoria Hotel is the only one on the north-western coast.

Every year, the parish celebrates St. Mark's Day with a fiesta at the end of April where local arts and crafts are displayed and various competitions are held. The annual harvest festival takes place every Whit Monday. At the end of June, the parish celebrates the Fisherman's Birthday, the Feast of St. Peter and St. Paul. Every year the small village of **Waltham**, about one mile (2km) north of Victoria, has the privilege of starting the celebrations, with priests blessing the fishermen, their boats and nets.

## Eating Out on the West Coast

**Patnoe Enterprises** $
Depradine St. Gouyave
☎ 444-8415
Ice cream and fast food

Close to Victoria and lying beside the road on the beach, there is a huge boulder with Carib markings and decorations which are clearly visible. **Gouyave** is the main town in the **parish of St. John**, and one can take the rather bumpy road up into the hills to the **Belvidere Estate**, where almost every plant and crop grown on the island can be seen. The first nutmeg to be grown on the island were also planted here. The **Dougaldston Estate** in the hills, can also be visited and one can visit the sheds where spices are processed and prepared for shipping. One can learn all about clove, cocoa, calabash, nutmeg, coffee and cocoa from informed guides who will also explain how each of the spices are handled. While they do not ask for any payment, it is customary to give them a small tip for their time and trouble.

The British tried to rename

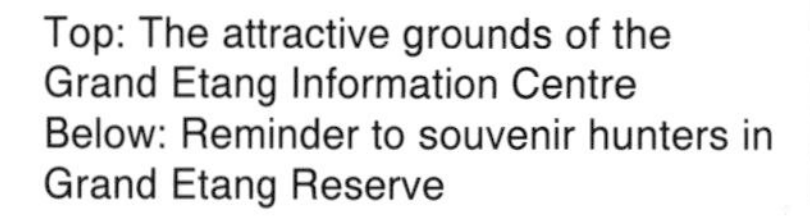

Top: The attractive grounds of the Grand Etang Information Centre
Below: Reminder to souvenir hunters in Grand Etang Reserve

Top: The sparkling Concord Falls at sundown.
Below: Youngsters enjoy a cooling dip at the end of a school day.

# The Calabash Hotel

The Calabash Hotel enjoys an enchanting, secluded bay setting on the verdant Caribbean island of Grenada. Intimate, private and relaxing, it offers suite accommodation, gourmet cuisine and high standards of personal service.

Choose between spacious whirlpool suites or romantic pool suites. All with balconies or patios for enjoying views of the flower-filled gardens and Caribbean Sea.

Breakfasts are served on your own private balcony by one of our friendly, attentive staff. Lunch may be a casual beachside affair — a prelude to the magnificent finale of a glorious day . . . a gourmet dinner in the candlelit restaurant.

Spend heady days relaxing on the powdery white sands of the beach with the warm waters of the sheltered bay lapping gently at your feet. A secluded freshwater pool, floodlit tennis court and gym are also available.

The Calabash Hotel,
PO Box 382, St. George's,
Grenada, West Indies
Telephone: (809) 444 4334
Fax: (809) 444 5050

Gouyave, Charlotte Town and both names appear on old maps. It has a nutmeg processing station and the town is the centre of a major fishing area, especially for yellow fin tuna which can weigh up to 160lb (72kg) and more. It has cold storage facilities and much of the catch is shipped to the United States. Each night the brightly-coloured fishing boats are pulled up on to the beach, known as the Lance, which is just north of the town.

It is worth visiting the nutmeg processing station in town where the nutmeg and mace are graded, separated, dried and sacked for shipping. There is a US$1 admission charge and guides, who should be tipped at the end of the tour, are on hand to show visitors round and explain the various processes. Afterwards, one can enjoy local cooking at one of Gouyave's eateries.

Just outside the village there is the small Mabuya Fishermens' Museum. There are no official opening hours but it is usually accessible from Monday to Saturday during the day. Continue south along the coast road to **Palmiste** where there is a New Life Organisation's Vocational Skills Training Centre. The project is run by four of Grenada's churches and teaches trades and skills to 16-23 year olds. The trainee carpenters and bricklayers have utilized these skills by helping expand the centre by building more classrooms and furniture. There is a small craft shop which sells items made at the centre. Behind the centre on a hillside, there is an artificial lake which makes a charming picnic spot.

There is a road which runs inland to **Mount Nesbit** and a small batik factory run by Thomas Sylvester. He creates the designs and his team, who he trained personally, produce them on beach wraps, scarves, bags and other products. Every design is drawn by hand making each item produced unique and collectable.

Further south the coast road runs through Grand Roy and Marigot and then there is another inland road which leads to **Concord Falls**. There are actually three falls in the series. The nearest, which can be reached by road, has changing rooms, washrooms and a small bar which serves drinks and light snacks. Visitors can swim in the pool at the foot of the falls. There are a number of stalls close to the falls selling souvenirs and local arts and crafts. The other two falls in the series are accessible via a forty-five-minute scramble along the river bank, but as the river has now been damned to provide clean drinking water, bathing in the Upper Falls is illegal. The third fall is the most spectacular with a 65ft (20m) cascade.

From the falls one can also continue inland for the fairly strenuous climb up to **Fedon's Camp** at 2,509ft (765m), and the volcanic **Mount Qua Qua**, part of the Belvidere Mountain Range. Julien Fedon, a Grenadian of Afro-French descent who owned the Belvidere Estate, made his headquarters here during the two-year uprising. Mount Qua Qua can also be reached by a trail which continues on to the Grand Etang, and from the summit at 2,300ft (701m) there are unsurpassed views of Crater Lake.

By returning to the coast road one can look or drive down to **Black Bay** which gets its name from its black, fine sand. There is an old water wheel beside the road leading down to the beach which was once used to crush the juice out of sugar cane. Beside the main road out of Concord, there is a memorial to a fatal accident on 16 January 1991, when a sixty ton boulder crashed down on a school bus, killing eight children and the driver. The boulder was so large that there was no lifting gear on the island capable of moving it and it finally had to be blasted apart.

The Fisherman's Birthday is the main event of the parish and takes place on 29 June. The fishermen, their boats and nets are blessed by local clergy, and the rest of the day is spent with boat races and other entertainments. Stalls selling food and drink are erected along the streets and the celebrations continue well into the night.

## The Interior

The best way of exploring the spectacular interior is to drive from St. George's north-east through the Grand Etang Forest Reserve, and then get out and walk one of the main hiking trails. Guides are available for visitors wanting to get the most out of their visit.

**Grand Etang Lake** was formed about 12,000 years ago, and is 1,740ft (530m) above sea level. The lake is surrounded by forest, and the nearby **Grand Etang Forest Centre** has information about the area's wildlife, forestry and vegetation, as well as the region's history and culture. Look out for monkeys, hummingbirds and shuffling armadillos which all live in the area. A dam has been built on the lake's outlet stream which has raised the level to supplement water supplies during the four driest months of the year. The **Annandale Waterfalls** are reached by the Beaulieu Valley, and are on the outskirts of Willis, about fifteen minutes drive from St. George's. The Concord trail leads to Mount Qua Qua, and the summit and if not shrouded in clouds, offers spectacular views of the surrounding area. A detour off the Concord trail leads to Fedon's Camp. Other walks from the forest centre include the easy, but interesting, Morne La Baye trail which although it takes only fifteen to twenty minutes, provides the opportunity to see much of the area's flora.

### The Grenadines

An arbitrary line drawn through the Grenadines as part of the Treaty of Versailles, determines the islands' sovereignty. The islands south of the line gives Grenada administrative responsibility for and sovereignty of Carriacou and Petit Martinique.

## Carriacou

### Getting There

There is a regular schooner service from Grenada which takes 3.5 to 4 hours, and day trips can be arranged to visit some of the offshore islands. Boats leave the Carenage for Carriacou on Tuesday, Wednesday, Friday and Sunday mornings and on Saturday and Sunday evenings, but times vary so it is advisable to check in advance. The fare is EC$20 for a single ticket and EC$30 for a return (EC$35 at weekends). Boats leave Hillsborough on Monday, Wednesday, Thursday and Saturday mornings and on Sunday at 5pm, but again, always check sailing times.

There are daily flights into the island's Lauriston Airport, with its 2,700ft (823m) long airstrip. The flight takes twenty minutes from Grenada.

Getting Around: There are many roads and hiking trails and minibuses run from Hillsborough to Bogles, Windward and Tyrrel Bays. The fare is EC$2 and taxis are also available.

Carriacou lies to the north, north-west of Grenada and covers an area of 13 sq miles (34 sq km). With a population of approximately 7,000, it is the most populated island of the Grenadines. It is believed that its name is derived from the Carib for 'land of reefs', and in the seventeenth and eighteenth centuries was spelt *Kayryouacou*. Many of the other islands in the chain are no more than islets or uninhabited rocks. Isle de Rhonde, however, about 8 miles (13km) north-east of Grenada, has a small resident community. The Grenadines are especially popular with yachtsmen because of the good year-round sailing weather and safe anchorages.

Carriacou was formed as a result of a volcanic eruption around twenty-six million years ago. Two thirds of the island is of volcanic origin, and one third fossil-bearing limestone. The vegetation is determined by the season and the amount of water available. In times of drought, especially during the first six months of the year, dry scrub and cactus predominate. There are large areas of scrub on the western side of the island, while the eastern beaches are fringed with coconut palms, manchineel and sea grape. There are well-established mangrove swamps at Petit Carenage Bay on the north coast, and this area also teems with birdlife. The most common tree on the island is the gumbo limbo, with its reddish bark. Both the dogwood and white immortelle are found on Carriacou but not on Grenada. Many species of cacti, tamarind, bougainvillea and flamboyant abound, as well as, coconut, almonds, sugar apple, limes and papaya.

The French were the first European settlers, and in 1750 when the island's first census was carried out, Carriacou had a population of 199. This statistic was made up of 92 whites, 92 'negroes' and 15 'mulattoes'; but by 1776 this had rocketed to 86 whites and 3,153 slaves on the forty-seven estates.

The Scots settled Dumfries on the south-eastern coast, which was until recently the site of a lime juice factory. The pressing plant was built in the early nineteenth century, and there are hopes it may be restored for its historical and architectural value — particularly its elaborate brickwork.

Carriacou has more than 80 miles (129km) of reasonable roads — a legacy from the French, who built them to enable easy movement of artillery around the island during their frequent hostilities with the British. Rapid Point on the northern tip of the island, is known locally as Gun Point because of the ordnance that used to be sited there. The fort overlooking the main town of Hillsborough, has been converted into a waterworks and the cannon that used to be sited there are now displayed on Hospital Hill which affords superb views out to sea.

A reef runs down much of the eastern shoreline, taking the brunt of the Atlantic breakers, and the sheltered waters between the reef and coast offer excellent anchorage, especially in Watering Bay, Jew Bay and Grand Bay. Tyrell Bay is the most popular anchorage along the western coast.

Windward on Watering Bay has a long boat building tradition and was founded by descendants of Glaswegian shipwrights who arrived in the nineteenth century. The skill of the shipbuilders is all the more impressive when one considers there were no power tools available, and almost all the work was carried out using axe, adze and drill and bit.

Most of the islanders, including the Scottish descendants, can trace their lineage back through many generations and those of African descent can trace their ancestry back to the African tribes from which they came. The 1750 census actually listed the slave's name followed by their African tribe.

Dancing is an important part of the

island's way of life, and many of the dances performed have changed little since they were first danced as part of tribal traditions and rituals in West Africa. As the descendants of the early slaves can still trace their ancestry back to their West African tribes, so the dances can still be identified as belonging to the Ibos, Moko, Hausam Chamba, Banda, Temne, and Arradah.

The most important dance is the Kromantin, which is a tribal dance from Ghana. Its other name is Chief Beg Pardon Dance, and it traditionally starts and ends most celebrations. The Big Drum Dance, or African Nation Dance, is a traditional West African dance performed on all special occasions, and it has also been adapted as a tourist entertainment. The drumbeat, singing and dancing at night helped the slaves overcome the tremendous hardship they endured daily. The drum was the symbol of the eternal spirit, which is why the missionaries, plantation owners and colonial officers tried so hard to ban it. The drums were traditionally carved from wood, but on Carriacou, it was not unusual to improvise using an old rum barrel with a goat skin stretched taut over the mouth. An example of this type of drum is in the Carriacou Museum. A cassette of drum music makes a memorable souvenir. Other dances have been adapted from old creole including the Bele dances, the Bongo and the Kalinder. Some have also been copied from European dances such as the Quadrille which was popular in England and France during the eighteenth century.

Carnival is held in February immediately before the start of Lent. Originally a two-day festival, it now lasts for at least a week and includes a costume and children's parade, election of the Carnival Queen,

Calypso King and the King and Queen of the Bands. It is a time for music, dancing and celebration, and even the most dance shy will find it difficult to resist the foot-tapping rhythms of the steel bands.

Maypole dancing is another old tradition that has survived on Carriacou, and each May Day schoolchildren dance round the pole plaiting the multi-coloured ribbons attached to it. Hillsborough plays host to an annual two-day regatta which starts on Caricom Day, the first Monday of August.

The Parang Festival is held just before Christmas and is another occasion for song, music and dance with street stalls offering a wide range of tasty foods and drinks.

After someone dies, the Tombstone ceremony takes place. It is believed that the spirit is not finally laid to rest until the tombstone is placed on the grave, whether this takes a few days or several years. All the relatives and friends of the dead person are invited to contribute to the tombstone. While the grave is prepared to receive the tombstone, the tombstone itself is placed overnight in the bed of the deceased so that relatives can speak to the dead person through it. The following day, amid much feasting, the tombstone is installed on the grave. This is a time of great celebration because the dead person's spirit is now at rest, and the festival is accompanied by singing, dancing and drumming.

Fishing and agriculture have been the island's mainstays, but tourism is now an important and growing income earner. There are more than a dozen locally-built sloops which fish daily from Carriacou and Petit Martinique, although most of the catch is sold to buyers from Martinique. A Government-built ice plant at Windward provides ice and fish storage facilities for the fishermen. Tree oysters, which grow on mangroves in the lagoon at Tyrrel Bay, and spiny lobsters caught offshore are local delicacies.

The *Carriacou Islander*, a 35ft (11m) motor powered catamaran, has a huge observation window in the hull which allows close up viewing of the coral reefs and fish around Carriacou and Petit Martinique. Saline and White Islands, just south of Carriacou, have the best reefs, while those near Sandy and Mabouya Islands off the west coast, are also spectacular.

## A Tour of Carriacou

**Hillsborough** is the main town, and Main Street runs parallel to the coast. It has shops, restaurants, banks, post office and a tourist information bureau. Monday is market day although there are some stalls open every day. The small **Botanical Gardens** has displays of tropical plants, flowers and trees, and the little museum in Paterson Street, run by the Carriacou Historical Society, has Amerindian and African artifacts as well as exhibits tracing the early British and French occupation of the islands. It is housed in a restored cotton gin mill and open Monday to Friday 9.30am-4.30pm and from 10am-4pm on Saturday. The airstrip is just to the south-west of the town, and overlooking the town is Hospital Hill with its disused cannon.

**Sandy Island** which lies due west in Hillsborough Bay is famous for its beauty, palm-fringed white, sandy beaches, clear blue waters and stunning coral reefs. It is a favourite anchorage for yachts and a popular diving and snorkelling site. The island is so pretty that it has often been featured as a backdrop for television advertisements.

At **L'Esterre**, one can visit the studio

of Canute Calliste, the island's most famous artist.

**Tyrell Bay** is south of L'Esterre and is a popular anchorage for yachts, as well as being famous for its boat-building, craft work, and the oyster beds among the mangrove swamps which can be visited by boats. The mineral waters at Amerindian Well, Harvey Vale, are reputed to have health giving qualities.

At **La Pointe** on the south-western tip, there are superb views of the ruins of an old French plantation house. The road then runs round the south coast past **Manchineel Bay** affording good views of White Island and Saline Island in the bay. **White Island** is a marine park because of its virgin reef and shoals of colourful tropical fish. The white sandy beaches make an ideal picnic spot and the surrounding waters are excellent for scuba diving and other watersports. **Dumfries** on the south-eastern coast of the island was one of the earliest settlements and has been declared an historical area exhibiting 200 years of history, including life on a plantation.

The road up the east coast runs past Grand Bay, Jew Bay to Point St. Hilaire. It then runs around Watering Bay passing close to Dover Ruins, the site of the first church on the island. The village of **Windward** is famous for its boat building and from here one can take the twenty-minute boat ride to visit Petit Martinique.

The road curves round the northern tip of the island at **Gun Point** and then back to Hillsborough along the west coast through **Anse La Roche**, the most scenic beach on the island with coral reefs just offshore. The beach which lies at the foot of the famous High North Range is secluded and unspoiled. **High North Peak**, at 955ft (291m), is the highest point on the island and is protected as a national park.

Continue south to the **Belair National Park** which offers fabulous views over the north of the island and beyond to Petit Martinique. **Belair** has old French and English ruins and there is an old sugar windmill. During the People's Revolutionary Government the area was used as an army camp. There are also superb views from Top Hill 775ft (236m), and from here it is a short run back into Hillsborough.

Other sights worth seeing include the **Anglican Rectory Garden** — once a Bousejour Great House — which is steeped in history and the **Ningo Well** which was the first well built on the island.

## Accommodation

There are two hotels on the island, the Caribbee Inn at Prospect, and the Silver Beach Resort at Hillsborough. A number of small guest houses, as well as villas and apartments can be rented.

There is excellent fish and shellfish available on the island and many traditional dishes to enjoy. Rum is, naturally, the island drink — especially Jack Iron which is distilled to a higher alcohol level than normal — and it makes a good souvenir.

## Eating Out On Carriacou

**Al's Snack Bar** $-$$
Tyrrel Bay
☎ 443-7179
West Indian cuisine

**Ali's Restaurant and Bar** $$
L'Esterre Bay
☎ 443-8406
West Indian cuisine

**Callaloo Restaurant and Bar** $$
Main Street, Hillsborough
☎ 443-8004
A quaint restaurant specialising in tasty seafood and local dishes.

**Kayak** $-$$
Hillsborough
☎ 443-8446
West Indian/creole

**The Pepperpot** $$
Caribbee Inn at Prospect
☎ 443-7380
The Caribbee Inn serves delightful creole cuisine with a definite hint of French influence. Situated in a charming old-world atmosphere with fine views along the coast. The hosts have created a fine blend of fresh home cooking which is an exquisite not-to-be missed experience.

**Poivre et Sel** $-$$$
Tyrrel Bay
☎ 443-8390
French

**Roof Garden** $$
Hillsborough
☎ 443-7204
West Indian

**Scraper's** $$
Tyrrel Bay
☎ 443-7403
seafood

**Silver Beach Resort** $$-$$$
Hillsborough
☎ 443-7337
The restaurant is situated on the water's edge and specialises in delicious Caribbean cuisine. The emphasis here is on fresh seafood, including lobster in season and fresh local vegetables and spices. The resort offers free hook-up to the dinghy dock and pick-up for visiting yachts in Tyrrel Bay.

**Talk of the Town** $$-$$$
Main Street, Hillsborough
☎ 443-7118
West Indian. Reservations necessary.

**What's the Scoop/Gramma'a Bakery** $
Patterson and Main Streets
Hillsborough
☎ 443-7256
Ice cream parlour and bakery

## Petit Martinique

The island can be reached by boat from Hillsborough. The crossing takes about twenty minutes.

About 900 people live on the island which covers 486 acres, (194 hectares) and is 3 miles (5km) east of the northern part of Carriacou. The island is really a large hill with some fine beaches on the western, leeward side. Like Carriacou, Petit Martinique was first settled by the French and many islanders have names of French origin.

The island also has a colourful history and long sea-going tradition. In the past, fishermen sold their catches in the free port of St. Marten and used the money to purchase duty-free goods which they brought home. This was never considered smuggling as there were no customs officers based on the island to pay duty to. Fishing and boat building are still the main occupations. Some corn and peas are grown and goats and sheep graze freely over the hills. Everything else has to be imported.

Although the island has electricity and telephones, the lack of rivers makes water a valuable resource, and all homes have a storage tank to collect rainwater running off the roof. Many of the island's roads are paved, although they mostly run along the western side of the island. There is a a post office, a school and a small Catholic Church. Other denominations usually hold outdoor services.

Cricket is hugely popular and the women's team regularly play against teams from the other Grenadine islands.

The island has its own Carnival, which is held during the two days before Lent. At Easter a two-day regatta is hosted which includes donkey races and the famous greasy pole competition.

# Grenada Fact File

## Accommodation

Price indications for hotels are usually the rates for single and double occupancy. Prices, unless clearly stated, do not usually include the eight per cent value added tax and ten per cent service charge.

$ Inexpensive accommodation
$$ Moderate
$$$ Luxury

**Blue Horizons Cottage Hotel** $-$$
Grand Anse
☎ 444-4316
32 rooms with kitchenettes, television, private patios, restaurant, bars, pool, jacuzzi, watersports and meeting room.

**Calabash Hotel** $$$
Prickly Bay, L'Anse aux Epines
☎ 444-4334
Situated in eight acres of tropical grounds in a delightful beach setting, the hotel has thirty suites, eight of which have private pools and twenty-two have whirlpools. Fine service and friendly staff ensure a rewarding stay. Excellent restaurant, bar, beach, pool, watersports, beach bar, fitness centre and conference facilities.

**Camerhogne Park Hotel** $
Grand Anse
☎ 444-4110
Twenty-five rooms with television and telephone. Restaurant, bar.

**Cedars Inn** $
True Blue
☎ 444-4641
A new hotel located in tropical gardens. Twenty rooms with television and telephone. Restaurant, bar, pool.

**Cinnamon Hill & Beach Club** $-$$
Grand Anse Beach
☎ 444-4301
A Spanish-style village condominium offering spectacular views. Fine restaurant, bar, pool, beach.

**Coyaba Beach Resort** $-$$
Grand Anse
☎444-4129
Forty rooms. Two restaurants, bars, water and land sports.

**Flamboyant Hotel & Cottages** $-$$
Grand Anse
☎ 444-4247
Thirty-nine attractively-decorated suites and apartments with air-conditioning, mini-bar, television and telephone. Each room has a private verandah offering spectacular views across Grand Anse Beach. Good restaurant, bar, pool, free diving equipment, conference facilities.

**Fox Inn** $
Point Salines
☎ 444-4123
The hotel is minutes from Port Salines International Airport. Twenty-two rooms. Restaurant, bar, pool.

**Gem Holiday Beach Resort** $-$$
Morne Rouge
☎ 444-4224
The hotel is located on the beautiful and secluded Morne Rouge Bay just fifteen minutes from the capital of St. George's. The hotel features self-contained apartments with full-equipped kitchens, living/dining rooms, telephone and terrace.

The lively Fantazia 2001 nightclub is air-conditioned and sound-proofed and offers dancing to good local bands.

**Grenada Renaissance Resort** $$-$$$
Grand Anse
☎ 444-4371
Luxury beachfront resort with 186 delightful rooms. Open-air restaurant, beach bar, cocktail lounge, poolside snack bar, water and land sports.

**Hibiscus Hotel** $
Grand Anse
☎ 444-4233
Close to the airport, this ten room hotel is conveniently situated for the beach. Restaurant, bar and pool.

**Horse Shoe Beach Hotel** $-$$
L'Anse aux Epines
☎ 444-4410
Set amid a tropical garden with its own private beach, the hotel features twelve villas all with king-size canopied beds, air-conditioning, private patio and fully-equipped kitchen. There are also six deluxe units and four elegant standard rooms. The dining room offers spectacular views across the bay in a romantic candlelit setting. Pool, lush tropical gardens, bar, barbecue.

**Hotel Amanda** $
St. George's
☎ 440-2409
Fourteen rooms. Restaurant and bar.

**La Source** $$$
Pink Gin Beach , Point Salines
☎ 444-2556
A luxury 100-room all-inclusive resort with private beach, watersports, nine-hole golf course and health/beauty treatments.

**Lance Aux Epines Cottages**
L'Anse aux Epines
☎444-4565
Charming one- and two-bedroom air-conditioned cottages situated directly on a secluded beach at Prickly Bay. The calm waters of the Caribbean Sea, the tranquil surroundings and welcoming staff combine to make an idyllic holiday hideaway.
Beach, boating, mini-market, watersports.

**Mahogany Run** $$$
Morne Rouge
☎ 444-3171
Fifty-one pretty rooms are situated in a Mediterranean-style property overlooking Morne Rouge Bay. Restaurant, piano bar, Grenada's only Olympic size pool, beach club, free scuba gear hire, bicycle hire.

**No Problem Apartment Hotel**
True Blue
☎ 444-4634
Twenty suites are located in this lovely garden setting five minutes from Grand Anse Beach. Rooms are equipped with kitchenette, television and telephone.
Pool, Conference facilities, boutique, mini-mart.

**Rex Grenadian** $$-$$$
Point Salines
☎ 444-3333, Fax: 444-1111
A luxury 212-room resort with a variety of elegantly-furnished rooms ranging from the magnificent Presidential suite, Royal suites, beachfront and garden view rooms. Panoramic views across the Caribbean Sea are afforded from the fabulous pool complex which is set on a rocky headland overlooking the tropical gardens, three-acre lake and sparkling waterfalls. The grounds are fronted by two white sandy beaches and guests are guaranteed a memorable stay by the warm, friendly staff.
Three restaurants, bars, terrace café, watersports, floodlit tennis and conference facilities.

**Sam's Inn** $
Dunfermline, St. Andrew's
☎ 442-7853
Twelve rooms in a small hotel just five minutes from Grenville. Excursions can be arranged to nearby places of interest, meals on request, close to beach.

**Secret Harbour** $$-$$$
L'Anse aux Epines
☎ 444-4548
A twenty-room hotel overlooking Mount Hartman Bay. Restaurant, bar, private beach, tennis, free watersports.

**Siesta Hotel** $-$$
Grand Anse
☎ 444-4645
Thirty-seven rooms in a Mediterranean-style property. Restaurant, pool and bar.

**Spice Island Inn** $$$
Grand Anse
☎ 444-4258
Fifty-six rooms. Fine hotel with restaurant, bars, beach, watersports, tennis, fitness centre, entertainment, free bicycles, conference facilities.

**Tropicana Inn** $-$$
Lagoon Road, St. George's
☎ 440-1586
Twenty rooms cater for both the business and leisure traveller. Close to the capital of St. George's. Restaurant, bar and conference facilities.

# The Flamboyant Hotel

PO Box 214, St. George's, Grenada Telephone: 809-444-4242 Fax: 809-444-1234

**True Blue Inn** $-$$
True Blue
☎ 444-2000
Ten delightful rooms welcome the visitor in this charming, secluded inn overlooking True Blue Bay. Comfortably-furnished cottages all have private balconies and air-conditioning. The unhurried and friendly atmosphere makes for a wonderful stay in an enchanting location.
Restaurant, bar, pool, yachting and yachting school, dock, swimming in the bay.

**Twelve Degrees North** $$-$$$
L'Anse aux Epines
☎444-4580
Once voted as one of the 'Best 100 Resorts in the Caribbean', this small, elegant hotel offers just eight apartments each with its own maid/cook. The resort is designed with guest privacy in mind and offers a wide range of watersports including windsurfers, sunfish and snorkelling.
Pool, tennis courts, beach.

**Victoria Hotel** $
Victoria
☎ 444-8104
Ten rooms. Restaurant, bar and beach.

**Villamar Holiday Resort** $
L'Anse aux Epines
☎ 444-4716
Twenty suites equipped with kitchenette, telephone, television and private patio. Restaurant, bar, pool and conference facilities.

### Carriacou

**Caribbee Inn** $-$$
Prospect
☎ 443-7380
This enchanting ten-bedroom country-style hotel guarantees visitors comfort and luxury in an idyllic escape from reality.
Restaurant, bar, cycling, hiking, nature trails, snorkelling.

**Silver Beach Resort** $-$
Silver Beach, Hillsborough
☎ 443-7337
Eighteen rooms. Restaurant, bar, beach, diving shop, full scuba and watersports facilities.

## Arrival, Entry Requirements & Customs

Passports are not required by British, US and Canadian citizens providing they have two documents proving citizenship, one of which must bear a photograph. Visas are not required by Commonwealth citizens, French and German citizens. Visitors from the United States and Canada staying less than six months can use their ID card to enter, but must have valid return tickets.

There is a departure tax of EC$35.

## Airport & Airlines

**Point Salines International Airport**
☎ 444-4167

**Aereotuy**
☎ 444-4732

**Airlines of Carriacou**
☎ 444-4425/2898

**American Airlines**
☎ 444-2222

**BWIA International**
☎ 440-3818
(In the USA 1-800-JET-BWIA)

**British Airways/LIAT**
☎ 440-2796
(On Carriacou ☎ 443-7362)

**Caledonian Airways**
☎ 440-2796

**Carib Express**
☎ 809-431-9200

**Helenair, Grenada**
☎ 444-2266/4101

## Banks

Banks are open from Monday to Thursday 8am-2pm, and Fridays 8am-12noon or1pm and 2.30-5pm. Banks are usually closed at weekends and on public holidays.

**Barclays Bank** has three offices:-
St. George's (☎ 440-3232)
Grenville (☎ 442-7220)
Grand Anse (☎ 444-1184)
There is also a branch in Hillsborough, Carriacou (☎ 443-7232).

**National Commercial Bank** (NCB) has eight offices:
St. George (☎ 440-3566)
Grenville (☎ 442-7532)
Gouyave (☎ 444-8353)
St. David (☎ 444-6355)
Grand Anse (☎ 444-2627)
Hillsborough, Carriacou (☎ 443-7829)
Petit Martinique.

**Grenada Bank of Commerce** has two branches:-
St. George's (☎ 440-3521)
Grand Anse (☎ 444-4919).

**Grenada Cooperative Bank** has three branches:
Church St.St. George's (☎ 440-2111)
Victoria St. Grenville (☎ 442-7748)
Main St. Sauteurs (☎ 442-9247).

**Grenada Development Bank** has two branches:
St. George's (☎ 440-2382)
Grenville (☎ 442-6464).

**Bank of Nova Scotia** has two branches:
Halifax St St. George's (☎ 440-3274)
Grand Anse Centre (☎ 444-1917).

## Beauty Salons and Hairdressers

There are several beauty salons in St. George's and one in Grenville.

## Camping

Camping is not encouraged, but is allowed in Grand Etang National Park, and in school grounds on Carriacou. Camping is not allowed on beaches.

## Car Rental

There are 750 miles (1,207km) of road on Grenada, most of them paved, and hire cars or four-wheel drive vehicles provide the best way of exploring the island. For visitors planning a trip during peak periods, it is advisable to hire a vehicle in advance through a travel agent. Cars can be hired, however, at airports, hotels or car hire offices on the island.

Hire car rates range from US$300 to $400 a week depending on the type of vehicle and the rental company. Average daily rates are around US$65 but this does not include insurance which is an additional $15-20 a day.

A temporary Grenada driving licence is required which can be obtained on production of your current driving licence on arrival at the airport, the police station or the car hire office. The cost for a temporary licence is EC$30 (US$11).

### Rules of the Road

Driving is on the left. The roads are generally good and there is a substantial road improvement programme underway. In rural areas, however, be on the look out for potholes, fallen branches, coconuts in the roads and other hazards. Do not speed because one never knows what may be round the next corner. The Grenadians love of cricket encourages them to play at every opportunity, and the road makes an ideal wicket!

Seat belts are not compulsory but it is advisable to wear them at all times. The speed limit is 40mph (48kph) or slower if signposted in town. There is no reason to drive very much faster out of town because you will not fully appreciate the scenery.

Drinking and driving is against the law, and there are heavy penalties if convicted, particularly if it resulted in an accident.

For visitors involved in an accident or breakdown, telephone your car hire company and they will usually sending out a mechanic or replacement vehicle.

If you get stuck at night, ensure that the car is off the road, lock it carefully and telephone a taxi to take you back to your hotel. Report the problem to the car hire company or police as soon as possible.

### Car Hire Companies

**Avis**
Paddock & Lagoon Roads, St. George's
☎ 440-3936
Collection and pick-up provided. Airport delivery available.

**Barba's Rentals**
Tyrrel Bay
☎ 443-7454

**Budget Rent-a-Car**
Point Salines Airport
☎ 443-7454
and St. George's ☎ 440-2778

**David's Car Rentals**
Four locations around Grenada
☎ 444-3038
Collection and pick-up provided. Airport delivery available.

**Island Rent-a-Car**
Westerhall
☎ 443-5624

**Jerry's Auto Service**
Lagoon Road, St. George's
☎ 440-1730

**Maffiken Car Rentals**
Grand Anse
☎ 444-4255

**MCR Car Rentals**
Paddock Road, St. George's
☎ 440-5398

**McIntyre Bros. Car Rentals**
True Blue
☎ 444-3944

**Ride Grenada**
Grand Anse
☎ 444-1157

**Sunshine Tours and Rentals**
Point Salines
☎ 444-4296

**C. Thomas & Sons**
True Blue
☎ 444-4384

**Thrift Rent-a-Car**
Grand View Inn, Grand Anse
☎ 444-4984

**Y&R Car Rentals L'Anse aux Epines**
☎ 444-4448

### Carriacou

**Martin Bullen** ☎ 443-7204
**John Gabriel** ☎ 443-7454

## Churches

The following denominations are represented: Roman Catholic, Anglican, Episcopal, Presbyterian, Methodist, Scots Kirk, Seventh Day Adventist, Jehovah's Witness, Islam, Salvation Army, Church of Christian Scientist, Church of Christ, Baha'i Faith, Mennonite Churches and Living Word World Outreach.

## Departure Tax

There is a departure tax of EC$35 for all passengers over 13 leaving the island (EC$17.50 for children 6-12).

## Dress Code

Dress is mainly casual, but one can be as smart or as cool as they wish. Beachwear is fine for the beach or pool areas, but it is recommended to cover up a little for the street.

## Embassies & Consulates

### Embassies and Consulates Abroad

**United States of America**
Embassy of Grenada
1701 New Hampshire Avenue NW,
Washington DC, 20009 USA
☎ 202-265-2561

**Canada**
High Commission of the Eastern Caribbean States
112 Kent Street, Suite 1610,
Ottawa, Ontario KIP 5P2
Canada
☎ 613-236-8952

**United Kingdom**
Grenada High Commission
1 Collingham Gardens,
Earls Court,
London SW5 0HW
☎ 0171-373-7808

**Rest of Europe**
Embassy of Grenada to the European Union
Avenue des Arts 24,
Box 2B 1040,
Brussels,
Belgium
☎ 011-32-2-230-6265

### Embassies & Consulates represented in Grenada

**British High Commission**
14 Church Street
St. George's
☎ 440-3536

**Embassy of the Republic of China**
Archibald Avenue
St. George's
☎ 440-3054

**The European Union**
Archibald Avenue
St. George's
☎ 440-3561

**Honorary Consul of France**
7 Lucas Street
St. George's
☎ 440-2547

**Consulate of the Cooperative Republic of Guyana**
Gore Street
St. George's
☎ 440-2189

**Consulate of the Netherlands**
Grand Etang Road
St. George's
☎ 440-2031

**Swedish Consulate**
PO Box 345
St. George's
☎ 440-1832

**USA Embassy**
Point Salines
St. George's
☎ 444-1173.

**Venezuelan Embassy**
Archibald Avenue
St. George's
☎ 440-1721

## Emergency Telephone Numbers

For police and fire ☎ 911
For coastguard ☎ 399
For ambulance:
☎ 434 in St. George's
☎724 in St. Andrew's
☎ 774 on Carriacou

### Hospitals

General Hospital, St. George's
☎ 440-2051

Princess Alice Hospital, St. Andrew's
☎ 442-7251,

Princess Royal Hospital, Carriacou
☎ 443-7400

## Festivals/Public Holidays *

**January**
1 January New Year's Day
Grenada Sailing Festival
Grenada Triathlon, Grand Anse
Spice Island Billfishing Competition

**February**
7 February* Independence Day
Carriacou Carnival
True Blue Indigo Yacht Race, True Blue Inn

**March**
St. Patrick's Day Fiesta, Sauteurs
Carl Schuster Round Grenada Yacht Race
Intercollege Sports Day, Queen's Park

**April**
Good Friday*
Easter Dinghy Races
Petit Martinique Regatta, Easter Weekend
Easter Monday*
St. Mark's Day Festival, Victoria

**May**
Labour Day*
La Source/Grand Anse Race
Whit Monday*

**June**
Corpus Christi*
Volley Ball Club Championships
South Coast Yacht Race
Fisherman's Birthday Celebrations

**July**
Venezuela Independence Day
Regatta — St. George's Harbour

**August**
Caricom Day *
Rainbow City Festival, Grenville
Grenada Carnival, held over the second weekend

**November**
Match Racing off Grand Anse

**December**
Carriacou Parang Festival
Christmas Day and Boxing Day *
New Year's Eve parties and gala dances
Midnight Marathon, New Year's Eve, a half marathon, Grenville.

## Fishing

Fishing is an island pursuit, and many Grenadians will fish for hours from harbour walls, the beach or river side.

Deep sea and game fishing is mostly for blue marlin and tuna which can weigh up to 1,000lb (450kgm), wahoo and white marlin, which can weigh more than 100lb (45kgm) and the fighting sailfish. Snapper, grouper, bonito, dorado and barracuda can all be found close to shore. There are a number of boats available for charter or which offer deep sea fishing.

**Boat Charter operators include:**

Captain Peter's Water Taxi Service
☎ 440-134,

*Bezo* — 32ft (10m) pirogue
☎ 443-5477

Evans Chartering Services
☎ 444-4422

*Havada* — 32ft (10m) pirogue
☎ 440-2198

Tropix Professional Sport Fishing
☎ 440-4961

## Health

The General Hospital is in St. George's near Fort George. The smaller Princess Alice Hospital is at Mirabeau in St. Andrew's and there is 24-hour emergency medical, surgical and pharmaceutical services available at the Black Rock Medical Clinic in the Grand Anse Shopping Centre.

Emergency dental treatment can be obtained at the Sun Smile Dental Care Clinic in the Le Marquis Complex at Grand Anse. The island has a decompression chamber available in case of diving accidents, air ambulance, 24-hour casualty department, and emergency dental facilities.

The Princess Royal Hospital serves Carriacou.

## Media

There are four island radio stations. Radio Grenada, with two channels, is broadcast by the Grenada Broadcasting Corporation, Spice Capital is privately owned, as is Young Sound FM.

Grenada Television broadcasts on channels 7 and 11, and Lighthouse TV, a privately-owned, non-profit making organisation, broadcasts mostly religious and family programmes. Channel 6 is a non-profit making community station offering mostly cultural programmes. Many hotels also have cable or satellite television.

## Nightlife

Places worth investigating include:

**The Boatyard Restaurant and Bar** at L'Anse aux Epines which features dancing after dinner on Wednesdays to a live band and on Fridays to a steel band.

**Cicely's at the Calabash Hotel** offers relaxing piano music on Monday, Wednesday and Saturday evenings and a steel band plays on Saturday night and Sunday lunchtime.

**The Dynamite Disco** at the Limes at Grand Anse features a variety of disco and reggae rhythms.

**Fantazia 2001** at Morne Route offers dancing to the latest international and local sounds.

**Island View** at Woburn offers local music on Friday and Saturday evenings.

Many hotels also hold beach or beach-side barbecues with steel bands, and these are generally open to non-guests as well. The Rhum Runners I and II offer evening cruises, including moonlight cruises with unlimited rum and all-night dancing.

## Pharmacies

Pharmacies are located in:

*Grenville*

**Beckwith's**
☎ 442-7312

**Parris**
☎ 442-7330

*Grand Anse*

**Gitten's**
☎ 444-4954

**Mitchell's**
☎ 444-3845

*St. George's*

**Gitten's** in Halifax Street
☎ 440-2165

**Grenada Pharmacy**, in Hillsborough Street
☎ 440-2345

**People's Pharmacy**, Church & Young Streets ☎ 440-3444

## Police

The police headquarters is in Fort George ☎ 440-1043

## Post Office

The Post Office (☎ 440-2526) is on Lagoon Road on the Carenage near the Customs House, St. George's. Post Office hours are 8.30am-4.30pm Monday to Friday. It is open during lunch but is closed on Saturday. There are post offices in all parishes. Stamps are on sale in most hotels and many shops.

## Shopping

Shops are usually open between 8am-4pm Monday to Friday, and from 8am-1pm on Saturday. Foodland on Lagoon Road in St. George's, and Gitten's Drug Mart in Grand Anse stay open until 8pm.

## SIGHTSEEING

A guided tour of Grenada has many advantages including a knowledgeable guide who will take visitors to the best location and provide them with an insight into the historical, geological or natural sights around the island.

**Arnold's Tours/Arnold's Hikes**
☎ 440-0531
Provides personal walking tours of the Saturday market in St. George's, all-day island trips incorporating mountain waterfalls, volcanic lakes and a sumptuous lunch at one of Grenada's elegant estate houses.

Arnold's also provides a unique opportunity to sample some of Grenada's fine dining on their *Dine Around* tour. Prices are all below US$43.00 per person including transfers to and from your hotel, dinner and all taxes.

**Caribbean Horizons Tours and Services**
☎ 444-1555. Fax: 444-2899
Arrange a wide range of guided tours and cruises including the rainforest and Balthazar River, complete island tours, fishing, sailing, picnic and sunset cruises as well as day trips to the Tobago Cays on a fabulous 52ft luxury yacht.

**Funseeker Tours**
☎ 444-1342
Offer standard tours around the island or individually-tailored trips to specific sights.

**Fun Tours**
☎ 444-3167. Fax: 444-2840
Enjoy a multi-island dive safari in the crystal-blue waters around Mayreau or Bequia in the Grenadines, or enjoy a tranquil day cruise to Carriacou to snorkel amidst the underwater coral gardens around Sandy Island.

Tailor-made excursions aboard luxury catamarans or yachts can be organised to transport visitors on an unforgettable experience through the fabulous Grenadine islands and the exquisite Tobago Cays.

**Happy Island Tours**
☎ 440-9069

**Henry's Safari Tours**
☎ 444-5313
Enigmatic Henry was born and raised on Grenada and with his knowledgeable team provides safe, reliable and ecologically-aware tours around the island. Visitors are transported around the island in comfortable air-conditioned vehicles to the heart of the countryside.

Visit the sparkling Concord and Annandale Falls and take a dip in their crystal-clear waters, or hike to the remote Honeymoon and Upper Concord Falls. All hikes lead through a wonderland of enchanting rainforest and rich flora and fauna.

Henrys also provides a dedicated shore team for yacht charters including laundry and shopping service, transport and repairs.

**Jolly Tours**
☎ 440-9822

**Q & K Spice Sunsation**
☎ 444-1656
Sunsation Tours provide a variety of fascinating tours around Grenada through rich forest vegetation to the undiscovered north-east of the island. Visit the River Antoine Rum Distillery and enjoy a delicious lunch at Mount Rodney Estate. Alternative tours visit nutmeg processing plants, Carib's Leap, or the delightful La Sagesse Nature Reserve.

**Raymond's Tour and Taxi Service**
☎ 444-1283

**Rhum Runner**
☎ 440-2198

**Starwind Enterprise**
☎ 440-3678

**Sunshine Cruises**
☎ 444-1852

## Sport

Cricket is the national game and it is played at every opportunity by both men and women throughout the countryside. Wicket-keeper Junior Murray made history on 2 January 1993 when he became the first Grenadian to represent the West Indies in Test Cricket.

Football is another favourite sport and in Victoria there is a football team called the Courts Hurricane. The team was established in 1958 to pull the community together after Hurricane Janet, and thus its name. The Hurricanes have won the national championship more times than any other team, including eight times consecutively!

For the visitor there is a wide range of sporting activities including swimming, scuba diving, horseback riding, golf, tennis, cycling, sailing, squash and fishing. The Atlantic coastline offers stronger swell for windsurfing and surfing, but the seas can sometimes be very rough and care should be taken.

Walking is great fun and there are lots of trails in the mountains, but one should wear sturdy, non-slip footwear. Protection against insects in advisable and carry adequate drinking water.

### Cycling

Bikes can be rented from Ride Grenada ☎ 444-1157

### Fishing

There is excellent game fishing for tuna, marlin, sail fish and billfish. Many anglers agree that the waters around Grenada offer some of the best fishing in the Caribbean, especially between November and June when migrating sailfish, white and blue marlin and yellow fin tuna are in the local waters.

Fishing trips can be organised through:

**Bezo Charters**
☎ 443-5021

**Captain Peters**
☎ 440-1349

**Evans Charter Services**
☎ 444-4422

**Sky Ride Watersports**
☎ 444-3333

**Sunshine Cruises**
☎ 444-2183

### Fitness Gyms/Health Clubs

There are a number of health clubs around the island including:

**Amada Marga Yoga Centre**
Near Tanteen Playing Field
St. George's
☎ 440-5880

**Body Image**
L'Anse aux Epines
☎ 444-3254

**Body Shop**
Grand Anse
☎ 444-4290

**Carriacou Fitness Club**
2nd Avenue
Hillsborough
☎ 443-8439

**Island Magic Massage Clinic**
Grenada Renaissance Hotel
☎ 444-3306

**Shamar**
Lucia Street
St. George's
☎ 440-6880

*On this sparkling gem of an island in th Caribbean Sea, this exquisite seventeen-roo air-conditoned apartment hotel with restauran beach bar, mini-mart and souvenir shop provid a luxurious stay for visitors wanting peac tranquility and first-class servic*

MORNE ROUGE BAY, ST. GEORGE S, GRENADA, WEST INDIES.
TELEPHONE: (809) 444-4224/3737 FAX: (809) 444 1189

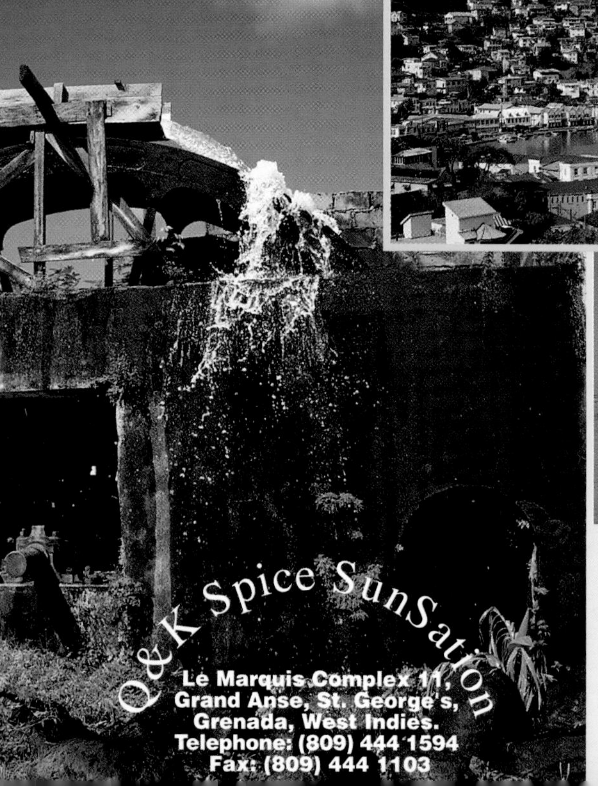

Q&K Spice SunSation
Le Marquis Complex 11,
Grand Anse, St. George's,
Grenada, West Indies.
Telephone: (809) 444 1594
Fax: (809) 444 1103


## SUNSATION TOU

Explore the historic Riv Antoine rum distillery, tour historic city of St. George's, take a day trip to the fabulo Tobago Cays for a day sunshine and snorkelli You choose Sunsation Tours are speciali in special experienc

## Golf

There is a nine-hole course at Belmont, near Grand Anse (☎ 444-4128). The club house is open to visitors and offers drinks and snacks. Clubs can be hired and caddies are available.

The Grenada Open Golf Tournament takes place in February.

There is also a private nine-hole course at La Source, and a new eighteen-hole course is being built.

## Horseback Riding

The Horseman, St. Paul's, offers a variety of horseback tours with an experienced guide
☎ 440-5368

## Parasailing

Sky Ride Watersports
☎ 444-3333

## Scuba Diving

The waters surrounding Grenada and Carriacou offer the most enchanting coral gardens with sea fans, gorgonians, sea horses, as well as a fascinating collection of reef fish. Most of the diving is based around Grand Anse and many of the best dive sites are within a thirty-minute boat ride. The best snorkelling is around Molinière and Dragon Bay, which are best reached by boat, while the headland of Morne Rouge Bay and the reef off Grand Anse can be reached from the land. Most hotels can arrange courses and qualified instructors are able to take pupils from beginner to advanced level during their stay. Equipment can be hired.

There are four main wreck sites that can be visited. The cruise ship *Bianca C* is believed to be the largest wreck in the Caribbean, and the top decks are about 90ft (27m) below the surface allowing divers to 'swim' in the liner's swimming pool.

The other wrecks are the *Buccaneer*, a two-mast sloop which sank in the 1970s and lies in 80ft (24m) of water, the *Three Part* wreck in 40ft (12m) of water, and the *SS Orinoco*, off La Sagesse Point, which went down on 1 November 1900. However, it is in rough waters and is only accessible to experienced divers.

Grand Mal Canyon and Red Buoy are the best wall dives and feature myriad corals and reef fish. There are also wall sites at Happy Hill, Halifax Bay, Flamingo Bay and Black Coral Wall. The main reef sites are Bass Reef, Grand Mal Reef, Spice Island Reef, Molinière Reef, Dragon Bay, Whibles Reef and Channel Reef.

The best dive sites off Carriacou are around Sandy Island, Sister Rocks, Pago Das Garden, Two Sisters on Ronde Island, Mabouya Island and Saline island.

The following companies offer diving instruction, diving trips and hire equipment:

**Aquarium Beach Club**
☎ 444-1410

**Dive Grenada**
☎ 444-1092

**Grand Anse Aquatics**
☎ 444-4129

**Karibik Diving**, Carriacou
☎ 443-7882

**Scuba World**
☎ 444-3333

**Silver Beach Diving**, Carriacou
☎ 443-7882

**Snagg's Watersports**, Carriacou
☎ 443-8293

**Sunshine Cruises**
☎ 444-1852

**Tanki's Watersports Ltd.**, Carriacou
☎ 443-8406

### Tennis

Almost all the resorts and many of the hotels have their own tennis courts which are usually floodlit.

### Watersports

A wide variety of watersports is available at all resorts and most large hotels. Dive Grenada offers windsurfing and sailing instruction, Grand Anse Aquatics offers windsurfing instruction, and Sail Grenada (☎ 444-2000) has sailing classes to suit all ages. Silver Beach Diving and Snagg's Watersports also offer water-skiing and windsurfing, and Sky Ride Watersports (☎ 440-9375) offer parasailing from Grand Anse Beach.

### Yachting

There are excellent marina facilities at Mount Hartman Bay on the south coast. Prickly Bay is the main yachting centre with a wide choice of charter boats and the Spice Island Boatyard and Marine Services. The Grenada Yacht Club, founded in 1954, also offers moorings to visiting yachts. The clubhouse was destroyed by Hurricane Janet, and a larger building on a new site was opened in 1960. The clubs hosts a number of regattas and events through the year, including the week-long Grenada Sailing Festival which attracts yachts from around the world.

On Carriacou there are many good anchorages, and Tyrrel Bay and Cassada Bay are two of the most popular, while Sandy Island is perhaps the most beautiful. There is also an anchorage and jetty at the Silver Beach Hotel, close to Hillsborough. Anchoring in Harvey Vale is not allowed.

On arrival, yachts should fly the yellow 'Q' flag and anchor at least 656ft (200m) offshore. Customs can also be cleared through Grenada Yacht Services, St. George's, and Spice Island Marina. Customs are open Monday to Friday 8am–4pm.

## Tourist Offices

**Tourist Information**
☎ 444-4140

**Grenada Board of Tourism**
PO Box 293
St. George's
☎ 440-2279

**Canada**
Grenada Board of Tourism
Suite 820
439 University Avenue
Toronto
Ontario
M5G 1Y8
☎ 416-595-1339

**Germany**
Liebigstrasse 8
60323 Frankfurt/Main
Germany
☎ 069 726 908

**United Kingdom**
Grenada Board of Tourism
1 Collingham Gardens
London SW5 0HW
☎ 0171 370-5164

**United States of America**
Suite 900D
820 2nd Avenue
New York NY 10017
☎ 212-687-9554

## Weddings

Requirements for getting married on Grenada are:

• Visitors must have been resident on the island for three working days before applying for a marriage licence.

• provide all documents in English or have translations into English certified by a notary.
• produce a certificate of non-marriage from a priest, lawyer or registrar on official note paper, attesting that neither party is married.
• produce final divorce documents if applicable.
• if under the age of twenty-one, complete a special form available from the Prime Minister's Office, St. George's, and have it signed by parents/guardian and notarised.
• produce passport and birth certificates.
• produce EC$25 worth of stamps (1 EC$10, and 3 EC$5 stamps) to cover Stamp Duty.

Once all the requirements have been met, all documents must be presented at the Registrar's Office in the Ministry of Health on the Carenage St. George's. The marriage licence which costs EC$10 is available from the Treasury Office.

Many hotels offer wedding packages and will make all the arrangements for you. The application must be filed at least five working days before the date of the wedding.

## Yacht Charter & Private Moorings

There is a huge range of charter vessels and crews available for sailing, sightseeing, fishing and diving tours.

Companies handling yacht charters include:

**Arnold's Tours**
☎ 440-0531

**Astral Travel**
☎ 440-5180

**Bezo Charters**
☎ 443-5477

**Carriacou Boat-Builders**
☎ 443-7542

**Club Mariner**
☎ 444-4439

**Evans Charter Services**
☎ 444-4422

**Fun Tours**
☎ 444-3167

**Moorings' Club Mariner Centre**
☎ 444-4439

**New Trend Tours**
☎ 444-1236

**Seabreeze Charters**
☎ 444-4924

**Sun Shine Cruises**
☎ 444-1852

**True Blue Inn**
☎ 443-5477

**Windward Islands Travel & Regattas**
☎ 444-4732

**There are marina services at:**

**Anro Agencies**
Grand Anse
☎ 440-2044

**Grenada Yacht Services**
Lagoon Road
St. George's
☎ 440-2508

**McIntyre Bros**
True Blue
☎ 440-2044

**The Moorings Marina**
Secret Harbour
☎ 444-4449

**Spice Island Marine Services**
Prickly Bay
L'Anse aux Epines
☎ 444-4342

# St. Lucia

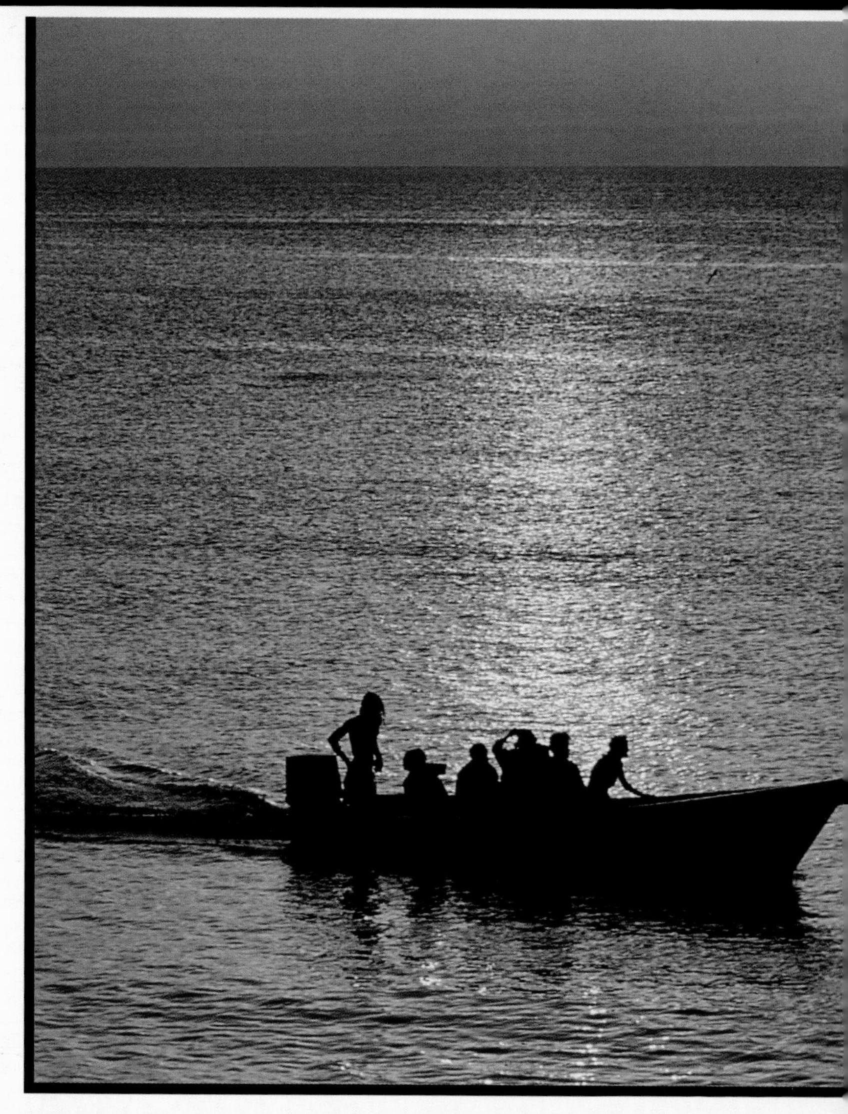

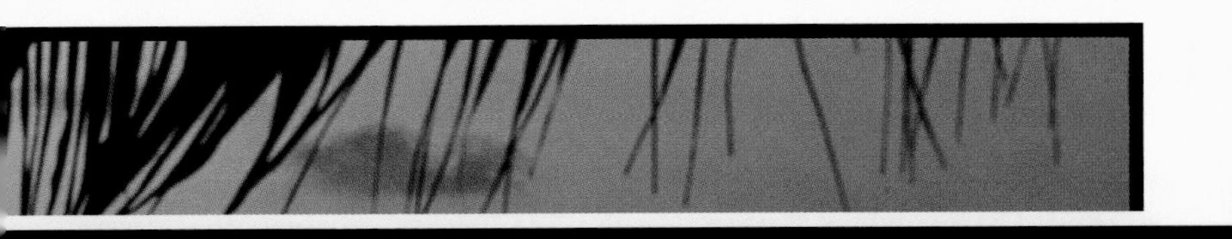

# St. Lucia

St. Lucia (pronounced St. Loo-sha), lies in the eastern Caribbean Sea about 21 miles (34km) south of Martinique and 26 miles (42km) north-east of St. Vincent. Both can be seen on clear days.

The island is the second largest of the Windward group, and is 27 miles (43km) long and 14 miles (23km) wide, covering an area of 238 sq miles (616 sq km), and with a population of around 150,000. The island is volcanic and the area around Soufrière in the south-west, has bubbling, hot mud pools and sulphur vents. The interior is wooded and mountainous with Mount Gimie 3,118ft (950m) the highest point. The Pitons — St. Lucia's 'pyramids' — in the south-west are another spectacular landmark. Gros Piton 2,619ft (798m) and Petit Piton 2,461ft (750m) are volcanic pinnacles rising out of the sea, which from a distance appear to be side by side. It is not until one gets closer that the distance between them and their magnitude, with their densely-forested slopes, is revealed. The rainforests are now largely restricted to the higher slopes of the mountains, and are primarily only accessible on foot. Lower slopes have been cleared for farming and forestry.

## Getting There

**By Air:** Hewanorra International Airport is just outside Vieux Fort near the southern tip of the island and about 40 miles (64km) from Castries and the main resort areas. Vigie Airport, just north of Castries, has domestic and regional flights, and some international flights from the USA on BWIA and American Airlines.

British Airways flies direct from London's Heathrow Airport three times a week. Caledonian Airways has a weekly charter from London Gatwick, and BWIA flies twice weekly. BWIA also serves other European destinations. There are also charter flights during the high season.

American Airlines flies to its Caribbean hub of San Juan in Puerto Rico, and then daily on to St. Lucia's Hewanorra airport. BWIA flies daily from Miami and New York to Hewanorra and Vigie, while American Eagle has daily flights between San Juan and Vigie Airport. Air Canada flies from Toronto and Montreal to St. Lucia. Amerijet International also flies direct during the high season.

LIAT flies regular services throughout the Caribbean from Vigie Airport. Most flights leave early in the morning.

*Note*: LIAT has a number of special air passes which offer some of the best deals on fares anywhere and allow visitors to island-hop at very low prices. It is often necessary to purchase these tickets before arrival in the Caribbean to make enquiries before your travel date.

Carib Express flies short take-off and landing jets between Barbados, Grenada, Dominica, St. Lucia (Vigie), St. Vincent, Tobago and Port of Spain.

Air Martinique operates between Martinique and St. Lucia. BWIA also operates services to many of the other Caribbean islands. Other operators include American Eagle, Helenair, Eagle Air and Eastern Caribbean Helicopters.

**By Sea:** Cruise ships are regular, almost daily visitors to St. Lucia. The main port of Castries and its cruise ship terminal at Pointe Seraphine has been modernised, and there are also port facilities at Vieux Fort and Soufrière.

There is a high speed catamaran service called the Caribbean Express which operates between the islands of St. Lucia, Martinique, Guadeloupe and Dominica. It stops at St. Lucia twice a week and the voyage from St. Lucia to Martinique takes one hour twenty minutes, to Guadeloupe five hours forty minutes, and to Dominica three hours twenty-five minutes. Tickets can be purchased through the travel agencies.

Hundreds of yachts also visit the island, and the main moorings are at Rodney Bay on the north-west coast, Castries Yacht Centre at the entrance of Castries Harbour, and Marigot Bay to the south.

## Getting around

There are around 465 miles (748km) of roads, about four-fifths of which are paved. Car or jeep hire is the best option for visitors planning to spend several days exploring. If not, use taxis or the island's 'bus' service.

Taxis are cheap and easily available. Taxi drivers attend special courses and make excellent guides. Taxis can be hired for the trip, the hour or day for tours, but ensure both the price and currency is agreed first. A taxi for four people from Hewanorra Airport to Castries costs around EC$120, and from Castries to Rodney Bay about EC$40. Expect to pay EC$40-50 an hour to hire a taxi.

Minibuses, privately owned Japanese vans, ply the main routes. They are a fun way of getting around but always check that the bus is heading in your direction before getting on. There are frequent services between Castries and Gros Islet in the north which run from early morning until 10pm, and later on Fridays, when the weekly 'jump up' takes place at Gros Islet. Services to the south are less frequent. Typical fares are EC$1.50 from Castries to Gros Islet, and EC$7 from Castries to Vieux Fort at the southern tip of the island.

Boats ply between Castries and Soufrière and these offer stunning views of the Pitons.

## CASTRIES

The island's capital is a charming, bustling city which gives little indication of its long and troubled past. Castries was fought over for 300 years, and has been devastated by four massive fires, the last of which in 1948 destroyed most of the commercial quarter. However, there are still many fine, old wooden buildings, with overhanging balconies and delicate filigree latticework. The rebuilding work which followed the fires accounts for the town's modern grid layout, which makes it simple to explore. Castries was named in 1785 after the French Minister of the Navy and the Colony Marechal De Castries. The name changed to Félicité during the French Revolution, but reverted back soon afterwards.

It is a city of contrasts with its ultra-modern cruise ship terminal at Pointe Seraphine, duty-free shopping and tourist centre, and the crowded side-walks of the streets overflowing with produce and goods from the tightly packed stores.

The only way to explore is on foot, and a good place to start is in **Derek Walcott Square** with its war memorial. On the eastern side of the square across Laborie Street is the 1897 **Roman Catholic Cathedral of the Immaculate Conception**, which contains paintings of numerous Biblical scenes, in which all the characters are black. Beside the cathedral is a massive 400 year-old saman tree, believed to be one of the oldest trees in the Caribbean, and certainly the oldest on St. Lucia. The main library is housed in an impressive Victorian building on the opposite side of the square, while the other two sides of the square feature

St. Lucia

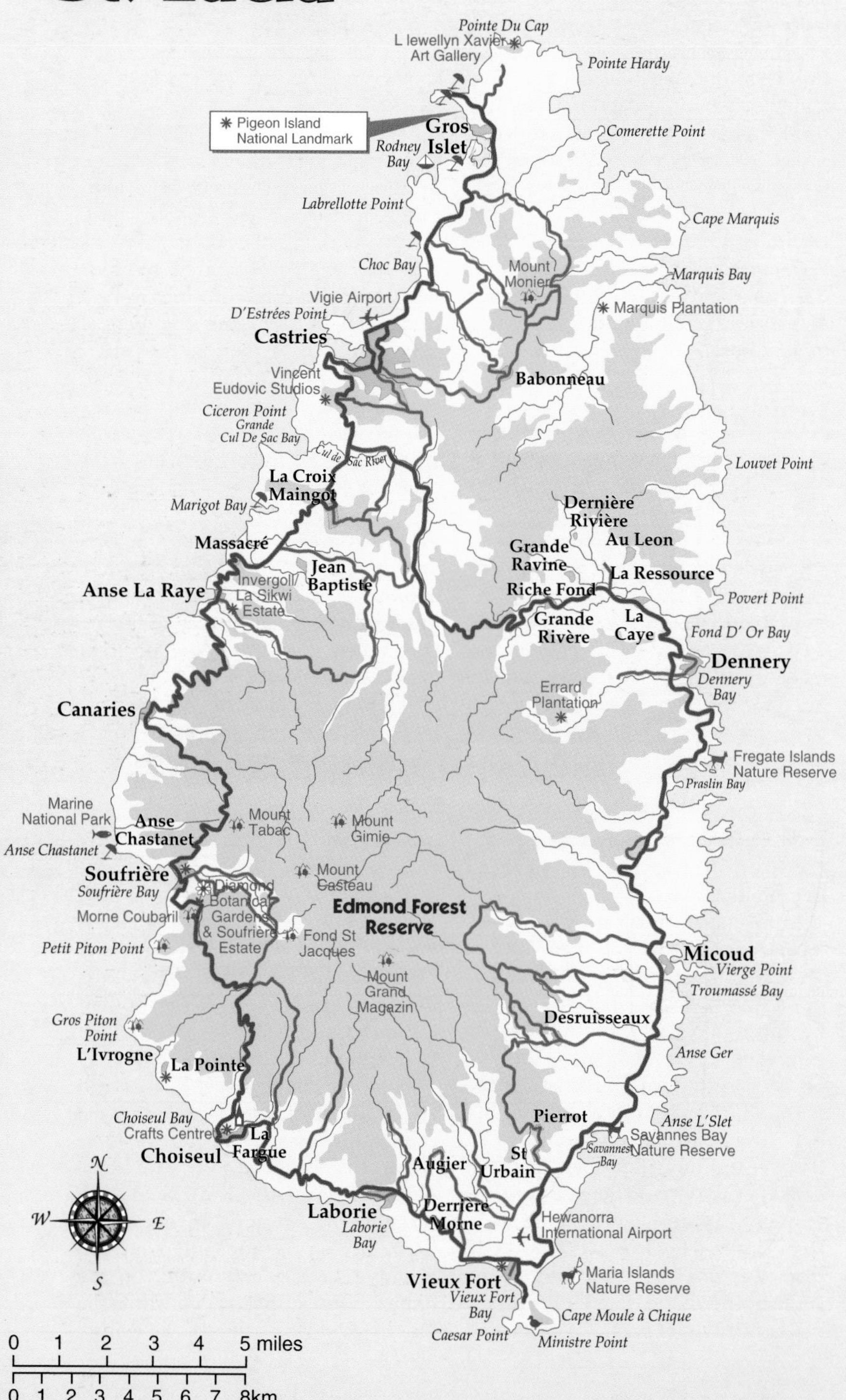
Pointe Du Cap
L lewellyn Xavier Art Gallery
Pointe Hardy
Pigeon Island National Landmark
Gros Islet
Rodney Bay
Comerette Point
Labrellotte Point
Cape Marquis
Choc Bay
Mount Monier
Marquis Bay
Vigie Airport
D'Estrées Point
Marquis Plantation
Castries
Babonneau
Vincent Eudovic Studios
Ciceron Point
Grande Cul De Sac Bay
Cul de Sac River
Louvet Point
La Croix Maingot
Marigot Bay
Dernière Rivière
Au Leon
Massacré
Grande Ravine
La Ressource
Jean Baptiste
Anse La Raye
Invergoll/La Sikwi Estate
Riche Fond
Povert Point
Grande Rivère
La Caye
Fond D' Or Bay
Dennery
Dennery Bay
Errard Plantation
Canaries
Fregate Islands Nature Reserve
Praslin Bay
Marine National Park
Anse Chastanet
Mount Tabac
Mount Gimie
Anse Chastanet
Soufrière
Mount Casteau
Soufrière Bay
Diamond Botanical Gardens & Soufrière Estate
Edmond Forest Reserve
Morne Coubaril
Fond St Jacques
Petit Piton Point
Micoud
Vierge Point
Mount Grand Magazin
Troumassé Bay
Gros Piton Point
Desruisseaux
L'Ivrogne
La Pointe
Anse Ger
Choiseul Bay Crafts Centre
Pierrot
Anse L'Slet
Savannes Bay Nature Reserve
Savannes Bay
La Fargue
Choiseul
St Urbain
Augier
N
W
E
S
Laborie
Laborie Bay
Derrière Morne
Hewanorra International Airport
Vieux Fort
Vieux Fort Bay
Maria Islands Nature Reserve
Cape Moule à Chique
Caesar Point
Ministre Point
0 1 2 3 4 5 miles
0 1 2 3 4 5 6 7 8km

Above: View of Castries and the Pointe Seraphine cruise ship terminal.

several charming old French wooden buildings.

The main downtown shopping area is bordered by Jeremie Street, Mandel Street, Peynier Street and Brazil Street. There are lots of shops and mini-markets to explore, offering a huge range of goods from fresh fruit, vegetables and spices, to island handicrafts, prints and the latest books and records.

After browsing through the shops, visit the new indoor two-floor market on Peynier Street beside the harbour. En route, notice the **Court House** on the left of Peynier Street, next to the small **Constitution Park**, and the **Town Hall** just beyond on the right. The new red tile-roofed market sells fresh fruits, spices and vegetables of all description and on Saturday, the busiest day, the market is swelled by people from outlying villages coming to sell their produce. There are market guides at the entrance who can show visitors round, identify the various goods on sale and explain their uses. Nearby, the old nineteenth century market with its large red gates, now houses the crafts market where woven baskets, mats, pottery, wood carvings, jewellery and other island wares are sold. Alleys which run behind the markets are packed with tiny eateries serving island specialities and snacks.

Walk along the John Compton highway, which hugs the harbour, to visit the **Pointe Seraphine** cruise ship terminal. The road passes the **Government Offices** on the right. The strange white building with its steeply-sloping roof, as you approach the terminal, is the home of the Alliance Francaise.

There are duty-free boutiques at Pointe Seraphine as well as a tourist information office, and the headquarters of the tourist board.

The terminal is on the southern shore of the **Vigie Peninsula**, which forms the northern side of Castries Harbour and is home of Vigie Airport. There can be few airports in the world where one can step out of the terminal, which recently doubled in size, cross the road and be on the beach.

Visitors can enjoy a snack or drink at the terminal, and if the walk back to town seems daunting, take one of the many taxis from there.

The northern shore of the peninsula has golden beaches and excellent views along the coast from the **Vigie Lighthouse**. Close by are the ruins of military buildings, a powder magazine built by the French in 1784, and the graves of troops who died there.

Other places to visit in Castries include the **Holy Trinity Church** and **King George V Gardens**, to the north-west of the new market. The area at the southern end of Chaussée Road has a number of fine old creole houses with overhanging balconies and ornately patterned eaves. West of Castries are the popular resort areas of Tapion and La Toc Bays.

## Eating Out in Castries

**Burger Plus** $ *
St. Louis Street
☎ 452-7018
A fast food establishment offering chicken, fish, burgers, fries and soft drinks.

**Caribbees** $$ ***
☎ 452-4767
Great creole food in this small, intimate restaurant. Lunch served from 12.30pm, dinner reservations necessary.

**Chez Paul** $$-$$$ ***
Brazil Street
Derek Walcott Square
☎ 452-3022
An excellent French restaurant in a former French colonial residence overlooking the main square. An exciting menu combining French haute cuisine and Pacific Rim, prepared by English masterchef Paul.

Open Monday to Friday from 8am-10pm and on Sunday from 11am-10.30pm. Make reservations for dinner.

**Green Parrot** $$-$$$ ***
Old Morne Road
☎ 452-3399
Fabulous views over Castries with an excellent, large fixed price menu offering speciality local dishes. The chef prepares all meals using the best local ingredients.

**Kimlan's** $-$$ ***
Micoud Street
☎ 452-1136
Offers good West Indian and creole dishes and many specialities.

**Natural Cafe** $-$$ **
Chaussée Road
☎ 452-6421
Vegetarian and 'healthy' Caribbean dishes, including fresh local produce.

**Paul's Place** $-$$ **
Bridge Street
☎ 453-1588
Enjoy European, creole and South Asian food. Specialities include Thai shrimp rolls, Indonesian satays and lobster thermidor. Great value for money, generous portions and daily changing lunch specials.

**Peppino's Pizza** $ *
Upper Bridge Street
☎ 452-3942
Pizzas to eat in, take out or have delivered, plus salads, burgers and baked potatoes.

**The Pink Elephant Grill & Bar** $-$$ **
William Peter Boulevard
☎ 453-2847
Specialities include grilled chicken, fish, beef and pork, and local specials are offered daily. Open Monday to Friday 9am-6pm, Saturday 9am-2pm.

**Subway** $ **
Brazil Street
☎ 452-2587
Good daily specials, creole dishes as well as giant sandwiches.

**Sunset Lodge Restaurant & Bar** $-$$ **
John Compton Highway
☎ 452-2639
A mixture of creole and Continental cooking with seafood, burgers and fresh fruit plates.

## A Circular Tour around The South Of The Island

The route heads south out of town across Morne Fortune with its many hairpin bends. If you are ascending observe the 'halt' signs on some corners because vehicles coming down the hill have to swing out to negotiate the tight bends. Approaching vehicles usually toot their horns.

There are a number of studios worth visiting, in particular the **Bagshaw Studios** (head for La Toc and follow the signs) where you can watch silk screens being created. They are open Monday to Saturday 8.30am-4.30pm and Sunday 8.30am-1pm. Further along take Old Victorian Road to visit **Caribelle Batik**, where silk and cotton batiks are produced in the centuries-old way. Opening times are Monday to Friday 8.30am-6pm and Saturday 8.30am-12.30pm. **Government House**, the official residence of the Governor General, stands on the Morne and is a fine example of late Victorian redbrick architecture.

The French started fortifying the Morne in the mid-eighteenth century, and the last defences were built by the English in 1905. Some military buildings have been restored and are now used as an educational complex.

From the Morne, the road runs south into Cul-de-Sac valley, a rich agricultural area with thousands of acres of bananas, formerly sugar cane, and an oil transhipment depot on the point, north of where the Cul-de-Sac river runs into the sea. The *Geest* freighter calls here once a week to collect bananas destined for the UK.

As the road descends into the valley, one encounters the studios of award-winning **Vincent Eudovic**, one of the island's most famous and talented sculptors.

He holds about three exhibitions of

Above: Marigot Bay is reputed to be one of the nicest anchorages in the Caribbean.
Below: The majestic Gros Piton near to Soufrière rises to 2,619ft.

his work each year using local woods for his abstract carvings. The main wood used is Laurier Canelle which is now extinct, but he uses old stumps and uncovered roots which are found deep in the forest. He and fellow artists also use mahogany, teak, Laurier Mabouey and red and white cedar. The studio is open Monday to Saturday from 8.30am-5pm, or 6pm and Sundays in the winter months.

From Cul-de-Sac valley, the winding, hilly road runs south towards Marigot Bay. One has to turn right for the bay, but it is worth the detour, and the road literally ends at the water's edge beside a police and customs station. Visitors can get a minibus from Castries to the bay but it drops passengers at the main road and they have to walk the last mile or so down to the water — and back later to get a bus into Castries. Marigot Bay is one of the most beautiful anchorages in the Caribbean, and was the setting of the film *Doctor Dolittle*, starring Rex Harrison. Scenes from Sophia Loren's **Fire Power** were also filmed here. Yachts bob up and down in the clear, turquoise waters, and the bay is surrounded on three sides by hills covered in lush tropical foliage. The water's edge is shaded by the overhanging fronds of swaying palm trees. Admiral Barrington evaded a French naval force in 1778 by sailing his squadron into the bay and camouflaging the vessels with palm leaves.

A free ferry plies across to Dolittle's Resort with its waterside restaurant. It is a delightful place for a beach lunch before continuing on the tour. There are also some good restaurants on the roadside of the bay, and once can normally watch islanders crafting hats and baskets from woven banana leaves, which are sold with other souvenirs by the water's edge.

From Marigot Bay, the road continues south through the **Roseau Banana Plantation**, and the small fishing village of **Massacre** with its community housing project, onto the fishing villages of **Anse La Raye** with its imposing church, and **Canaries**. There is a crossroads just before the bridge in Anse La Raye and a small sign to the **Invergoll Estate** (sometimes known as La Sikwi Estate) to the left. Turn here, bearing right at the junction and stop at the new footbridge over the river (which replaced one of many destroyed in the September 1994 flood). The bridge provides access to the 120 year-old, 400-acre (160 hectares) Invergoll Estate, which grows bananas, cocoa and some coffee. The tour includes the old sugar mill with its 40ft (12m) water wheel made in Glasgow, Scotland in 1878, and milling machinery made by Fletchers of Derby, England. There is a bar and a theatre set in the botanical garden. There are also tours to the **Anse La Raye waterfalls** and rainforest. Visitors can make reservations through their hotel or alternatively through Carib Touring. ☎ 452 1141

The new road between Anse La Raye and Canaries affords a good view of the **Pitons** (Spikes) across Soufrière Bay. These huge natural pyramids rise from the sea, and from a distance seem to be side by side. Petit Piton is the nearer of the two, with Gros Piton almost one-and-half miles (2km) beyond across Anse des Pitons.

The road hugs the western flanks of the mountain, which rise up into a vast area of rainforest. One can only visit the forest, now a protected area, with a guide but it is worth the visit and makes a fascinating and unforgettable day trip.

The road then descends towards the coast and the village of Soufrière. Before turning into Soufrière, it is worth detouring along the bumpy road that leads to the Anse Chastanet Resort. It is said the road is not repaired to discourage too many visitors, but it is worth taking because as it climbs up the hill there are stunning views of the Pitons behind. One can also take great photographs from across the water of the two mountains clearly separated by the sea.

## Eating Out South of Castries

**Bon Appetit** $$ ***
Morne Fortune
☎ 452-2757
Fabulous views, intimate atmosphere, attentive, personal service and great food. There are only five tables so book in advance for dinner. The restaurant is run by Renato and Cheryl Venturi. All soups and starters are home made, and the house speciality is freshwater crayfish.

**Dolittles Resort** $-$$ ***
☎ 451-4230
On the north side of Marigot Bay and accessible by private boat or ferry. Great atmosphere, great views and very good food. The restaurant serves an excellent selection of local and international cuisine.

**Eudovic's** $$ **
Goodlands
☎ 452-2747
Fabulous setting perched on the hill overlooking spectacular scenery. The restaurant is owned by one of the island's most famous sculptors and guests dine surrounded by many of his hand carvings which are available for purchase. Visitors may purchase the sculptures after eating.

**J J's Restaurant & Bar** $-$$ **
Marigot Bay
☎ 451-4076
West Indian, French and local speciality dishes are served in the restaurant which is a leisurely ten minute stroll from the bay. There is even free transport for those who can not face the walk.

Open from 7.30pm until the last guests leave. There is a great party atmosphere on Friday nights when J J's throws its weekly jam.

**Kimono's** $$$ **
Sandals St. Lucia,
La Toc Bay
☎ 452-3081/9
An intimate forty-seat restaurant on the hillside overlooking the bay. Guests are greeted at the door and dressed in a kimono, and each table has its own chef to prepare the chosen dishes.

Desserts and tea are served in the lounge. Open nightly except Friday 6.30pm-10pm. Reservations required.

**Les Pitons** $-$$ **
Sandals St. Lucia
La Toc Bay
☎ 452-3081/9
Authentic creole and Caribbean dishes freshly-prepared and served in casual but elegant surroundings. Open Tuesday to Thursday and weekends 6.30pm-10pm. Reservations required.

**The Pavilion** $$-$$$ ***
Sandals St. Lucia
La Toc Bay
☎ 452-3081/9
The resort's main dining area is situated by the pool and delightful for dinner. The cuisine is a mix of international with strong Italian influences. A beach barbecue is held weekly, two nights feature an Italian buffet. There is an international buffet once a week.

Breakfast is served from 7.30am to 10am. Lunch is served from 12.30pm to 2.15pm and dinner between 6.30pm and 10.15pm.

**Restaurant La Toc** $$$ ***
Sandals St. Lucia
La Toc Bay
☎ 452-3081/9
An elegant French restaurant offering excellent food and attentive, efficient service. A carving trolley serves special entrées and there is a flambé cart serving delicious entrées and desserts. Open Tuesday and Thursday to Sunday 6.30pm-10pm. Reservations required.

**Rusty Anchor** $$ **
Marigot Bay Resort
☎ 451-4357
Good food in a fabulous setting overlooking the bay. Always a good selection of fresh fish plus steaks.

**San Antoine** $$-$$$ ****
Morne View
☎ 452-4660
The restaurant occupies a historic house, in 11 acres (4 hectares) of tropical gardens, which once played host to famous figures such as Somerset Maugham. There are wonderful views and owners Michael and Alison Richings ensure truly elegant dining and excellent international cuisine. There is an extensive à la carte menu, daily set price menu, and a very good accompanying wine list. Dinner reservations are recommended. A complimentary taxi service is offered to and from hotels for parties of four or more.

**Tapion Reef Hotel** $$-$$$ **
Tapion Bay
☎ 452-7471
The restaurant has a good à la carte menu featuring West Indian and creole dishes. Noted for its seafood and freshwater crayfish. The restaurant and bar overlook historic Tapion Rock. Dinner reservations recommended.

## Soufrière

Soufrière is still a picturesque fishing town, even though it no longer enjoys the prosperity of a century ago when it was a busy port. It nestles in the shadows of the Pitons, with Soufrière Bay to the west and the sulphur gushing volcanic crater which gives it its name, inland to the south-east.

The first settlers were Amerindians and there are many petroglyphs in the area, particularly at Stonefields, and the rock terraces at Belfond are believed to be their work.

The French established huge plantations here and slaves were shipped from Africa to work them. In 1746, Soufrière was the first town to be established in St. Lucia, and it has been an important trading and farming centre ever since.

By 1775, there were more than 100 estates producing sugar or coffee, and Soufrière was 'the bread basket of St. Lucia'. It was badly hit in 1780 by a hurricane and the town had only just started to recover when it became embroiled in the French Revolution of 1789. The Revolutionary Council in Paris ordered that Soufrière be renamed La Convention. A guillotine was erected in the Town Square and some of Royalist planters lost their heads, while others fled.

Slaves, freed by order of Paris, joined with deserters from the French army and battled for three years in the Brigand War with the authorities. The town's strong French heritage can still very much in evidence. Many family names are of French origin, as are many of the places and geographical features nearby such as Anse Mamin, Etangs, Fond St. Jacques and Terre Blanche.

On 10 September 1994, the area was hit by a ferocious storm and the worst flooding in seventy-five years. In three-and-a-half hours, 11 inches (28cm) of rain fell. Rivers flooded, washing away homes and bridges, and landslides destroyed months of work on new projects including the new Castries to Soufrière road. Although it was the worst storm in living memory, only six people lost their lives.

Today, the town has a peaceful atmosphere and Soufrière Bay offers a sheltered anchorage for yachts. The jetty accommodates boats offering sightseeing and trips to and from Castries.

The long sandy beach is lined with coconut palms, beneath which sit the open fishing boats after a day at sea. The waterfront is a centre of activity in the afternoon as the fishermen sell their daily catch, and people from surrounding villages bring produce for sale at the Saturday market.

The Soufrière River divides the town, and most of the shops, craft centres, restaurants and guesthouses

Above: The waterfall at Diamond Estate Botanical Garden.
Below: The area around Soufrière is made up of verdant coconut plantations.

are found in the two or three streets inland from the jetty, including the police station and post office.

Soufrière is also noted as the home of Marie-Josephe-Rose de Tascher de la Pagerie, better known as Empress Josephine, wife of Napoleon Bonaparte. Although born at Morne Paix Bouche in the north of St. Lucia, she spent much of her childhood at Malmaison, her father's estate on the outskirts of Soufrière. One can visit the estate with its massive iron water wheel used to crush the sugar cane, and iron crucibles in which the sugar juice was boiled. There is also a copper press where lime oil was extracted, and copra sheds where coconuts were cut in half and laid out to dry. Women still husk the coconuts by hand ready for drying, and can be seen removing beans from the cocoa pods.

Just to the north at **Anse Chastanet**, a fabulous coral reef rich in marine life has been designated a Marine National Park. Divers claim it to be one of the most beautiful reefs in the region because of its multi-coloured corals, sponges and shoals of dazzling, tropical fish. It is an area rich in brain coral, sea fans and the fish include angel fish, blue-headed wrasse, parrot fish and flying gurnards.

The Anse Chastanet Hotel is a delightful forty-eight room hotel situated on a lush 500-acre (200 hectare) estate. Guests are accommodated in unique and stylish rooms. The bedrooms, bathrooms and tropical hardwood furniture have been personal designed by the architect-owner and all blend delightfully with the surrounding environment. The owner, Nick Troubetszkoy first arrived in St. Lucia in 1970 and stayed onto transform Anse Chastanet into the peaceful haven it has become. With his wife Karolin, they run the hotel in a most hospital and elegant fashion. Thirty-six open treehouse-style deluxe rooms are situated on a hillside adorned with spectacular trees and twelve rooms are situated directly on the beach.

Guests can leave behind the cares of the world and enjoy candlelit-dinners in either the open-air restaurant located in the shadow of the magnificent sugar-loaf peaks of the Pitons, or dine in the enchanting Trou au Diable restaurant situated right on the beach.

The two Pitons, **Gros Piton** to the south at 2,619ft (798m), and **Petit Piton** to the north at 2,461ft (750m), can be climbed, but the ascent is rated as difficult, and a full day is needed for the round trip. Guides are available.

The road south of town leads to St. Lucia's drive-in **Soufrière volcano**. The giant crater was formed about 40,000 years ago. The eruption was so massive that it blew the top of the mountain into the sea to the west.

Knowledgeable guides explain the geological history of the area and how the lunar-like landscape was created. There are sulphur vents and twenty-four cauldrons of bubbling mud boiling at around 171°C (340°C). The volcano is dormant because most of the subterranean pressure has been released. During the oil crisis in the 1970s, an attempt was made to harness the boiling thermal waters so they could drive turbines. The scheme failed because the lava is so acidic that it corroded the drilling pipes and well-head caps.

Large areas of the crater are covered with vegetation and it is amazing that sixty people actually live within its perimeter, earning their living either farming or selling souvenirs.

It is essential to keep within the boundary fences and ropes, as the ground around the boiling mud pools is very dangerous.

There are also sulphur springs on the Diamond Estate, founded in 1784 for the troops of King Louis XVI of

France so that they could benefit from its therapeutic waters. The king granted funds to construct the main building and twelve stone baths. In 1930 Andre Du Boulay, owner of both the Soufrière and Diamond estates, decided to restore two baths for his own use. Later the outside pools were built and opened to the public for a small fee. There are changing cubicles.

In 1983 after the death of M. Du Boulay, his daughter Joan Devaux decided to landscape the natural gorge, which is the main feature of Diamond, as an historical garden. Today, it is a blaze of colour with hibiscus, ixora, orchids, heliconias and scores of other plants and trees.

The gardens are beautifully maintained and landscaped with pergolas, gazebos, rockeries and arbours. Labels make it easy to identify the various plants, and there are several displays showing the appearance of various fruits and plants after their shells or outer casings have been removed.

The path leads to the two outdoor Diamond Mineral Baths and changing area, and then continues along a fern-lined walk to a glade with a sparkling waterfall that tumbles into a rock pool. The gardens are open daily from 10am-5pm. ☎ (809) 452-4759.

The **Soufrière Estate** was originally part of a 2,000 acre (800 hectare) land grant by King Louis XIV to three Devaux brothers from Normandy, France. The brothers arrived in 1742 to establish their plantations, and the family still owns them today. The young Empress Josephine played with the children on the Soufrière Estate which was close to her father's **Mal Maison Plantation** which is open daily from 10am-4pm. Tours of the plantation offer an insight into the harvesting and processing of crops such as copra and cocoa. The mini zoo features local animals such as agouti, manicou and boa constrictors. The plantation is open daily from 10am-4pm. Another nearby estate which is open daily 9am-5pm is **Morne Coubaril Estate**. It overlooks Soufrière and was fortified by the French to protect the bay. It is about one mile (2km) out of town on the Choiseul road. It is a working estate, and guided tours show visitors around the copra oven which is used for reducing coconuts, the cocoa processing house, the manioc house and authentic reconstructions of Carib and African slave huts.

Almost opposite the gates to Morne Coubaril is the entrance to the Jalousie Plantation Resort and Spa — one of the island's most exclusive resorts situated on a spectacular beach between the two Pitons. Many companies offer full-day boat trips from Castries and its nearby resorts to Soufrière.

Inland, the road climbs steeply through dense, lush vegetation into one of the island's few remaining areas of tropical rainforest. There are spectacular views from the rough **Fond St. Jacques** road back over the Pitons and Soufrière, and the forest is home to hundreds of exotic birds, animals, plants and insects, including the vivid orange flambeau butterfly, St. Lucia oriole, St. Lucia forest thrush and St. Lucia blackfinch — all endemic to the island. Once can also sometimes catch a glimpse of the rare and colourful St. Lucia parrot, the island's national bird.

The foliage and heady aromas which fill the air are breathtaking. The giant tree ferns, bamboo stands, and giant gommier, mahogany and cedar trees, wild orchids and air plants which cling to the bark of their host trees, are an incredible sight. Walks through the **Edmond Forest Reserve** can be arranged through tour guides, or through the Forestry and Lands Department in Castries. The drive back from Soufrière to Castries takes about one-and-a-half hours.

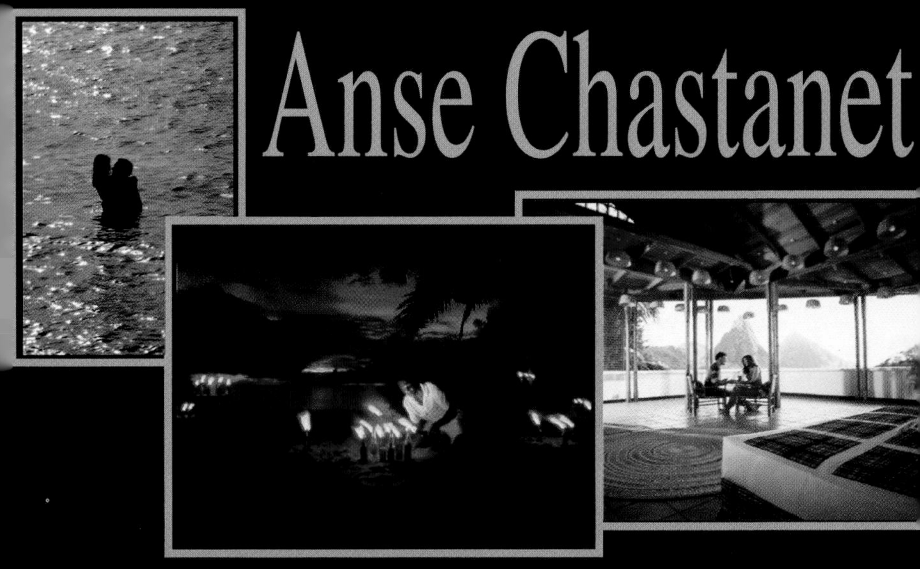
Anse Chastanet

Above: The picturesque fishing village of Soufrière.

## Eating Out in Soufrière

**Anse Chastanet Hotel** $-$$ **
☎ 459-7354
The beach restaurant has a varied menu using fresh and delicious local produce served in mouthwatering creole-style sauces. The romantic open-air Piton Restaurant offers memorable cooking from French chef Jacky Rious and his team while guests relax and sit in the shadow of the magnificent Pitons. The set five-course menu offers an excellent and varied choice.

**Bang** $$ ***
Soufrière
☎ 459-7864
Located on the waterfront and an eating adventure. The restaurant and rum shop consist of a number of relocated country homes, and offers delicious local dishes, including a traditional Caribbean barbecue.

**Camilla's Restaurant and Bar** $-$$ ***
Bridge Street
☎ 459-5379
A great place to eat or enjoy a drink in a very relaxed atmosphere. There are daily lunch specials featuring international and creole dishes and there are gourmet, à la carte and dinner menus. The bar is noted for its cocktails! Open Tuesday to Sunday from 8am to late.

**Dasheene** $$-$$$ ****
Ladera Resort
☎ 459-7850
Exciting food combining new-wave Californian and traditional Caribbean dishes. One of the finest restaurants on the island with an impressive wine list, and an even more impressive view.

The restaurant is perched 1,000ft (305m) up on the mountain side and offers spectacular views of the elegant pool deck across to the Pitons. Open daily.

**The Humming Bird Beach Resort** $-$$ **
☎ 459-7232
The waterside restaurant serves great seafood, always fresh and prepared to order.

**Jalousie Plantation** $$-$$$ ***
Near Soufrière
☎ 459-7666
There are four restaurants in this all-inclusive resort near Soufrière. The Verandah offers breakfast, the Pier specialises in seafood and creole dishes, the Plantation Room offers French gourmet cuisine, and the Bayside Grill offers lighter fare such as grills and sandwiches.

**Jacquot Restaurant and Bar** $-$$ **
☎ 459-5161
The restaurant serves Caribbean and international dishes, with some Chinese entrees. Try the specialities such as creole curries and rotis.

**The Still** $-$$ ***
La Perle and Ruby Estates
☎ 459-7224
A family owned restaurant offering genuine St. Lucian dishes in a delightful plantation setting. There is an impressive lunch buffet of island specialities. Open daily from 8am to 5pm and for dinner by reservation only.

## Soufrière to Vieux Fort

From Soufrière the new road climbs into the mountains and rainforests past the Pitons on the right, and then drops down to the coast. There are several side roads to the coast. A detour to La Pointe is worthwhile, and if by taking the road for La Pointe and L'Ivrogne, which follows the L'Ivrogne River, one can also take in the **nature trail** along the way. The gravel-paved looped trail takes about one hour to walk. Most of the tree species — such as mahogany and Caribbean pine — are still used commercially on the island and provide cover for many of the bird species, especially singing warblers, finches and hummingbirds. There is a medicinal herb garden and an interpretive centre with information about endangered species, vegetation zones and the rainforest by day and night.

The fishing village of La Pointe is the centre of the island's pottery industry. Here local clay is shaped into mainly functional products, such as massive coal pots and traditional cooking pots. From La Pointe take the coast road south instead of returning to the main highway.

The tiny fishing village of **Choiseul** with its church almost on the beach, features a crafts centre whose weavers produce functional items such as baskets, mats, sewing boxes, fans and laundry baskets. At one time, almost all St. Lucian babies slept in these locally-woven bassinets. It is open Monday to Friday from 8am-4pm and Saturday 10am-4pm. The village also has a flourishing furniture industry, producing mostly chairs from cedar, with screw-pine fibre-woven backs.

Choiseul is a charming village with its old gingerbread houses on stilts overlooking the bay. The road then follows the coast to **Laborie**, another pretty little fishing village, and Vieux Fort at the southern end of the island, close to the international airport.

**Vieux Fort** was named after a fortress which used to look across to St. Vincent in the distance. In the second half of the eighteenth century it was the centre of the island's sugar industry, but its fortunes declined as the sugar plantations closed. A new lease of life came during World War II when the Americans built and airstrip as a refuelling stop for the aircraft flying between the USA and Europe. The expanded airstrip is now **Hewanorra International Airport.**

Island Windsurfing is based in Vieux Fort and operates in **Anse Sables**, and they hire equipment and give lessons. Their Reef Beach Cafe includes a video lounge where beginners can learn about the sport before getting their feet wet.

**Ministre Point** is the most southerly point on the island at the end of the Moule à Chique Peninsula. Apart from the lighthouse perched on the rocks and the incredible views across to St. Vincent and the Grenadines, the cliffs are home to thousands of seabirds. This whole area is a bird-watcher's paradise, and the two islands to the east off Vieux Fort — Maria Major and Maria Minor — make up the **Maria Islands Nature Reserve** which contains many rare species of plants and birds. Maria Major is the only place in the world where the harmless kouwes grass snake is found. The islands are also host to the unique zandoli te ground lizard. The reserve is closed during the breeding season but tours can be arranged at other times.

## Eating Out In and Around Vieux Fort

**Chak Chak Cafe** $-$$ **
☎ 454-6260
Close to Hewanorra Airport and offering continental and creole daily specials.

**Il Pirata Ristorante Italiano** $-$$ **
☎ 454-6610
An Italian beach restaurant offering relaxed dining and authentic cuisine, with a good range of Italian wines. Open daily except Monday from 7am-9.30pm.

**Ocean Hideaway Beanfield** $$ ***
☎ 454-5253
Good creole home cooking is served in the converted barracks once used by USA troops during World War II. There are lunch specials, weekend barbecues and nightly dancing in the air-conditioned disco. Open Monday to Thursday 8.30am-11pm, weekends from 8.30am-2.30pm.

**The Reef Beach Cafe** $-$$ ***
Anse du Sables
☎ 454-7400
The cafe is situated on the beach and offers Caribbean and international dishes.

**Sandy Beach Restaurant and Bar** $ ***
Anse du Sables
☎ 454-7416
Good food, good service and a fun place, especially on Friday night which is Caribbean night. Open daily from 10am-10pm, except Wednesday 10am-5pm. Evening reservations are recommended.

**Skyway Inn** $$ **
Close to Hewanorra Airport
☎ 454-7111
The air-conditioned restaurant offers breakfast, lunch and dinner. Specialities include freshly-caught seafood cooked island-style.

## Vieux Fort To Castries Along The East Coast

From Vieux Fort, the new road follows the Atlantic coast north past Savannes Bay, the **Savannes Bay Nature Reserve** and Point de Caille to Micaud. Along the way there are spectacular coastal views. When the breeze picks up, the waves come pounding in which makes this a very popular area for experienced windsurfers and surf boarders. There are many bays along this stretch of coastline, such as **Anse L'Slet**, **Anse Ger** and **Troumassé Bay**. There are usually steep roads down to these coves, and the last section often has to walked. Between the two fishing villages of Micoud and Dennery, and just after the small fishing village of Praslin, you can see the Fregate Islands just offshore. The tiny islands are the nesting site of frigate birds, and tours can be arranged through the St. Lucia National Trust (☎ 452 5005/453 1495).

**Dennery** has a long tradition as both a fishing and boat building community. The fishing boats are all hand-built and were traditionally made from trees felled in the rainforests. Efforts are being made, with some success, to encourage the boat builders to use fibreglass for construction to protect the trees.

Just beyond Dennery one can visit

FOR AIRPORT TRANSFERS AND SCENIC FLIGHTS
Telephone:
(809) 453 6952
Fax:
(809) 453 6956
After hours and weekends
(809) 453 2171

the working **Errard Plantation** which is open daily. This is a private estate and it is advisable to seek permission before progressing along the rough road to reach the small **Errard Waterfall** at the end of a short trail. Alternatively, take one of the organised day trips to the estate for a conducted tour by the owner in a four-wheel drive vehicle.

The main road then continues through La Caye and Grand Rivère, before winding its way north back into Castries. It is 33 miles (53km) from Vieux Fort to Castries along the east coast route.

## North of Castries

The road north out of Castries passes Vigie Airport, Vigie Beach, Vide Bouteille Point and Choc Bay with its many resort hotels and the nearby Gablewoods Shopping Mall. Situated off the beach is the curiously named Rat Island, a former nunnery which is now being considered for an artists' colony. This stretch of coastline between Vigie and Pigeon Island in the north has many of St. Lucia's finest beaches, and is the major resort area.

The road past Gablewoods Mall runs through the huge Marisule Estate and then leads to **Rodney Bay** — one of the most popular moorings for yachts in the Caribbean. The beautifully-landscaped marina has restaurants, bars, shops, a yacht chandlery and invariably, hundreds of moored vessels. Rodney Bay is now one of the leading charter centres in the Caribbean and several charter companies are based there. Across Rodney Bay is the fishing town of **Gros Islet** with its large Catholic church, and historic Pigeon Point over the bay.

Gros Islet is most famous for the Friday night 'jump up' — a huge party which spills out into the street and attracts scores of merrymakers for the carnival-like festivities. The party starts around 9pm to the sound of deafening music. Scores of stalls line the streets selling local specialities, such as crispy fried fish, conch, fish cakes, roast corn and little cakes. The bars set up tables and chairs in the street, and the concept is to mingle while moving from bar to bar enjoying a few beers, and a lot of talking and dancing. The party continues until the early hours of Saturday morning so ensure you have arranged transport home.

During the rest of the week, the town with its few streets of tiny clapboard houses, returns to fishing — its major source of income, although tourism is increasingly important because of nearby Pigeon Island.

### Pigeon Island National Historic Park

Pigeon Point, formerly Pigeon Island, is one of the region's most famous historic sites. It is open daily 9am-5pm and an admission fee is charged. It was from here in 1782 that Admiral Rodney set sail to intercept the French fleet. The ensuing Battle of the Saints prevented the French from making their rendezvous with the Spanish and saved Jamaica for the British Empire.

Pigeon Island is no longer an island because it is connected to the mainland by a causeway built from earth removed during the excavation of the ill-fated Rodney Bay Development, a tourism project that foundered in the 1970s. There is a spectacular drive along the causeway to the parking area at the entrance of the huge fortified area. The site features gun batteries and the remains of military buildings, and even for those not interested in history, it is a delightful place to visit.

Pigeon Point covers 44 acres (18 hectares) of sloping grasslands, dry

## The Battle of the Saints

In 1778 the English captured St. Lucia from the French during the American War of Independence. A naval base was established in Gros Islet Bay protected by the heavily fortified Pigeon Island. There were frequent clashes between the English and French navies, but the most decisive battle occurred on 12 April 1782 in the Battle of the Saints, so named because it was fought off the Isles des Saintes, between Guadeloupe and Dominica. The French fleet in Fort Royal, Martinique, planned to connect with the Spanish fleet at Cap François in Haiti, before launching an attack on Fort Charles in Jamaica. Jamaica was at the time under the command of Admiral Horatio Nelson. If successful, the combined French and Spanish attack could well have driven the English out of the Caribbean.

Look-out posts on Pigeon Island monitored the French build up at Fort Royal, and on 8 April, Admiral Rodney received a signal that the French fleet consisting of more than 150 ships and an army of 10,000 men, had set sail. Within two hours, the English fleet was in pursuit.

Anxious to avoid a confrontation until they could link up with the Spanish fleet, the French eluded Rodney for three days, but their ships slowed down on the evening of 11 April because of the calmer winds in the lee of Dominica. English squadrons led by Hood, Rodney and Drake closed in. Although the battle raged all day, Admiral de Grasse on his flagship *Ville de Paris*, struck his colours in surrender just before sunset.

tropical forests, and two peaks, connected by a saddle, which made excellent observation posts. The new museum and interpretation centre, in the restored officers' quarters, has electronic multi-media displays on the fort and the Battle of the Saints. There are botanical gardens, beautiful sandy beaches, a restaurant and a 200-year-old English tavern. Take care to avoid the low arches! The park has a wedding gazebo and its own wedding coordinator to ensure everything goes smoothly.

The 40-acre (16 hectare) park was officially opened by Princess Alexandra on 23 February 23 1979, to commemorate the island's independence attained the previous day.

From Pigeon Island drive north to **Pointe Du Cap**, the northern tip of the island where the exclusive Cap Estate has many fine beaches and coves, a golf course, and some of St. Lucia's most expensive homes. Martinique can clearly be seen on the horizon.

One can either return to Castries along the coastal road, enjoying a leisurely lunch at one of the beach grills and a swim in the sea, or take the inland road south of Gros Islet which runs past Mount Monier to Barbonneau and then west back into Castries. Just south of Mount Monier, the road runs close to what used to be the Morne Paix Bouche Estate, where Empress Josephine was born in 1763. An interesting detour from the inland road is to the **Marquis Plantation**, with its impressive stands of mahogany, teak, coffee and cocoa trees. Boat trips run along the Marquis River to

Above: The historic site of Pigeon Island is a 40-acre national park.
Below: Rodney Bay is one of the most popular haunts in the Caribbean for yachts.

Marquis Bay for a swim in the Atlantic. There are a number of organised tours to the estate where visitors are greeted by one of the owners — and a large reviving glass of rum punch.

There are a number of other accessible bays on the north-eastern coastline including the sweeping Grande Anse and Anse Lavoutte.

## Eating Out

**Gablewoods Shopping Mall**
El Burrito $-$$ *
☎ 451-7924
Mexican restaurant serving burritos, fajitas and national dishes.

**Kafe Kools** $ *
☎ 451-7052
An ice cream parlour, crèperie and bar offering sandwiches, main dishes, as well as savoury crepes, ice cream.

**Miss Saigon** $-$$ **
☎ 451-7309
A wide range of oriental-style cuisines are available including Chinese, Indian, Thai, Malaysian and Indonesian.

**Peppino's Pizza** $ *
☎ 451-6970
Pizzas to eat in, take out or have delivered. Try one of the unusual combinations like Hawaiian pizza with ham, pineapple and sweet pepper toppings.

### *North of Castries*

**Bayside Sandals Halcyon** $$-$$$ ***
Choc Bay
☎ 453-0222
Offering breakfast, lunch and dinner beside the pool of this delightful hotel. There is an international buffet on Friday evenings and nightly music and entertainment.

**Beach Haven International** $$-$$$ ***
Orange Grove Hotel
Vigie Beach
☎ 452-0065
International cuisine and daily specials are offered in the Beach Haven seaside restaurant, plus a fast-food section.

**Cafe Clementine** $-$$ ***
Orange Grove Hotel
Bois d'Orange
☎ 452-0021
A beautiful hilltop setting in an old plantation house overlooking St. Lucia. Dine on the balcony and enjoy good West Indian and international cooking in a relaxed atmosphere. Open daily for breakfast, and lunch between 11am and 3pm, and dinner from 7pm to 10pm.

**Cafe Tropical** $-$$ **
Pointe Seraphine
☎ 452-7411
A fast-food cafe offering snacks, hot meals and fast foods, as well as ice cream and draught beer.

**Chung's** $-$$ **
Choc Bay
☎ 452-4795
A good Chinese restaurant offering relaxed, casual dining.

**Coal Pot** $-$$ ***
Vigie Marina
☎ 452-6811
Although the menu changes constantly, it concentrates on local produce and traditional island cooking. Lunch specialities include crab back and callaloo served with local bread. Prices are very reasonable and servings generous.

**Coral Reef Restaurant** $$-$$$ ***
Windjammer Landing Resort
☎ 452-0913
A Caribbean buffet is served every Thursday accompanied by a steel band and floor show. There are also Mexican and seafood evenings with live music. Open Monday to Saturday 6.30pm to 10.30pm. Children eat half price.

**D's Restaurant** $$ **
Edgewater Beach Hotel
Vigie Beach
☎ 453-7931
Creole and international dishes served for lunch and dinner. There are daily lunch specials, and guests dine on the terrace on excellent seafood, and specialities including sautéed chicken livers in sherry, and chicken *picatta* with mint and yoghurt.

**Friendship Inn** $-$$ **
Sunny Acres
☎ 452-4201
Charming little restaurant serving breakfast and dinner. Good value for money, There are poolside barbecues on Saturday nights.

**Island Bar and Bistro** $-$$ **
Windjammer Landing Villa Beach Resort
☎ 452-0913
Great views of Labrelotte Bay, Castries and on clear days, Martinique. A bistro-style menu with all dishes prepared to order, and served by the pool. Open daily 11am to 11pm. Happy hour daily from 5pm to 6pm.

**Jammers Beach Bar** $-$$ **
Windjammer Landing
☎ 452-0913
Enjoy snacks, pasta, seafood or burgers in a relaxed informal atmosphere located between the delightful pool area and the sea. Open daily from 9am to 1am. Happy hour 5 to 6pm.

**Jammers Restaurant** $$-$$$ ****
Windjammer Landing
☎ 452-0913
A great place for Sunday brunch which is served to the sounds of a steel band. A mixture of creole and international cuisine with à la carte and daily table d'hôte menus available. Open daily from 7.30am to 10.30pm. Sunday brunch from 11am to 2.30pm.

**Jimmie's** $$-$$$ ***
Vigie Cove
☎ 452-5142
Deservedly renowned for its mouth-watering creole and seafood dishes. Try salt fish and green fig, the national dish, which features on the Friday and Saturday lunch menus. Open all day.

**Labrelotte Beach Barbecue** $-$$ **
Windjammer Landing
☎ 452-0913
A wide range of barbecue foods always available. A favourite for families with children, or visitors wanting a leisurely open-air lunch by the the blue waters of the Caribbean Sea. Open daily from 12noon to 3pm.

**Laurell's** $-$$ **
Bois d'Orange
☎ 452-8547
Creole cuisine served in an informal setting.

**Mario's** $$-$$$ ***
Sandals Halcyon
Choc Bay
☎ 453-0222
Gourmet restaurant offering the finest of Italian fare, with excellent fresh pasta dishes and a good selection of Italian wines. Open for dinner only.

**Palm Grill** $-$$ **
Wyndham Morgan Bay Resort
Choc Bay
☎ 450-2511
Beach grill offering lunch and dinner.

**Pierhouse** $$-$$$ ***
Sandals Halcyon
Choc Bay
☎ 453-0222
Dine in elegance and splendour in the restaurant which is built out over the sea. The restaurant offers the best of island cooking. Reservations required.

**The Tradewinds** $$ **
Wyndham Morgan Bay Resort
Choc Bay
☎ 450-2511
Open for breakfast, lunch and dinner serving continental and American cuisine.

**Vigie Beach Hotel** $ **
☎ 452-5211
Excellent-value buffet lunches and selection changes daily.

## *Rodney Bay/Gros Islet*

**The 'A' Pub and Restaurant** $-$$ **
Rodney Bay
☎ 452-8725
Close to the Rex St. Lucian Hotel, the pub serves good steaks, seafood and sandwiches.

**Banana Split** $-$$ **
Gros Islet
☎ 450-8125
A mix of creole and continental cuisine, good seafood.

**The Bistro** $-$$ ***
Rodney Bay Marina
☎ 452-9494
Lively, waterfront setting offering a wide range of dishes from bistro-style meals to pub food and light dinners. Open daily from 5pm, but closed on Thursday during the summer. Happy hour is between 5 and 6.30pm and dinner reservations are recommended. Docking is available.

**Capone's** $-$$ **
Rodney Bay
☎ 452-0284
Fun 1930's Art Deco 'speakeasy' restaurant with barmen dressed as gangsters, offering good Italian fare. Pizzas, sandwiches and spit-roasted chicken served in the adjoining parlour and pizza garden.

**Charthouse** $$-$$$ ****
Rodney Bay
☎ 452-8115
Good food in a luxurious greenhouse-setting beside the water. Noted for its charcoal broiled- steaks, hickory smoked spare ribs and fresh, locally-caught seafood. Open Monday to Saturday from 5pm with last orders at 10.30pm. Reservations are recommended.

**Eagles Inn** $-$$ ***
Rodney Bay
☎ 452-0650
Famous for seafood and West Indian lamb dishes. The waterfront inn is open for lunch and dinner and serves snacks during the day. Specialities include callaloo, curry and accras (fish cakes). There is nightly evening entertainment including a creole dance night and traditional barbecue. Sunday is 'eat all you can' family day. Open Sunday to Thursday from 10am, Friday 10am to 5pm, and Saturday from 5pm.

**The Flamingo Restaurant** $$-$$$ ***
Rex St. Lucian
Rodney Bay
☎ 452-8351
Elegant dining offering a mixture of continental and West Indian cuisine, and famous for its flambées, thus its name. Discreet live music on Sunday, Tuesday and Friday. Open nightly from 7pm to 9.45pm.

**Frosties** $-$$ **
Rex St. Lucian,
Rodney Bay
☎ 452-8351
A fun place to indulge oneself on chocolate mint surprise, St. Lucian banana boat, peach cardinal or ice cream floats. Toasted sandwiches are also served along with juices and coffee for a quick breakfast or snack. Open daily from 7am to 10pm.

**Ginger Lily** $$ **
Rodney Bay
☎ 452-8303
Authentic and good value Cantonese and Chinese cuisine served in delightful surroundings. Specialities include the almond chicken ding with baby corn, and lobster in a ginger sauce. Open for lunch Tuesday to Saturday from 11.30am to 2.30pm and dinner from 6.30 to 11.30pm. Happy hour is 6 to 7pm on Monday and Friday, and there are luncheon specials from Tuesday to Saturday.

**The Golden Apple** $$ ***
Gros Islet
☎ 450-0634
Only creole and seafood specialities, including lobster, barbecued lambi and chicken, are offered in this small, intimate restaurant which opens for dinner. Try the conch, flying fish and rotis.

**The Great House Restaurant** $$-$$$ ****
Cap Estate
☎ 450-0450
Super French and creole food, elegantly presented in a great setting under the control of Chef Xavier. The dinner menu changes daily to ensure that only fresh ingredients are used. Traditional afternoon tea is served between 4.30 and 5.30pm, Sunset Happy Hour is between 5.30 and 6.30pm and dinner is served between 7pm and 10pm. Reservations are recommended.

**The Hummingbird** $$ ***
Rex St. Lucian
Rodney Bay
☎ 452-8351
Relaxed dining with a nightly eat-all-you-can buffet offering a wide range of dishes, except Wednesday when it is à la carte. There is gentle live music nightly.

# San Antoine

Elegant à la carte restaurant in an historical Great House situated in eleven acres of lush tropical gardens overlooking Castries Harbour.
A four-star rated restaurant serving exquisite cuisine in an unparalled setting.
For a celebration or simply a taste of the Caribbean at its finest.

**Open for lunch Monday to Friday:**
**11.30am - 2.30pm**
**Open for dinners Monday to Saturday:**
**6.30pm-10.30pm.**

PO Box 157, Castries, St. Lucia, West Indies.
Telephone (809) 452-4660

# Spinnakers

Situated on the beautiful Reduit Beach in front of the St. Lucian Yacht Club, we serve delicious breakfast, mouthwatering lunches and fabulous dinners.

Excellent prices in the finest location.

Enjoy a selection of dishes ranging from simple snacks to fine prime rib or fillet steak. Lobster cooked in a delicious garlic sauce or a varied selection of salads.

Open daily
Tel: (809) 452-8491

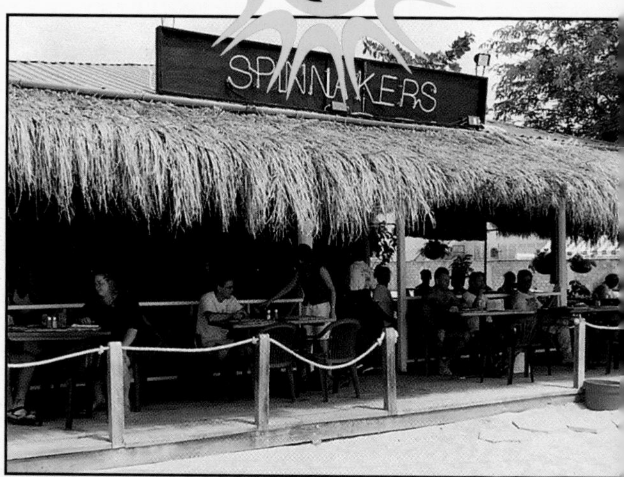


**St. Lucia's only Beach Ba**

**The Islander** $$ ***
Rodney Bay Marina
☎ 452-0255
Open daily for breakfast, lunch and dinner. A buffet is served on Monday evening, Tuesday to Thursday is à la carte from the continental and creole menu, and Friday is open air barbecue night.

**Key Largo** $-$$ **
Rodney Bay Marina
☎ 452-0282
Pizzas cooked the traditional way in wood-fired ovens, plus good salads, great coffee and an interesting Italian wine list. Happy hour is between 5.30pm and 6.30pm.

**La Nautique** $$-$$$ ***
Royal St. Lucian
Rodney Bay
☎ 452-9999
A delightful, informal restaurant serving meals throughout the day, with huge breakfast buffets, sandwiches, fresh seafood and local specialities for lunch, and creole and West Indian dishes alongside continental cuisine for dinner. Open daily from 7am to 10pm.

**L'Epicure Restaurant and Mistral Lounge** $$-$$$ ***
Royal St. Lucian
Rodney Bay
☎ 452-9999
Beachside restaurant offering seafood and West Indian dishes. The Monday night Caribbean buffet features local specialities accompanied by a steel drum band. After dinner guests can enjoy cocktails while listening to the Royal's resident jazz band. Open daily from 7pm to 10pm. Le Mistral Lounge is open until midnight.

**The Lime Restaurant and Bar** $$ ***
Rodney Bay
☎ 452-0761
Good value food, great setting and one of the fun places on the island. You can enjoy an excellent value for money creole buffet lunch or bar snacks, and a delicious dinner before working it off on the dance floor. The Late Lime, the nightclub, offers a wide choice of music from classical, reggae and calypso to country and jazz. Friday and Saturday are disco and Sunday jazz night.

**Marina Steak House** $$ ***
Rodney Bay
☎ 452-9800
A lovely waterfront setting to enjoy seafood dishes or steaks. Open Monday to Saturday from 6pm to midnight.

**Memories of Hong Kong** $-$$ **
Reduit-Gros Islet Highway
☎ 452-8218
Authentic Cantonese and Chinese cooking prepared by their resident chef from Hong Kong. There are lots of speciality dishes, including a vegetarian bird's nest soup, and delicious freshly made desserts. Open Monday to Saturday 5.30 to 10.30pm.

**Miss Saigon** $-$$ **
Rodney Bay
☎ 451-7309
A mix of Southeast Asian and American cuisines. The restaurant is open for breakfast, lunch and dinner Monday to Saturday between 8am and 8pm. Reservations are suggested.

**The Mortar & Pestle** $-$$ ***
Harmony Marina
☎ 452-8756
Good food and a fun place at night. The waterfront restaurant offers 'Haute Cuisine des Caraibes' — the very best West Indian cuisine. Caribbean specialities include Guyana Casareep soup, lobster creole a la Guadeloupe, Lambi St. Lucia, and red snapper Martinique. Open for breakfast, lunch and dinner. There is live music several nights a week.

**Peppino's Pizza** $ *
Gros Islet
☎ 450-9778
Pizzas to eat in, take out or have delivered. Try their Jamaican patties.

**Spinnakers Beach Bar and Grill** $-$$ **
St. Lucia Yacht Club
Reduit Beach
☎ 452-8491
The beach restaurant serves breakfast, lunch and dinner with great views of the bay. Apart from the excellent carvery, the blackboard menu offers a good choice at very reasonable prices, and you can enjoy Happy hour is from 6pm to 7pm.

# St. Lucia Fact File

## Arrivals, Immigration and Customs

British citizens and visitors from European Community and Commonwealth countries need a valid passport for entry, but a visa is not required. Visitors from the United States and Canada staying less than six months can enter on an ID card but must have a valid return airline ticket.

## Accommodation

The free and widely available 'Road Map St. Lucia' gives the location for all hotels and resorts on the island.

In the information provided, the symbols stand for the following:-

$ Inexpensive accommodation
$$ Moderate
$$$ Luxury

**Anse Chastanet Beach Hotel** $$$
PO Box 7000
Soufrière
☎ 459-7000
Near the famous Pitons with spacious hillside and beachside accommodation, offering two restaurants and bars, two beaches, scuba diving, boutiques, free hiking programme for walkers and nature lovers, watersports, airport transportation, tennis and organised trips. Children under the age of two are not accommodated.

**Beach Haven Hotel** $
PO Box 460
Vide Bouteille
Castries
☎ 453-0065.
An elegant, small, comfortable hotel on the beachfront. Facilities include restaurant, bar, fast-food area, sundeck and beach.

**Candyo Inn** $
Castries
☎ 452-0712
A small, friendly twelve-room inn near to Reduit Beach. Facilities include restaurant and pool.

**Caribbees Hotel** $
PO Box 1720
Castries
☎ 452-4767
The twenty-room hotel is just inland of Castries on La Pensée. It features the Olive Garden restaurant, bar, pool, conference room for 250 people, tennis, basketball and volleyball courts and fitness centre. There is free transportation daily to Castries and transfers to and from the beach.

**Chesterfield Inn** $
PO Box 415
Bridge Street
Castries
☎ 452-1295
This small, family run inn was originally a plantation house built in the 1880s. It overlooks Castries harbour, and was once owned by one of the first English settlers to the island. The property retains many of its original features. Facilities include a small dining room offering home cooking and bar. The inn makes a good base for exploring Castries or for visitors with only a short time on the island.

**Club Med** $$
Vieux Fort
☎ 454-6547
The Club has recently been completely renovated, and the 250-room waterside property has a number of features including night club. Facilities include restaurant, pool, beach, watersports and tennis. There is horse riding nearby.

**Club St. Lucia** $$$
(all inclusive)
PO Box 915
Castries
☎ 450-0551
UK ☎ 0372-66944,
USA ☎ 212-545-8437
Canada ☎ 416-968-9500
On the northern tip of the private Cap Estate, the resort has over 370 bungalows dotted around the scenic hillside gardens. Facilities include a racquet club with courts, gym, squash court and pool. The resort offers two restaurants and bars, beach bar, three pools, two beaches, tennis, boutiques, drug store and children's club. Rates include accommodation, drinks, meals, water and land sports, tennis, nightly entertainment.

**E's Serenity Lodge Mini Hotel** $
Sunny Acres
Castries
☎ 452-1987
Overlooking Choc Bay, the hotel is 3 miles (5km) from Castries and close to the beaches and restaurants. Facilities include bar, breakfast and dinner on request.

**East Winds Inn** $$-$$$
(all inclusive)
Labrelotte Bay
PO Box 193
Castries
☎ 452-8212
A small twenty-six chalet resort set in tropical gardens between Castries and Cap Estate. A beautiful beach which is protected by a reef and therefore ideal for snorkelling. Facilities include restaurant, clubhouse, bars, pool with sunk-in bar, sun terrace and snorkelling equipment.

**Foxgrove Inn** $
Mon Repos Post Office
St. Lucia
☎ 454-0271
A new comfortable twelve room inn with magnificent views of Praslin Bay on the eastern Atlantic coast. Twenty minutes drive from Hewanorra Airport. Facilities include fine restaurant, bars, pool, tennis. clubhouse, horse riding, nature walks.

**Friendship Inn** $
Sunny Acres
PO Box 1475
Castries
☎ 452-4201
A small hotel 3 miles (5km) from Castries and within easy walking distance of the beach, shops and restaurants. Facilities include restaurant, bar and pool.

**Glencastle Resort** $
PO Box 143
Massade
Gros Islet
☎ 450-0833
A recently-opened hotel in the hills overlooking Rodney Bay, close to two beaches and with conference facilities for the business traveller. Facilities include pool and gazebo bar and restaurant.

**Green Parrot Inn** $-$$
Castries
☎ 452-3399
A lively fifty-five room inn with fabulous views from its vantage point on the Morne. Facilities include a nightclub and pool.

**Harbour Light Inn** $
City Gate
c/o La Clery Post Office
Castries
☎ 452-3506
On Vigie Beach and close to downtown Castries. Facilities include restaurant and bar, with beaches and shopping nearby.

**Harmony Marina Suites** $$
PO Box 155
Castries
☎ 452-8756
An exclusive and family owned luxury all-suite hotel at Rodney Bay in a secluded waterfront location. Close to shops, bars, restaurants and nightclubs. Honeymoon suites include jacuzzi, four-poster beds and sheepskin rugs. The hotel is two minutes from the fabulous Reduit Beach. Facilities include the Mortar and Pestle Restaurant, bar, pool, minimarket, windsurfing, canoes and nearby boat mooring.

**Humming Bird Beach Resort** $$
PO Box 280
Soufrière
☎ 459-7232
A small resort set in tropical gardens running down to the beach. Facilities include restaurant, bar, pool, beach and batik studio.

**The Islander Hotel** $-$$
PO Box 907
Castries
☎ 452-0255
Close to Reduit Beach and offering rooms and kitchenette-equipped apartments. Facilities include open-air restaurant, terrace cocktail bar, pool, with supermarket, gifts shop, disco and watersports nearby, and free shuttle to the beach.

**Jalousie Plantation** $$$
(all inclusive)
PO Box 251
Soufrière
☎ 459-7666
UK ☎ 0800-22-761
USA and Canada ☎ 800-392-2007
Set in the mountains amid lush tropical gardens, this elegant resort is quite stunning. Rates include luxury accommodation, meals, snacks, all drinks, sports activities and instruction, spa and fitness centre, supervised children's activities, airport transfers, and all taxes and service charges. Facilities include restaurants, bars, watersports, dive shop, tennis, deep sea fishing and sightseeing tours.

# THE REX ST. LUCIAN

## MAKING DREAMS COME TRUE

Just fifteen minutes north of Castries and Vigie Airport, the Rex St. Lucian has everything it takes to turn all your desert island holiday dreams into reality. Located on St. Lucia's finest palm-fringed Reduit beach where only the magnificent sunsets overshadow its fabulous setting.

The Rex St. Lucian's 260 finely-appointed rooms, all with private balcony, offer excellent views of the lush, tropical gardens and are tastefully furnished to the highest standard.

Whether your dream is to relax on miles of golden sandy beach; or enjoy superb sporting activities including sun fish, snorkelling, tennis, sailing, water-skiing; or dance to the sounds of local and international rhythms; or sample fine

cuisine in tropical surroundings and sip exotic cocktails in the shadows of the evening sun . . . look no further . . . the Rex St. Lucian will provide an unique and unforgettable stay.

Reduit Beach, P.O. Box 512, Castries, St. Lucia, West Indies.
Tel: (809) 452-8351 • Fax: (809) 452-8331
Reservations: UK/Europe: 44-181-741-5333 USA/Canada: (305) 471-6170

**Kimatrai Hotel** $
PO Box 238
Vieux Fort
☎ 454-6328
A small, friendly hotel with twelve double rooms, six apartments and three bungalows just a few minutes drive from Hewanorra Airport. Facilities include restaurant, bar, laundry service and television lounge.

**Ladera Resort** $$$
PO Box 225
Soufrière
☎ 459-5156
USA and Canada ☎ 1-800-841-4145
A small luxury resort of handcrafted villas and suites set in tropical gardens, and all positioned to provide fabulous views of the Pitons and the Caribbean Sea. Villages have their own pools and gardens. Facilities include the excellent Dasheene restaurant, bar, pool, library and nearby watersports, and transport to and from Hewanorra, Soufrière and the beach.

**Le Sport** $$-$$$
(all inclusive)
PO Box 437
Cariblue Beach
Castries
☎ 450-8551
USA and Canada ☎ 1-800-544-2883
UK ☎ 0800-590-794
A beautiful beach resort at the north-west tip of the island, with the emphasis on health and activity, as well as relaxation. Facilities include restaurant, bar, three pools, beach, floodlit tennis, cycling, volleyball, archery, hiking, fencing, weight training, golf, aerobics, yoga, stress management and T'ai Chi.

**Marigot Bay Resort** $$
Marigot Bay
PO Box 101
Castries
☎ 451-4357
Nine miles (14km) from Castries with pretty cottages set in the hills behind the marina. Facilities include dive shop, day sailing, pool, water-taxi, watersports, yacht charter, restaurants, bars, boutiques and provision store.

**Marlin Quay** $$-$$$
Rodney Bay Marina
☎ 452-0393
A popular waterfront resort with luxury one to three-bedroom suites, apartment and villas.

**Oasis Marigot** $$
PO Box 387
Castries
☎ 451-4185
USA and Canada ☎ 800-263-4202)
A small, intimate resort of twelve sea houses with stunning views on the hillsides close to Marigot Bay. Each house has direct access to the small palm-fringed beach. Facilities include restaurants, bars, dive shop, day sailing to Soufrière, Rodney Bay and Martinique, water-taxi service to deserted beaches, watersports and boutiques.

**The Orange Grove Hotel** $
Bois d'Orange Village
Gros Islet
☎ 452-0021
A recently renovated plantation-style hotel suitable for both business people and holidaymakers. Facilities include pool, trips to the beach, restaurant and barbecue nights.

**Rendezvous Resort** $$$
(all inclusive)
Malabar Beach
PO Box 190
Castries
☎ 452-4211
(USA 1-800-544-2883)
A chic, couples-only resort with luxury cottages set in 7 acres (3 hectares) of tropical gardens alongside a sandy beach. Rates include meals with wine, drinks, daily activities, sports equipment, cruises on the hotel's catamaran, airport transfers and all taxes and service charges. Facilities include restaurants, bar, tennis, gym, jacuzzi, sauna, watersports, pool with swim-up bar and beach bar.

**Rex St. Lucian** $$
Reduit Beach
PO Box 512
Castries
☎ 452-8351
USA ☎ 1-800-255-5859
UK ☎ 0181-741-5333
A luxury resort set in 10 acres (4 hectares) of tropical grounds alongside on of St. Lucia's finest beaches. The 260 room hotel is a fifteen-minute drive from Castries. Recently refurbished luxury rooms are set admist gardens of palm trees and exotic flowers.

Facilities include shopping arcade, tours, activities desk, car rental, restaurants, bars, disco, snorkelling, scuba diving, pool, tennis and beach.

**Royal St. Lucian Hotel** $$$
Reduit Beach
PO Box 977
Castries
☎ 452-9999
USA ☎ 1-800-255-5859
UK ☎ 0181-741-5333
The magnificent Royal St. Lucian is situated on the fabulous Reduit Beach and provides the sophistication and elegance of a truly luxury resort. The classical entrance hall with its cool marble interior, tropical plants and cascading fountain offers a delightful welcome to the weary travellers. Leading through the entrance hall, guests can glimpse the lush foliage of the exotic gardens with its fabulous pool and swim-up bar. All the suites offer separate bedrooms and living accommodation with exquisite bathrooms and elegant terraces overlooking the gardens and sparkling waters of the Caribbean sea.

The stylish bar is cool and relaxing for pre-dinner drinks which are served to the sounds of a relaxing classical pianist or to soft jazz rhythms. The grace and charm of the staff in L'Epicure is surpassed only by the beautiful surroundings and delicious menu.

Facilities include two restaurants, watersports, cable television, telephone, swim-up pool bar, beach, pool and floodlit tennis courts.

**Sandals Halcyon** $$$
(all inclusive)
Choc Bay
☎ 453-0222
USA ☎ 1-800-SANDALS
UK ☎ 0171-581-9895
A couples-only luxury resort with cottages set in beautiful gardens alongside a sandy beach. Facilities include four restaurants, seven bars and swim-up bars, pools, entertainment, daily activities, airport transfers, gift shops, body shop, car rental, disco, fitness centre and health club complex, golf, scuba, tennis, tours and watersports.

**Sandals St. Lucia** $$$
(all inclusive)
La Toc
PO Box 399
Castries
☎ 452-3081
USA ☎ 1-800-SANDALS
UK ☎ 0171-581-9895
A luxury resort with pastel-coloured villas set in tropical gardens on a hillside which descends to a crescent shaped, half mile (1km) long beach. Facilities include watersports, pools, four restaurants and bars, beachgrill and bar, laundry service, tennis, golf, watersports, fitness centre, gift shop, beauty salon, nightclub and beach vendors market.

**Sea Horse Inn** $-$$
Marigot Bay
PO Box 1825
Castries
☎ 451-4436
Close to a secluded beach with rooms and waterside cottages. There are several restaurants nearby. Continental breakfast is included. Facilities include eco-tours, fishing and golf.

**Skyway Inn** $$
PO Box 353
Vieux Fort
☎ 454-7111
Two minutes from Hewanorra Airport, and close to Lonely Tree Beach and the Windsurfing Centre. Five minutes from Vieux Fort. Facilities include restaurant and bar, open-air rooftop lounge, gift shop, beach, shuttle and windsurfing.

**Still Plantation and Beach Resort** $$
PO Box 246
Soufrière
☎ 459-4224
Set in lush, tropical gardens, the resort offers the chance to experience life on a real tropical plantation. There are self-contained apartments and studios, and beachfront accommodation. Facilities include an excellent restaurant serving island specialities, bars, beach, laundry service and pool.

**Tapion Reef Hotel** $
The Morne
PO Box 370
Castries
☎ 452-7471
Convenient small hotel with self-contained apartments overlooking Castries and the harbour. Facilities include restaurant, bar, pool and daily bus service.

**Top of the Morne Apartments** $
Morne Fortune
PO Box 376
Castries
☎ 452-3603
Apartments with kitchens, patios and spectacular views. It is ten minutes drive to the beach, and eight minutes into Castries. Facilities include self-drive cars, pool.

**Tropical Haven Mini Hotel** $
PO Box 615
Castries
☎ 452-3505
Situated on the La Toc coastline overlooking Castries with ten comfortable rooms and private patios. Castries, shopping and the nearest beach are all within walking distance. Facilities include restaurant, bar and sundeck.

**Villa Beach Cottages** $
Choc Beach
PO Box 129
Castries
☎ 452-2691
Five lovely cottages set in tropical gardens, a few yards from the beach. Facilities include restaurant and bar, maid service, laundry service, baby-sitting, supermarket with nearby shopping.

**Windjammer Landing Villa Beach Resort** $$-$$$
Labrelotte Bay
PO Box 1504
Castries
☎ 452-0913
USA ☎ 1-800-743-9609
Canada ☎ 1-800-267-7600
UK ☎ 0800-373-742
Luxury fully-equipped villas with private plunge pools suitable for families and honeymooners alike. Facilities include three restaurants, bars, pools and childrens pools, supervised children's activities, tennis, watersports, car rental, health and beauty centre.

**Wyndham Morgan Bay Resort** $$-$$$
Choc Bay
PO Box 2167
Gros Islet
☎ 450-2511
USA ☎ 1-800-WYNDHAM
UK ☎ 0181-367-5449
A four-star hotel on Choc Bay with eight 3-storey buildings in delightful gardens running down to the beach. Facilities include restaurants, bar, boutique, health club, watersports, tennis and floodlit courts, lawn games, table tennis, pool and kid's club.

## Airlines

**Air Canada**
☎ 452-2550/454-6249.

**Air Martinique**
☎ 452-2463

**American Airlines**
☎ 453-2970/454-6777

**American Eagle**
☎ 452-1820

**BWIA International**
☎ 452-3778/454-6249.
In the USA 1-800-JET-BWIA

**British Airways**
☎ 452-7444/454-6172

**Carib Express**
☎ 431-9200/451-8235

**Eastern Caribbean Helicopters**
☎ 453-6952

**Helenair**
☎ 452-7196

**LIAT**
☎ 452-3051/454-6341/452-2348

## Banks

Banks are open Monday to Friday between 8am-3pm, and until 5pm on Fridays. Banks are generally closed at weekends and on public holidays, although Barclays, National Commercial Bank and the Royal Bank of Canada have Saturday morning hours.

**Bank of Nova Scotia**
William Peter Boulevard
Castries
☎ 452-2292

**Barclays Bank** has seven locations:
La Clery ☎ 452-4395
Rodney Bay Marina ☎ 452-9384
Jeremie Street, Castries ☎ 452-4041
Bridge Street, Castries ☎ 452-3306

Vieux Fort ☎ 454-6255
Soufrière ☎ 459-7255
Micoud ☎ 454-4244

**C.I.B.C.**
William Peter Boulevard
Castries
☎ 452-3751
*also at*
Vieux Fort ☎ 454-6262

**National Commercial Bank of St. Lucia** has six locations:
John Compton Highway, Castries
High Street, Castries
Pointe Seraphine, Castries
Vieux Fort
Gros Islet
Soufrière

**Royal Bank of Canada**
William Peter Boulevard
Castries
*also at*
Rodney Bay Marina ☎ 453-9921

**St. Lucia Cooperative Bank**
Bridge Street
Castries
☎ 452-2881
*also at*
Rodney Bay ☎ 452-2882

**St. Lucia Development Bank**
Bridge Street
Castries
☎ 452-3561

## Beaches

Popular beaches include Reduit Beach in Rodney Bay, Labrelotte Bay, Vigie Beach, La Toc and Marigot Bay. Around Soufrière there are a number of small beaches, including the delightful, sheltered Anse Chastanet and Anse Mamin.
Beaches on the windier Atlantic Ocean coast tend to have choppier seas but offer excellent surfing and windsurfing.

## Car Rental

Hire car rates range from US$300 to $400 a week depending on the type of vehicle and the rental company. Average daily rates are US$65 but this does not include insurance which costs an additional US$15-20 (EC$37-50) per day. A temporary St. Lucia driving licence is required which can be obtained on production of a current driving licence on arrival at the airport, the police station in Castries or the car hire office. The cost is EC$30.
Seat belts are not compulsory, but it is advisable to wear them at all times. The speed limit is 30mph (48kph) in Castries, and there is no reason to drive any faster out of town because you may miss some of the beautiful scenery.

Hire companies include:

**Avis Rent a Car**
☎ 451 6976

**Budget Rent a Car**
☎ 452 0233

**Cool Breeze Jeep Car Rental**
☎ 454 7898

**Courtesy Rent a Car**
☎ 452 8140

**CTL Rent a Car**
☎ 452 0732

**Economy Car Rental**
☎ 451-7997

**Sun Fun Car Rental** (*Hertz*)
☎ 452 0680

**Inter Island Car Rental**
☎ 453 1086

**National Car Rental**
☎ 450 8721
**St. Lucia Yacht Club Rental**
☎ 452 5057

**Wayne's Motorcycle Centre**
☎ 452 2059

## Churches

The following denominations are represented: Roman Catholic, Anglican, Baptist, Church of Christian Science, Methodist, Pentecostal Assemblies, Seventy-Day Adventist.

## Departure Tax

There is a departure tax of EC$27 (US$11) for departing passengers.

## Embassies and Consulates

**British High Commission**
24 Micoud Street
Castries
☎ 809-452-2484
Open: Monday to Friday 8.30am-12.30pm

**Federal Republic of Germany Consulate**
6 Manoel Street
PO Box 195
☎ (809) 452-2511
Open: Monday to Friday 8am-12.30pm and 1.30pm-4.30pm

**French Embassy**
Vigie
Castries
☎ (80) 452-2462
Open: Monday to Friday 8.30am-12.30pm and 1.30pm-4pm

**Italian Consulate**
Reduit
PO Box GM 848
☎ (80) 452-0865
Open: Monday to Friday 1pm-4pm

**Netherlands Consul**
M & C Building
Bridge Street
PO Box 1020
Castries
☎ (809) 452-2811
Open: Monday to Friday 8am-4.30pm

**Organisation of American States**
Vigie
Castries
☎ 809-452-4330
Open: Monday to Friday 8.30am-12.30pm and 1.30pm-4.30pm

## Emergency Telephone Numbers

For police, fire and ambulance ☎ 999
Air and sea rescue ☎ 452-2894/452 1182/453 6664

## Festivals/Calendar of Events

| | |
|---|---|
| **1/2 January** | New Year's festivites |
| **22 February** | Independence Day |
| **Feb/March** | Carnival — a two-day extravaganza prior to Lent |
| **March/April** | Good Friday<br>Easter Sunday |
| **May** | International Jazz Festival |
| **29 June** | Fisherman's Day |
| **29 August** | Feast of St. Rose of Lima<br>Flower Festival |
| **22 November** | St. Cecilia's Day. Island musicians celebrate the patron saint of music |
| **13 December** | St. Lucia's Day, National Day |
| **25 December** | Christmas Day |

## Fishing

Operators include:
**Mako Watersports**
Rodney Bay Marina
☎ 452-0412

**Captain Mike's Watersports**
Vigie Marina
☎ 452-7044

Above: The elegant Brig Unicorn runs regular visits to Soufrière.

## Hospitals

There are four hospitals on the island.

**Victoria Hospital**
☎ 453 7059

**St. Jude's Vieux Fort**
☎ 454 6041

**Soufrière**
☎ 459 7258/5001

**Dennery**
☎ 453 3310

## Police

The police headquarters is in Bridge Street, Castries
☎ 452 3854/5

## Post Offices

Post Office hours are 8.30am-4.30pm Monday to Friday and Saturday 8am-12noon. There are post offices in most towns.

## Sea trips

(see also Yacht Charter under Sport)

**Brig Unicorn**
The ship was used in the film *Roots* and sails from Vigie Cove each Monday and Friday morning for Soufrière and area visit. Includes buffet lunch, rum punch, snorkelling, swimming and visit to Marigot Bay. Arrives back around 4.30pm ☎ 452-6811

**Endless Summer I and II**
Two 56ft (17m) catamarans offering full-day sail tours to Soufrière and nearby area. Trips include Marigot Bay, buffet lunch, rum punch, snorkelling. Sunset cruises also provided ☎ 450-8651

**Motor Yacht Vigie**
A private luxury yacht offering day cruises along the west coast, visits to Soufrière and area. Leaves from Rodney Bay Marina ☎ 452-3762

**Surf Queen**
A 41ft (12m) trimaran offering trips to Soufrière and area, lunch in a private home and afternoon swimming and snorkelling in Anse Chastanet Bay.
☎ 452-8351

## Service Charges and Taxes

There is a Government tax of eight per cent on all hotel and restaurant bills, and a service charge of ten per cent is usually added. Menus and tariffs sometimes include these charges so check to make sure they have not been added twice. In shops, the price on the label is what you pay. When buying in markets and from street vendors, try haggling over the price.

## Shopping

Shops usually open between 8.30am and 12.30pm and 1.30pm to 4pm Monday to Friday, and between 8am to around 12noon on Saturday. The Castries Market is a fun place to shop for locally-produced souvenirs. The Pointe Seraphine cruise terminal has a number of elegant boutiques selling a wide variety of clothing, jewellery and gifts. Gablewoods Mall is open from 9am to 7pm Monday to Saturday although some shops stay open later.

The Rodney Bay Marina Shopping Arcade has a selection of shops and restaurants. Many hotels also have their own shops and boutiques.

## Sightseeing

Sightseeing and island tours by land or sea can be organised through hotels, tour representatives or one of the many specialist tour companies on the island. These include:

**Barefoot Holidays**
☎ 450 0507

**Barnards Travel**
☎ 452 2214

**Carib Touring**
☎ 452 1141

**Cox & Co**
☎ 452 2211

**Minville & Chastanet**
☎ 452 2811

**Solar Tours**
☎ 452 5898

**Spice Travel**
☎ 452 0866

**St. Lucia Reps**
☎ 452 7922

## Sport

### Fitness Gyms/Exercise Centres

**Body Inc**
Gablewoods Mall
☎ 451-9744

**Fitness Palace**
Marisule, Gros Islet Highway
☎ 452-0822

**Laborde's Gym**
Old La Toc Road, Castries
☎ 452-2788

**St. Lucia Racquet Club**
Club St. Lucia, Cap Estate
☎ 450-0551

### Golf

**Cap Estate Golf Course**
☎ 450-8523

### Horseback Riding

**International Riding Stables**
Beausejour, Gros Islet
☎ 452-8139

**Trim's Riding Stables**
Cas-en-Bas
☎ 452-8273

### Squash

**St. Lucia Yacht Club**
Reduit Beach
☎ 452-8491/8350

**St. Lucia Racquet Club**
Club St. Lucia
Cap Estate
☎ 450-0551

### Scuba Diving

**Buddies**
Vigie Marina
☎ 452-5288

**Dolphin Divers**
Rodney Bay Marina
☎ 452-9485

**The Moorings Scuba Centre**
Club Mariner
Marigot Bay
☎ 451-4357

**Scuba St. Lucia**
Anse Chastanet and Rex St. Lucian
☎ 459-7355

**Windjammer Diving**
Windjammer Landing Beach Resort
☎ 452-0913

### Tennis

Almost all the resorts and many hotels have their own floodlit tennis courts.

### Watersports

A variety of watersports are available at all resorts and most large hotels.

**Parasailing St. Lucia** is based at the Rex St. Lucian
☎ 452-8351

**Island Windsurfing**
Anse de Sables beach
Vieux Fort ☎ 454-7000

### Yacht Charter and Private Moorings

There is a huge range of vessels and crews for charter for sailing, sightseeing, fishing and diving. Marigot Bay and Rodney Bay, both on the northwestern coast, are the two most popular marinas.
Companies offering yacht charters are:

**Destination St. Lucia**
☎ 452 8531

**Escape to Paradise**
☎ 452 0344

**Moorings St. Lucia**
☎ 452 4256

**Sun Sail**
☎ 452 8648

**Brig Unicorn**
☎ 452 6811

**Cahoni**
☎ 452 0693

**Endless Summer**
☎ 450 8651

**Surf Queen**
☎ 452 8351

**Motor Yacht Vigie**
☎ 452 3762

## STAMPS

The St. Lucia Philatelic Bureau is located at the General Post Office in Bridge Street, Castries (☎ 452-3774).

The bureau offers the island's commemorative stamps for sale. Commemorative sets are issued every year and they feature St. Lucian history, wildlife, celebrities and special occasions. The island's first air mail letters were sent on 22 September 1929, aboard a Pan American Airways flight piloted by Captain Charles Lindbergh.

# THE ROYAL ST. LUCIAN

## IN A CLASS OF ITS OWN

The 98-ocean view suites of the Royal St. Lucian have been exquisitely designed to provide the ultimate in deluxe accommodation.
Each suite comprises an elegant bedroom with private patio and luxurious bathroom. They are also equipped with a private bar, cable television and direct-dial telephone.
L'Epicure Restaurant serves the finest international cuisine in an elegant beachside setting, and the spacious Le Mistral lounge serves exotic tropical cocktails to the sound of soft jazz rhythms each evening.
Welcome to the majestic Royal St. Lucian where your stay is guaranteed to be a magical and unforgettable experience.

**PO Box 977, Castries, St. Lucia, West Indies**
**Telephone: 809 452 9999**
**Fax: 809 452 6939**
**Reservations: UK/Europe 44-181-741-5333**
**US/Canada: 305-471-6170**

## Tourist Information

The tourist information office at Pointe Seraphine is open from 8am-4.30pm Monday to Friday. The office opens on Sunday for half a day if a cruise ship is in port on Sunday or a public holiday. The office in Soufrière is open 8.30am-4pm from Monday to Friday, and 8.30am-12.30pm on Saturday.
There are also information centres at Jeremie Street, Castries
☎ 452-2479

Vigie Airport
☎ 452-4094

Hewanorra Airport
☎ 454-6644

**United Kingdom**
St. Lucia Tourist Board
421a Finchley Road
London NW3 6HJ
☎ 0171-431-4045.
Fax: 0171-431-7920

**Canada**
4975 Dundee Street West
Suite 457, Etobicoke D
Islington
Ontario M9A 4X4
☎ 416-236-0936

**France**
A.N.I.
53 rue Francois 1er,
Paris 75008
☎ 47-23-09-65

**Germany**
Postfach D-61293
Bad Hamburg
Germany
☎ 06172-304431

**United States of America**
820 2nd Avenue
New York
NY 10017
☎ 212-867-2950

## Tour Operators & Travel Agents

There are many tour operators on the island and all offer a number of trips and excursions, or can tailor make itineraries to suit you. Many of the tours sound the same, so check to see that you are getting value for money, or getting something special.
Main operators are:

**Barefoot Holidays** (St. Lucia)
Rodney Bay Industrial Estate
☎ 450-0507

**Barnard's Travel**
Micoud and Bridge Street, Castries
☎ 452-1615

**Carib Travel**
Micoud Street, Castries
☎ 452-3176
*and at*
Clarke Street, Vieux Fort
☎ 454-6450.

**Carib Touring**
☎ 452-1141

**Conference and Incentive Services**
☎ 252-7058

**Cox & Co**
William Peter Boulevard, Castries
☎ 452-2211

**Eastern Caribbean Helicopters**
Rodney Bay
Castries and Soufrière
☎ 453-6952

**Hibiscus Travel**
Soufrière
☎ 459-5218
*and at*
Bourbon Street, Castries
☎ 453-1527

**International Travel Consultants**
Bourbon House
Bourbon Street
Castries
☎ 452-3131

**M&C Tourist Department**
Bridge Street, Castries
☎ 452-2811

**Pitons Travel Agency**
La Clery
☎ 452-1227

**St. Lucia Helicopters**
Pointe Seraphine
☎ 453-6950

**St. Lucia International Travel Service**
Micoud Street, Castries
☎ 452-1293

**St. Lucia Representative Services**
Micoud Street, Castries
☎ 452-3762

**Solar Tours & Travel**
Bridge Street, Castries
☎ 452-5898

**Spice Travel**
Reduit Park, Rodney Bay
☎ 452-0866

**Sun Fun Tours**
☎ 453-1472

**Sunlink International**
Reduit ☎ 452-8232
Club St. Lucia ☎ 450-0842

**Toucan Travel**
Rodney Bay Marina
☎ 452-0896

**Travel World**
John Compton Highway, Castries
☎ 451-7443

## Weddings

Requirements for getting married on St. Lucia are:

• Visitors must have been resident on the island for two working days before applying for a marriage licence. This application can be made through a local solicitor to the Attorney General.
• provide all documents in English
• produce a certificate of non-marriage from a priest, lawyer or registrar on official note paper, attesting that neither party is married.
• produce final divorce documents if applicable.
• produce passport and birth certificates.

Many hotels also offer wedding packages and will make all the arrangements for you. The application must be filed at least four working days before the date of the wedding. Most denominations of church weddings can be arranged in advance, and registrars usually charge a fee plus travel costs. Valentine's Day is a very popular day for weddings, and registrars are usually very busy rushing around conducting marriage after marriage.

## Youth Hostels

Limited youth hostel-style accommodation is available through the National Research Development Foundation in Castries (☎ 452-4253). It has about eight multi-bed rooms to accommodate students, and can also recommend a number of small guest houses offering friendly, budget accommodation.

# St. Vincent and th

# Grenadines

St. Vincent and the necklace of islands that make up the Grenadines are some of the most unspoiled islands in the Caribbean. The Grenadines boast some of the most exclusive holiday islands in the world and have long attracted the very rich and famous.

St. Vincent is 21 miles (34km) southwest of St. Lucia, and 100 miles (160km) west of Barbados. It lies to the north of the Grenadines, and altogether, there are thirty-two islands spread out in a sixty mile long arc reaching down to Petit St. Vincent just a stone's throw from Petit Martinique which is part of Grenada. It is 18 miles long (28km) long, and at its widest 11 miles (17 km) across. It covers an area of 134 sq miles (347 sq km). Bequia lies 9 miles (14km) south of St. Vincent and is the largest of the Grenadines covering an area of about 7 sq miles (11 sq km). The other main islands are Union Island which covers 3.2 sq miles (5 sq km), Canouan with an area of 3 sq miles (4.8 sq km), Mustique covering 2 sq miles (3 sq km), Mayreau one sq mile 1.6 sq km), Palm Island and Petit St. Vincent both about 110 acres (44 hectares). There are many other tiny uninhabited islands including the idyllic Tobago Cays. In total the territory of St. Vincent and the Grenadines covers almost 150 sq miles (388 sq km.)

St. Vincent is a lush volcanic island with mountains running north to south down the centre of the island. These mountains have steep, densely-wooded slopes with many fast moving streams flowing down them. The volcano Soufriere is St. Vincent's highest peak at 4,048ft (1,234m), and last erupted in 1979. This eruption was not as severe as the two major eruptions which occurred in 1812 and 1902. These eruptions have, however, deposited a layer of rich fertile ash which has produced the lush vegetation which covers most of the island, particularly in the Mesopotamia Valley. The eastern coast has cliffs and largely rocky beaches with choppy seas and surf due to the onshore winds, while the western, sheltered coastline has fine beaches and safe swimming.

## Getting there

**By air**: The main airport is on St. Vincent but there are also small airports on Bequia, Canouan, Mustique and Union Island.

There are no direct international flights to St. Vincent and the Grenadines, but there are same day connections with LIAT through the main gateways of Barbados, Grenada, Martinique, St. Lucia, San Juan and Trinidad, serviced by Air Canada, Air France, American Airlines, BWIA and British Airways.

LIAT also have scheduled flights from St. Vincent and Union Island to many eastern Caribbean islands.

Carib Express operates short take-off and landing jets between St. Vincent and Barbados, Grenada, Dominica (Melville Hall), St. Lucia (Vigie), Tobago and Port of Spain.

Air Martinique also flies scheduled services to Mustique and Union Island and several Caribbean destinations, while Mustique Airways flies between Barbados, Mustique and St. Vincent.

SVG Air provide a reliable air-charter service from St. Vincent to most Caribbean islands, as well as a scheduled service to Canouan and Union Island twice a week.

**By boat**: Cruise ships dock at Kingstown in St. Vincent and often visit the other Grenadines. There are regular ferry services between St. Vincent and the Grenadines. For visiting yachts there are ports of entry at Kingstown and Wallilabou Bay on St. Vincent, and entry formalities and registration can also be undertaken on Bequia, Mustique and Union Island.

## Getting around

**By hire car**: For visitors planning to spend several days on the island it is advisable to hire a car or jeep in order to explore the area thoroughly. For those planning just an occasional trip, use taxis or the island's 'bus' service. All towns and villages are connected to the main highways, and even though these side roads may be rough and pot-holed they are usually passable with care.

**By taxi**: Taxis are cheap and easily available. They can be ordered by telephone from any hotel or picked up at the taxi ranks at the airport or in Kingstown. All fares are fixed, but prices are negotiable for visitors wishing to hire a taxi for sightseeing or longer periods. Taxi drivers make excellent guides, but it is advisable to agree the fare first and agree which currency you are paying in. Expect to pay around EC$40 an hour if hiring a taxi for a tour. The fare is EC$15 between Kingstown and the airport, EC$10 from Kingstown to Fort Charlotte, and EC$35 from Kingstown to Mesopotamia. A full list of fares is available from the tourist office and the dispatcher at the airport.

**By minibus**: Minibuses, privately-owned Japanese vans, ply the main routes on the island, generally carrying up to ten passengers. Always check that the bus is heading the right way before boarding. Most drivers have adopted flamboyant names which are boldly printed across the front of the vehicle, and music is generally played at near-deafening volumes inside. Buses leave Kingstown from around the market area, and en-route can usually be flagged down if there are empty seats. Most buses transport people into Kingstown to work, and run until they have taken them back again. They tend not to run in the evenings and are scarce on Sundays. Fares are fixed and typical fares from Kingstown are: EC$2 to Layou, EC$2.50 to Mesopotamia, EC$4 to Georgetown, and EC$5 to Sandy Bay.

**By boat**: There are regular ferry services between St. Vincent and Bequia, and between St. Vincent and the other Grenadine islands down as far as Union Island. All ferries leave Kingstown from the Grenadines Ferry Jetty, which is located to the south of the deep-water dock.

There are three ferries on the St. Vincent-Bequia run. From Monday to Friday and on Sunday, the first boat from St. Vincent to Bequia sails at 9am. On Saturday the first boat to Bequia leaves at 12.30pm. The last ferry sails at 7pm each evening. From Bequia to St. Vincent, the first ferry leaves at 6.30am from Monday to Saturday, and at 7.30am on Sunday. The last ferry leaves at 5pm every night. Fares are collected on board and cost EC$10 for a single ticket between Monday and Saturday, and EC$12 on Sunday. The crossing takes approximately one hour, but be warned, this can sometimes be rough, especially when one leaves the lee of the island and the Atlantic breakers hit the ferry side on.

The mail boat, the *MV Snapper* sails from St. Vincent at around 10am three times a week on Mondays, Thursdays and Saturdays, and stops at Bequia, Canouan, Mayreau and Union Island. The trip from St. Vincent to Union Island including stops at the other ports of call takes just over five hours depending on the seas. The ferry returns on Tuesday and Friday after an all-night stopover on Union Island leaving at 7am and arriving back in St. Vincent at noon.

On Saturday the ferry docks for less than two hours before leaving for St. Vincent at 5.30pm and arriving at 10.30pm. It is recommended to always ring to confirm the times of sailings.

The *MV Snapper* offers a great way

of visiting the islands and for visitors only able to take the Saturday sailing to spend just an hour or so on Union Island, there are still some fabulous views on the cruise through the Grenadines. The fare from St. Vincent to Bequia is EC$10 (EC$12 at night and weekends), to Canouan EC$13, to Mayreau EC$15 and Union Island EC$20.

**By air:** Liat and Mustique Airways fly scheduled services within the islands. LIAT offers a number of sightseeing flights and day tours from St. Vincent, and both Mustique Airways and SVG Air are available for charter.

# St. Vincent

The island is small and fun to explore although most trips take longer than one would imagine from the map. There are about 300 miles (483km) of road but some are only suitable for four-wheel drive vehicles.

Although Richmond is only 15 miles (24km) by road up the west coast from Kingstown, one should plan on spending at least three hours just to get there and back. It is necessary to allow more time if you are going to stop several times on the way to take photographs, do a little exploring, and perhaps swim or have something to eat and drink.

The island is not a typical tourist paradise and the main attraction is its natural beauty, the warmth and friendliness of the people who live here, and the year-round sunshine.

While most of the west coast and all of the south and east coasts are accessible by vehicle, much of the interior is not, and the only way in is on foot. There are many beautiful walks, sparkling waterfalls and rich, tropical rainforests to enjoy on the walks which are the essence of natural St. Vincent at its best.

## Kingstown

This is a typical west Caribbean waterfront town: bustling, noisy, full of hooting traffic, and a busy market that also serves as the main bus station.

It is a small, compact town which is easy to explore on foot. There is a lot of modernisation and rebuilding work going on, including the new Government offices on the waterfront. However, there are some fine old buildings, many of which date back to the nineteenth century. There are cobblestone streets, tiny alleys and sidewalks with overhanging upper storey balconies supported by wooden pillars, which offer pedestrians some protection from both sun and rain.

The heart of downtown Kingstown is concentrated in about a dozen blocks between Upper and Lower Bay Streets which run along the waterfront, and Tyrrell, Grenville and Halifax Streets which together form a continuous road and run parallel with them. There are many shops and stores to browse around selling a good selection of goods including duty-free items, local handicrafts and batik wear, preserves. The old fruit and vegetable market and the new fish market make for a fascinating visit.

### Walking tour of Kingstown

The **ferry boat jetty** makes a good starting point for a walking tour of Kingstown. It is a bustling, lively place as the ferries load up and disgorge their passengers, and schooners take on cargo for delivery to the other Grenadine islands. Many of the warehouses were built from bricks brought out from England as ballast in the vessels which returned laden with molasses and sugar.

From the ferry jetty, turn left on to **Grenadines Wharf**, with its many old

# ST VINCENT

Commantawana Bay
Fancy
Owia
Falls of Baleine
Sandy Bay
Soufriere Mountain
Larikai Bay
Overland Village
Waterloo
Wallibou Beach
Trinity Falls
Richmond Beach
Richmond
Petit Bordel Bay
Chateaubelair
Richmond Peak
Georgetown
Troumaka Bay
Troumaka
Cumberland Bay
Black Point Tunnel
Wallilabou Bay
Colonarie
Barrouallie
Colonarie Bay
Grand Bonhomme
Sans Souci
Peter's Hope Beach
Union
N.Union Bay
Montreal Gardens
S.Union Bay
Layou
Vermont
Biabou
Layou Bay
Biabou Bay
Buccament Bay
Mesopotamia
Peruvian Vale
Campden Park Bay
Argyle Beach
Yambou Head
KINGSTOWN
Kingstown Bay
Stubbs
Glen
Villa
Belvedere
Villa Beach
Calliaqua Bay
Calliaqua
Blue Lagoon
N
W
E
S
0 1 2 3 4 5 miles
0 1 2 3 4 5 6 7 8Km

warehouses and nineteenth century buildings, including an old arrowroot store. The road then leads into Upper Bay Street. The new multi-storey building on the waterfront beyond the deep-water wharf, are the **Government Offices** and headquarters of the National Bank. It also houses the tourist board. Just beyond this is the imposing red-roofed, stone police headquarters with its immaculate officers on duty outside. The building was constructed in 1875. Take a look at the historic Cobblestone Inn on Bay Street which was built in 1813 and is reputed to be where King JaJa of Opobo in Africa is said to have stayed while in exile. Retrace your steps and turn left into South River Road. On the corner of South River Road and Upper Bay Street is Noah's Arkade which sells books, detailed maps and an excellent selection of island handicrafts and souvenirs.

The LIAT offices are at the top of South River Road. At the junction with Halifax Street turn left past the General Post Office and many of the banks, including Barclays, and the offices of Cable and Wireless on the right. The **Court House** was built from local stone in 1798 and is situated just across the junction from Hillsborough Street. Turn left into Hillsborough Street past the **Cenotaph** towards the **market**, which lies between Hillsborough and Bedford Streets. The market provides the opportunity to see the wide variety of agricultural produce grown on the island, as well as items on sale including preserves and spices. The jovial women selling their wares sit on boxes shouting items of news and gossip to each other, whilst trying to persuade passers-by to buy their goods. There is also find a wide range of arts and crafts to be found. Around the market there are also plenty of opportunities to sample local dishes from the stalls.

From the market, take Lower Bay Street along the waterfront past the new fish market which was built largely with Japanese financing — hence the area's local name of 'Little Tokyo' — to the Philatelic Bureau, where one can purchase the island's colourful, commemorative stamps. From here back track a little and take Higginson Street up to Grenville Street. For a spot of lunch, visit Sid's on Grenville Street which is on the first floor and is packed with cricket photographs—many of which feature the owner. The two televisions are usually tuned in to cricket if there is a match on. The pub offers excellent West Indian food including special dishes of the day. Aggie's just up the street, and also an upstairs spot, is famous for its seafood in spicy creole sauces, and its traditional scouse.

On the corner of Higginson and Grenville Streets is the **Methodist Church.** It was dedicated in 1841, although the belfry was not added until 1907. The interior is very light and there is a very elaborate and large pipe organ.

Turn left into Grenville Street and almost opposite is the **Anglican Cathedral of St. George's**, with its striking clock tower. The nave and lower parts of the tower date from around 1820, and the church was built largely from money raised by the sale of Carib lands after the Second Carib War. The two transepts were added in the 1880s and are pure Victorian, and there is a fine Georgian galleried interior, and some beautiful stained glass windows.

One window showing the famous 'Red Angel' was commissioned by Queen Victoria for St. Paul's Cathedral in London, and was supposed to depict an angel dressed in white. The artist misunderstood and portrayed the angel in red garments. The Queen refused to have the window installed, and it was stored in the basement of the Cathedral. It was here that Bishop Jackson spotted it, and asked Dean Inge of St. Paul's if he could take it back to St. Vincent for his cathedral. The chandelier in the cathedral was also originally destined to be hung elsewhere. It was bound for Brazil, but the ship carrying it grounded off St. Vincent, and the chandelier was saved for the church. Beneath the chandelier lies the stone plaque to Major Leith.

A little further down the road, just after North River Road, is the unusual **St. Mary's Roman Catholic Cathedral**. The first church on the site was built between 1823-28, but was extended in 1877 when the steeple and sanctuary were added, and enlarged again in 1891. In the late 1930s and early 1940s it was totally renovated by the Flemish Dominican Charles Verbeke. This cycle of building has resulted in a fascinating combination of architectural styles, although the building is still largely Romanesque with heavy Gothic overtones and a very ornate interior. Next door is the Cathedral School and Presbytery.

## Other Places to Visit

**Fort Charlotte** stands 600 feet (183m) above the sea on the promontory known as Berkshire Hill, just north of Kingstown and with great views over the town and surrounding countryside. It was started in 1763 and completed in 1806 but never saw action. It is now used as a coastguard lookout. From the fort which was named after George III's queen, there are good views along the coast across to the Grenadine islands to the south. The former officers' quarters have been turned into a small pictorial museum, with a number of paintings of historical scenes from Black Carib history by Lindsay (Linzee) Prescott.

One can walk or drive to the fort and it is a perfect place for either a lunchtime picnic, or to relax and watch a spectacular sunset out at sea. The walk to the fort which is uphill all the way, will take between thirty and forty minutes — but at least it is downhill on the way back.

The **St. Vincent Botanical Gardens** are a delight. Admission is free and one can spend hours wandering around the beautiful grounds. The gardens are on the western outskirts of town and are open from dawn to dusk. On arrival at the entrance numerous guides descend on visitors offering to show them around. Do not let this put you off, as it really does pay to have an individually-conducted tour. The guides are generally well informed and will ensure visitors do not miss a thing. It is advisable to agree a fee before setting off, but visitors are welcome to walk around on their own if preferred. The gardens are the oldest in the western hemisphere, and were founded in 1765. They originally covered thirty acres, but in 1828 three acres were set aside for Government House after which the gardens went through a period of decline. Today twenty glorious well-tended acres remain and contain a wealth of tropical plants, shrubs and trees. Plants destined for the Royal Botanic Gardens at Kew in England were cultivated here and their growth monitored to ensure they were disease-free before being sent on to England. The gardens contain many rare species, including the Bermuda Cedar, now extinct in their natural habitat. At the far end of the gardens, there is a massive breadfruit tree. The plaque beneath states that the tree was grown from one of the original plants brought to St. Vincent by Captain Bligh on *HMS Providence* in 1793.

There is also a fine specimen of the Soufriere Tree — the last one if its species in the world. It was one of

Above: The St. Vincent Botanical Gardens are a delight to wander around.
Below left: Stained glass window in the Cathedral of St. George's, Kingstown.
Below right: Colourful tee-shirts on sale in Kingstown market.

several brought from the slopes of the volcano and planted in the gardens in 1812, but it is the only one surviving today. All the trees in the wild were wiped out following the various eruptions of Soufriere during the past 150 years. The Soufriere flower is the national flower.

The scene looking across the water-lily pond towards the gazebo beyond is a much photographed one, and the gardens, especially Hibiscus Alley with fifty different varieties on display, are a favourite location for newlyweds to have their wedding photographs taken.

In a far corner of the gardens, there is an aviary where one can see the endangered St. Vincent parrot. The aviary is running a breeding programme to release young birds back into the wild.

The Governor General's Residence stands in splendid isolation overlooking the Botanical Gardens. The house which was built in 1886 is set in its own landscaped gardens and is reached by a private gateway leading from the gardens.

The **Archaeological Museum** is in the Botanical Gardens, in what used to be the Gardens Curator's House, built in 1891. The museum specialises in the pre-Columbian history of the island with fascinating displays of Arawak and Carib artifacts, stone axes, pottery and jewellery. There is a small admission fee.

After leaving, take time to look at **Isaac's House**, near the entrance. The house was built at the beginning of the twentieth century for Sydney Barber Isaac, a Kingstown magistrate.

The **St. Vincent Craftsmen's Centre** is on the outskirts of the town on the airport road. It is a short walk from the centre of the town and is clearly signposted. Visitors can often watch artisans at work, weaving straw, creating jewellery, moulding clay or sculpting in wood, coconut and other materials. Of particular interest are the hand-made West Indian dolls dressed in traditional costumes.

## Eating Out in and Around Kingstown

**Aggie's Restaurant and Bar** $-$$
Grenville Street
Kingstown
☎ 456-2110
Excellent West Indian and seafood

**Amor's Restaurant and Bar** $-$$
Sharpe Street
Kingstown
☎ 456-2359
Healthy cuisine

**The Attic** $-$$
Corner of Melville & Grenville Streets
Kingstown
☎ 457-2558
West Indian and continental cuisine, live music and nightly entertainment.

**Basil's Bar & Restaurant** $-$$
Bay Street
Kingstown
☎ 457-2713
International cuisine is served in this lively atmosphere located downstairs at the Cobblestone Inn. A buffet lunch and candlelit dinners are a daily feature of the restaurant. Chinese buffet on Fridays.

**Bella Vista Inn** $-$$
Kingstown Park
☎ 457-2757
Creole

**Bounty Restaurant** $-$$
Halifax Street
Kingstown
☎ 456-1776
Fast food and local specialities

**Chung Wa Restaurant & Bar** $-$$
Bay Street
Kingstown
☎ 457-2566
Chinese

**Cobblestone Roof Top Restaurant** $-$$
Bay Street
Kingstown
☎ 456-1937
Fast food and West Indian specialities

**D-Tunnel** $-$$
Camden Park Industrial Centre
☎ 457-8606
West Indian and international dishes served in an open terrace restaurant.

**Horseshoe Restaurant and Bar** $-$$
Grenville Street
Kingstown
☎ 457-2042
West Indian specialities

**Joyce's Snackette** $
Bay Street
Kingstown
☎ 456-2823
West Indian fast food and specialities

**Kentucky Fried Chicken** $
Grenville Street
Kingstown
☎ 457-2612
Fast food

**Le Cafe** $-$$
Halifax Street
Kingstown
☎ 457-2791
International

**Moore's Delight** $
Corner Middle & Egmont Streets
Kingstown
☎ 456-1928
West Indian specialities

**Nice Foods Unlimited** $-$$
Heron Hotel complex
Kingstown
☎ 456-1391
West Indian and international

**Sid's Pub** $-$$
Grenville Street
Kingstown
☎ 456-2315
Excellent West Indian and creole specialities. Sports pub with a lively atmosphere.

## The West Coast

This road leads along the coast through several small, picturesque fishing villages which also offer some of the island's best scuba diving. The Leeward Highway starts in Kingstown and runs past the Botanical Gardens and over the hill, from the summit of which there are fine views back across Kingstown and ahead to Campden Park Bay.

The road runs inland around the beautiful **Petit Byahaut** bay. It is only accessible by boat and is one of the most exclusive retreats on the island. It is set in a fifty-acre valley which runs inland from an exquisite, secluded bay. Petit Byahaut is a private place with comfortable tented accommodation, complete with fresh water and solar power, for a maximum of fourteen people. The seaside bar serves delicious candlelit dinners prepared from fresh local produce in this most romantic of settings. The valley boasts mango, sugar apple, guava, banana, soursop, citrus and coconut trees, as well as fabulous flowering plants such as hibiscus, frangipani, morning glory and allamanda. The turquoise waters which lap the white sandy beach teem with brightly-coloured tropical fish, and an underwater wonderland of corals and sponges. Visitors are guaranteed a delightful stay in this exquisite retreat from reality.

At **Buccament** there is a government banana collecting and packing station, and beside the road which runs through the Cane Grove Estate to the sea, there are a number of rocks bearing Carib petroglyphs, carved many centuries ago by Arawak or Carib Indians.

At Cane Grove Estate there is a feeder road running inland along the Buccament Valley through Peniston to

**Vermont**. At the head of the valley there are nature trails into the rain-forest. One is dwarfed by massive trees with canopies blocking out the light and draped with massive hanging vines. The lucky visitor may spot the rare St. Vincent parrot, and the best chance for this is first thing in the morning shortly after dawn, or late in the afternoon when they come out to feed. Another secretive rare bird which is occasionally spotted is the whistling warbler, also only found on St. Vincent. More common species include the red-capped green tanager, cocoa thrush, crested hummingbird and black hawk.

There are two well-marked trails, which split just after the bridge not far from the start. The longer trail takes two hours and the shorter one about an hour, although one could spend the whole day here taking a picnic lunch into the bargain. A short distance downstream from the bridge at Table Rock, there are sparkling pools and small waterfalls. Just inland from Layou is the Emerald Valley Hotel and Casino — the only casino on the island.

**Layou** is a pretty fishing village with brightly-coloured fishing boats sitting on the beach beneath the shady palm trees. The village, with a small police station, is noted for its crucifix with a black Christ, which is in the cemetery by the church.

Most of the open boats fish using nets with one end secured on land. The boats are rowed out into the bay while the net is fed out. The fishermen then make a loop which brings them back to the beach. The other end of the net is handed ashore, and then it is all hands to the ropes as the net, hopefully with a full catch of fish, is pulled in.

Visit the old **Rutland Vale Sugar Works** to see how elaborate and ingenious the nineteenth-century engineers had to be in providing power for the sugar mills. A huge

Above: There are many black sand beaches on the west coast of St. Vincent.
Below: Old sugar mill set amidst verdant coconut groves near to Layou.

aqueduct was built to bring in water to power the massive water wheels which provided the power for the mill rollers used to crush the cane.

St. Vincent's most famous petroglyphs can be seen just past Layou, on a huge twenty-foot rock along the river bank about a quarter of a mile inland from the road. The ten-minute walk is across private land so obtain prior permission if not accompanied by a guide. There is also a rock carving on the Calendar Stone at Mount Wynne, next to the black sand beach.

There were many large estates along this stretch of road, including the Peter's Hope Estate which used to process copra for oil and cassava.

The highway runs from Layou to Richmond through several delightful coastal villages such as Barrouallie, Troumala and Chateaubelair. There are also many black sand beaches en route where one can stop and relax in the sun or swim in the sea. Visitors should ensure their vehicle is safely parked off the road.

**Barrouallie** (pronounced Bar-elly) is a small fishing village with little houses and boats pulled up on to the beach. Fishermen here have traditionally hunted blackfish — the small pilot whale — in open boats powered by oar and using hand-held harpoons.

There are more petroglyphs in the grounds of the school on the hill. The stones are set in a lawn and can be visited with prior permission from the school office.

The village of Barrouallie has considerable French influence which can be seen in the architecture and its traditional town square. The police station dates from the 1700s and is one of the oldest buildings on the island. The cemetery contains many graves of victims of the cholera epidemic which swept up the coast in 1854.

**Wallilabou Bay** is a popular anchorage for visiting yachts, and just inland one can visit the Wallilabou Falls and take a dip in the pool beneath the cascading falls.

**Chateaubelair** is the most northerly town on the west coast and the French are reputed to have built a castle here overlooking the bay. However there is no trace of it, but it could help explain the name which translates as either 'castle of beautiful air', or 'castle of fair wind'.

The road then runs on to **Richmond** where there is another Government banana reception and packing plant. Visitors can swim safely from either Richmond Beach or nearby Wallibou Beach. Inland the landscape is dominated by Richmond Peak with Soufriere further to the north.

The road ends here but there is a path to **Trinity Falls**, so named because there are three falls with water warmed by the many hot pools in the area. The falls, considered by many to be the most beautiful on the island, are in a deep volcanic canyon, reached by a forty-five minute walk from the road through tropical forest. One can swim here but it is inadvisable for anyone but a strong swimmer as the falls and warm water combine to create strong, swirling currents similar to a giant jacuzzi. There are, however, several other calm water pools in the area. Guides are available for the hike.

Further up the coast are the spectacular **Falls of Baleine** where the waters plunge in a sheer drop about 60ft (18m) to the pool below. The falls can be reached after a very strenuous hike from Fancy at the end of the Windward Highway, or from the end of the Leeward Road via the Wallibou Dry River. The best, and easiest way in, however, is to take a boat from Kingstown or one of the fishing villages along the coast, so that after landing there is only a short walk to the falls.

## Eating out on the West Coast

**Emerald Valley Casino** $-$$
Penniston Valley
☎ 456-7140.
Light meals and drinks are served in the casino. The pool-side restaurant offers West Indian and international dishes.

**Stephen's Hideout** $-$$
Cumberland Bay
☎ 458-2325
Seafood and West Indian specialities

**Wallilabou Anchorage** $-$$
Wallilabou Bay
☎ 458-7270
West Indian specialities

## The South Coast

Take the airport road from Kingstown to Arnos Vale for a drive up to the summit of Dorsetshire Hill.
**Dorsetshire Hill** was the site of the last battle in the Second Carib War, during which the Carib Chieftain Chatoyer, was killed in hand-to-hand fighting. An obelisk marks the spot where he died. There are splendid views from the summit across the town, harbour and surrounding countryside. One can reach the hill by taking Queen's Drive, which starts close to the airport in Arnos Vale with its sports complex and cricket ground, and return down Sion Hill.

The road inland runs to Mesopotamia also known as the Marriaqua Valley (see West Coast section), while the road south continues to the magnificent **Calliaqua Bay**. Many of the island's hotel and resorts are along this stretch of coastline which has good sandy beaches and warm, safe waters. It has also developed as a highly fashionable residential area.

The small village of **Villa** has expanded in recent years because of the number of hotels in the area, and is located close to Villa Beach and Indian Bay Beach, among the best on the island.

Offshore lies Young Island, a private island resort. Just beyond is **Fort Duvernette**, which stands atop a towering 190ft (58m) rock. The rock is part of the Young Island estate, and used to be known as Young's Sugar Loaf because of its shape. Permission should be sought to visit the fort, although it is easy to swim out to it. There are also usually one or two rowing boats whose owners will take visitors across — and collect them. The fortress was built at the beginning of the nineteenth century to defend Calliaqua Bay and the island's old capital. It had two gun batteries, one on the summit and one forty feet below this. The summit is reached by steps hewn out of the rock.

**Calliaqua** is on the south-western corner of the island, and used to be the old capital of St. Vincent. Like Marriaqua, it had its origins in a Spanish name. It was originally called Calliagua, meaning 'calm waters'. Just beyond Calliaqua one can take the road inland to **Ribisti** and visit the old Harony Hall sugar mill. Blue Lagoon nestles in the corner of the island from where one can walk around the headland overlooking Sharp's Bay and Cable Hut Bay, with Mulligan Cay just offshore.

## Eating out around the South Coast

**A La Mer Restaurant** $-$$
Indian Bay Beach Hotel
☎ 458-4001
West Indian and international cuisine

**Argyle Nature Resort** $-$$
Overlooking Argyle Beach
☎ 458-0992
International and seafood specialities

**Beachcombers** $-$$
Villa Beach
☎ 458-4283
West Indian and international food is served in this open-air beachfront setting.

**Chicken Roost** $
Arnos Vale
☎ 456-4932
Fast food

**The Coral Room** $-$$
Sunset Shores Hotel
Villa Beach
☎ 458-4411
This delightful family-run hotel restaurant features an extensive à la carte menu serving steak, fish, lamb and fresh seafood prepared in mouthwatering sauces.

**Dolphins** $-$$
Villa Beach
☎ 457-4337
A charming restaurant in a great location. An great menu specializing in seafood, creole and continental cuisine all prepared with local herbs and spices. The bar features live music at weekends.

**French Restaurant** $-$$
Villa Beach
☎ 458-4972
This must rank as one of the finest restaurants in the Caribbean. Located in a charming open-air setting, the chef combines delicious French cuisine with a distinctive West Indian flair.

**Grand View Restaurant** $-$$
Villa Point
☎ 458-4811
West Indian and international cuisine

**Lagoon Hotel and Marina** $-$$
Blue Lagoon
☎ 458-4308.
Situated on a delightful terrace above the water's edge, this restaurant serves a fine blend of international dishes with excellent seafood specialities.

**Lime 'N' Pub** $
Villa Beach
☎ 458-4227
West Indian and seafood dishes.

**Pizza Party** $
Arnos Vale
☎ 456-4932
Pizza, barbecued chicken and snacks. Pizza delivery to yachts.

**Villa Lodge** $-$$
Villa Lodge Hotel
Villa Point
☎ 458-4641
Seafood and West Indian specialities are served in this charming restaurant overlooking Indian Bay.

**Young Island Resort** $$-$$$
Young Island
☎ 458-4826
Seafood and continental. Reservations required.

## Mesopotamia and the East Coast

Drive south from Kingstown and take the Vigie Highway inland to the Marriaqua Valley, better known as Mesopotamia, or 'Mespo'. Three rivers running down the hills merge to form the Marriagua, (Spanish for 'married waters'), although this name altered over the years to become Marriaqua. This is a vast fertile valley surrounded by hills on all sides and carpeted with verdant, lush vegetation. It is believed that the hills actually form the rim of a massive volcanic crater which erupted millions of years ago.

The valley was not really developed until after the Second Carib War of 1795-6, because it had been a Carib stronghold until that time. There was a Carib camp at Vigie (French for 'look out') during the Second Carib War, and after the war, the land was sold to English settlers. It was one of the first places planted with the breadfruit trees brought by Captain Bligh. The main crops are bananas, coconut, cocoa and nutmeg, but almost every other fruit and vegetables found on the island is grown here. Most of the farms are small holdings, with the farmer and his family living in little houses nestling on the sides of the valley. Terraces have been carved out on the hills for crops, and altogether there are twenty-three small agricultural villages in the valley.

**Mesopotamia**, with its small Roman Catholic Church, is at the mouth of the valley where the three rivers merge, before running into the Yambou River which then tumbles its way down to the eastern coast along the Yambou Gorge. The highest point around Mesopotamia is Grand Bonhomme, 3,181ft (970m), and the smaller peak, Petit Bonhomme, is just over 2,000ft (610m).

**Montreal** is at the end of a rough road to the north west of Mesopotamia in the mountains. **Montreal Gardens**, formerly part of a plantation around the Great House, specialises in the commercial production of tropical American flowering plants, especially anthuriums. One can visit the Muscovado Sugar Factory and the remains of the arrowroot factories at Farm and Escape village near the **Yambou Gorge** where there are also a number of petroglyphs to be seen.

The Mesopotamia road reaches the sea at the village of **Peruvian Vale**, where one can turn right and head back south around the coast via Argyle Beach and Arnos Vale.

On this route there is a giant rock off shore the pretty **Argyle Beach**, and an imposing church up on the hill. Argyle beach, with its crashing surf, is one of the places the islanders come to party, and cook out under the stars. Just inland up the valley is the Argyle Nature Resort, a small hotel with a pool and some of the prettiest rooms on the island.

Turn left at the coast and head north to the village of **Biabou**, with its Anglican church built on the promontory. There are the remains of many old arrowroot factories and sugar mills along this coastal highway. The road then leads past **Grant's Bay** and **South** and **North Union** to **Sans Souci**. The origin of this place name, which in French means 'without care', is unknown. There was a French plantation here, and it has been suggested, that the name was given because the estate was so dilapidated. In Union one can visit the flower centre established by Victor Hadley, which specialises in growing ginger lilies, orchids and anthuriums.

The Windward Highway, another spectacular drive, continues to **Colonaire**. There is good walking in this area either following the river valley inland or along the cliffs to find a secluded beach. The stretch of highway to Georgetown offers spectacular sea views along the way and there are also many good black sand beaches. At **Black Point** there is a man-made cavern where rum used to be stored before being rowed out into the bay to the waiting ships at anchor. Today the cavern is home to large numbers of bats.

**Georgetown**, named after King George III, did not really develop until the opening of the Black Point Tunnel in 1815. The 200 foot long tunnel, engineered by Colonel Thomas Browne, was literally carved through the mountain, which sloped steeply down into the sea. Until the tunnel — built by Carib and slave labour — was opened there was no road between the north and south of the island, and boat was the only means of travel. After the tunnel opened, Georgetown became the sugar capital of the island, and the Mount Bentinck factory, which finally closed in 1984, was the last operating sugar plant on the island.

After Georgetown, the road deteriorates the further north one drives, and if you are heading for Fancy, the journey is best continued in a four-wheel drive vehicle. If you only want to reach the Sandy Bay area, however, the journey can be undertaken in an ordinary car, but care must be taken, especially after wet weather.

Shortly after Georgetown one crosses over the huge Rabacca Dry River which was formed by the flow of volcanic ash from Soufriere during the 1902 eruption.

For most of the year, the dry river, which is several hundred feet across, looks more like a huge gravel pit through which the road snakes, but after heavy rain it becomes a raging torrent and crossings should not be attempted. At least two lorries and a tractor have been swept into the sea by the fast flowing waters.

Rabacca Farms used to be known as Orange Hill Estate and ran from near the coast to the slopes of Soufriere, making it one of the world's largest coconut estates, extending across almost 3,200 acres. It has now been divided into a number of small farms as part of the Government's Rural Development Project, but still produces bananas, coconuts, citrus and spices, as well as aubergines and cola nuts, used for flavouring what must now be the world's most popular carbonated drink. Arrowroot grows by the roadside, and there are ruins of several sugar and arrowroot mills.

The best way of getting to **Soufriere** is from a track which starts in the banana and coconut plantations of Rabacca Farms. There is a huge sign for the trail by the side of the road and one should take the left turning to drive to the trail head. Visitors can hike around the rim of the huge volcano, more than a mile across, and then either return to the east coast, or continue down to the western coast. The hike to the west coast follows a gulley carved out by lava flowing from Soufriere into the Caribbean Sea, and one can reach the coast either at Richmond Vale or further south at Chateaubelair. It is advisable to have a guide for this trip and arrangements in place for a car or boat to pick you up if you plan to cross the island.

Soufriere, because of its frequent eruptions, is one of the most studied volcanoes in the world. There were major eruptions in 1718 and 1812, when a cloud of volcanic ash blocked out the sun as far away as Barbados. The huge crater was formed after the 1902 eruption, and the last eruption was on Good Friday, 13 April 1979 — although the many vents and bubbling hot pools show that there is still a lot of subterranean activity.

The trail is quite steep and steadily climbs volcanic ridges for just under three-and-a-half miles until it reaches the summit 4,048ft (1,234m) above sea level. The landscape is quite startling and stark in comparison with the lush, tropical vegetation further south and encountered on the walk in. After walking around the volcano one can either return on the same route, making a round trip of about seven and a half miles, or carry on to the west coast. The western route is a good 10 miles (16km) to the coast making the whole trip is about 15 miles (24km) in total. A good day's walking in view of the heat, ascent and terrain.

Back on the Windward Highway, the road runs into **Sandy Bay**, where native Caribs were settled after the Carib Wars, and then it is a short drive to **Owia**, another Carib village on the north-eastern tip of the island. It is noted for its arrowroot processing mill and the salt ponds, both of which can be visited.

St. Vincent has traditionally been one of the world's major suppliers of arrowroot, and the discovery that arrowroot improved the quality and traction of computer print-out paper gave the industry a massive boost.

Above: The Falls of Baleine where the icy waters plunge about 60ft (18m) to the pool below.

The **Owia Salt Ponds** form a natural swimming pool beside the sea because of a series of volcanic ridges just off the coast. There is an impressive series of steps down the cliff to the water. From the cliffs St. Lucia can be seen about 20 miles (32km) to the north west.

After **Commantawana Bay**, one reaches the tiny village of **Fancy**, another Carib village, and the end of the road. There is a trail which starts here and travels west around the coast to the Falls of Baleine, but it is a very strenuous hike. It is not advisable unless you are a very fit, experienced walker and a guide is essential. The best way to see these falls is by boat as described on the west coast route.

## Eating out on the East Coast

**Ferdie's Restaurant and Bar** $-$$
Georgetown
☎ 458-6433
West Indian specialities

# BEQUIA

Bequia is the largest of the Grenadine islands and was known by the Caribs as Becouya — the 'Island of the Cloud'.

Bequia, pronounced beck-way, can be reached by boat and air, and although only nine miles (14km) from Kingstown, the ferry crossing can sometimes be a little rough. However, on a calm day it is a delightful journey as the ferry makes its way down the west coast of the island to Port Elizabeth. A good indication of the island's popularity is that many St. Vincentians choose to holiday there every year.

The airport, which was completed in 1992, is on the south coast and is served by LIAT, Mustique Airways, SVG Air, Air Carriacou and Air Martinique.

Among the first English settlers were the Warners, and their plantation at Spring became so successful that others came to the island to grow sugar cane using slave labour. After emancipation, however, this type of estate was no longer economic to run. Many of the population left the island and the land was divided into many smaller farms. Around this time the Wallace family arrived from Scotland, and in 1830 Sir William Wallace managed the Friendship Estate. One of his sons, Bill, founded the whaling industry with Frenchman Joseph Ollivierre, who had purchased the Paget Farm Estate.

Bequia is still one of the few places in the world where whaling is legal, although there is only one open 18ft (6m) wooden boat still engaged in this practice. On average one whale per year is killed. There is a small whaling museum in the Paget Farm home of Athneal Ollivierre, who is known as the 'Last Harpooner', and is grandson of Joseph. The entrance from the road to the blue and white painted house leads under a pair of huge whale bones. Fishing is still the main occupation and a new fish processing plant has been built on the south coast.

Ferries dock at the jetty in Port Elizabeth which lies in the great sweep of **Admiralty Bay**. As the ferry rounds the headland to enter the bay it passes the Battery which was built on the cliffs in the late eighteenth century at Hamilton. It also has to negotiate the reefs offshore, most notably the Devil's Table Reef. The tourist information office is close to the jetty with the police and customs station located just to the left. Taxi drivers will descend on visitors in droves offering lifts to any destination. Expect to pay around US$15 an hour to hire a taxi for a sightseeing tour or to drop you at one of the beaches.

**Anchorage Bay** is a large sheltered natural harbour which has attracted yachts from around the world for many years. The Bequia Yacht Marina was reopened in 1993 and every year it services yachts from around the world. While repairs are being carried out, sailors can usually be found relaxing in the Harpoon Saloon which overlooks the harbour.

The small **Port Elizabeth** waterfront is usually busy and packed when a ferry is docked. At night, it is extremely picturesque with several small bars and restaurants and the twinkling lights of the anchored yachts moored in the bay.

Admiralty Bay is divided into a number of beaches, including **Princess Margaret Beach,** — named because she bathed here in 1958 — and Lower Bay, a 2 mile (3.5km) walk from Port Elizabeth, with a small fishing village. Palm-fringed **Friendship Bay** is due south of Port Elizabeth on the southern coast, and is the longest beach on the island. Offshore one can see Petit Nevis, where there a whaling station, and Ile de Quatre. **Hope Bay** lies to the east on the Atlantic Ocean side. Port Elizabeth was named in 1937 to commemorate the Coronation of the present queen's parents.

Roads run across the island to Hope Bay, where there is a working coconut plantation, and up the eastern coast as far as Spring, where there are a number of sugar mill ruins just beyond the Spring Bay Hotel and further north at Brute Point. There is a lovely walk from Port Elizabeth to **Spring Bay** where there is a 200-year-old working plantation and delightful small hotel, overlooking the ocean. The restaurant largely uses produce grown on the estate or caught just offshore. The old sugar mill was working until 1905. In Industry, about one mile (1.5km) further on, where there are trails to Bequia Head and across the island to Anse Chein on the north-west coast.

The road also runs south along Admiralty Bay to Lower Bay, and to the Friendship Bay area and along the south coast for a short distance. The former British Prime Minister, Sir Anthony Eden, used to own a property on Friendship Bay. There is also a road up to **Mount Pleasant**, one of the best vantage points on the island.

The many boutiques, shops and art galleries on Bequia are open between 8am and 12noon, or 9am and 1pm, and again between 2pm to 6pm. The island is noted for its beautiful model boats. The three banks in Port Elizabeth are open Monday to Thursday from 8am to 1pm, and on Friday from 8am to 1pm and 3pm to 5pm. The Post Office is open Monday to Friday from 9am to 12noon and 1pm to 3pm; and on Saturday between 9am and 11.30am. The Bequia Casualty Hospital is in Port Elizabeth (☎ 458-3294), and there are five churches on the island.

St. Mary's Anglican Church in Port Elizabeth dates from 1829 and contains some fascinating memorial tablets. It is built of local limestone and bricks brought in as ships' ballast. This church was built to replace the first church which was blown down in 1798.

Beaches are usually secluded, and always sandy, and there are thirty-five major dive sites around the island, none more than fifteen-minutes away by boat. There is, however, no shore diving. One can visit the wreck of the *MS Lireco*, a 110-foot freighter that was specially sunk in 1986 as a facility for divers.

Watersports are available from Dive Bequia at the Plantation House (☎ 458-3504), Sunsports at the Gingerbread complex (☎ 458-3577), Dive Paradise at the Friendship Bay Hotel (☎ 458-3563), and Bequia Dive at Friendship Bay (☎ 458-3248). De Reef Aquasports in Lower Bay and Paradise Windsurfing in Friendship also offers windsurfing.

There is accommodation to suit all tastes from the excellent Plantation House with its fine restaurant — one of the Caribbean's rising gastronomic stars — to small, comfortable guest houses.

## Eating out on Bequia

**Cafe King Fisher** $
☎ 458-3575
Snacks and specialities

**Coco's Place** $
Lower Bay
☎ 458-3463
Local specialities. Good value and meals served all day

**Cool Spot Restaurant and Bar** $-$$
Back Street
Port Elizabeth
☎ 458-3586
West Indian and seafood

**Crescent Inn Beach Bar** $-$$
Industry Beach
☎ 458-3400
Seafood and West Indian specialities

**Daphne's** $-$$
Port Elizabeth
☎ 458-3271
West Indian specialities and seafood

**Dawn's Creole** $-$$
Lower Bay
☎ 458-3154
Creole specialities and seafood

**De Reef** $-$$
Lower Bay
☎ 458-3447
West Indian cuisine

**El Mirador** $-$$
Hamilton
☎ 457-3080
Seafood and Spanish foods and wine

**Flame Tree Restaurant** $$
Blue Tropic Hotel
☎ 458-3573
Local dishes and fine steaks a speciality

**Frangipani Hotel Restaurant** $-$$$
Admiralty Bay
☎ 458-3255
West Indian and international

**Gingerbread Cafe** $
Admiralty Bay
☎ 458-3800
Snacks and delicious home baked cakes

**Gingerbread Restaurant** $-$$
Admiralty Bay
☎ 458-3800
Seafood and continental

**The Green Boley** $
Belmont Beach
☎ 458-3247
Snacks and fast food

**Harpoon Saloon** $-$$
Port Elizabeth
☎ 458-3272
Seafood, creole and continental cuisine

**Julie's Guest House** $-$$
Back Street
Port Elizabeth
☎ 458-3304
West Indian and creole specialities

**Keegan's** $-$$
Lower Bay
☎ 458-3245
West Indian specialities

**Le Petit Jardin** $$
Back Street
Port Elizabeth
☎ 458-3318
French and international. Good wine list.

**Maranne's Ice Cream** $
Belmont Beach
☎ 458-3041

**Ocean View Restaurant** $-$$
Friendship Bay Resort
☎ 458-3222
West Indian, seafood and international with a good wine list

**Old Fig Tree** $-$$
Belmont Beach
☎ 458-3201
Seafood and West Indian specialities

**Old Fort Restaurant** $-$$
Old Fort Hotel
☎ 458-3440
West Indian and creole

**Plantation House Restaurant** $$
Belmont
☎ 458-3425
International

**Spicy 'n Herby Beach Bar** $-$$
Friendship Bay Resort
☎ 458-3222
West Indian, seafood and light meals.

**Spring on Bequia Hotel Restaurant** $$
Spring
☎ 458-3414
Seafood and creole specialities

**Theresa's** $-$$
Lower Bay
☎ 458-3802
West Indian specialities

**The Whaleboner** $-$$
Port Elizabeth
☎ 458-3233
West Indian and creole specialities

Above: The charming harbour at Port Elizabeth on Bequia.
Below: The stunning Macaroni Beach on the exquisite island of Mustique.

# MUSTIQUE

This gem of an island has often been in the headlines because of the rich and famous who own homes here or regularly drop in — most notably Princess Margaret.

Named by the French after the mosquito swarms first found there, the island is now one of the most exclusive resorts in the world. It has been beautifully developed by Colin Tennant, whose aim was to establish it as an international community. He bought the island in 1959 and it is now run by the Mustique Company who represent the property owners. It is a tiny island of green, gently sloping hills surrounded by white sandy beaches and sparkling turquoise seas, making it an ideal tropical hideaway. There is excellent snorkelling along the west coast at **Endeavour**, **Plantation**, **Britannia** and **Lagoon** bays, and good water-skiing in Britannia Bay.

Offshore there are many coral reefs, protecting the twelve miles (19km) of coastline. **Britannia Bay** on the south coast and **Macaroni Bay** on the north coast are among the island's best beaches.

The island is ten minutes flying time from St. Vincent, six hours from New York and ten hours from London. By sea, it is about two-and-a-half hours from Kingstown, and the Mustique Company boat provides transportation to neighbouring islands.

There is an airstrip, church, cricket pitch, riding stables, nature reserve and fully-equipped doctor's clinic. Most of the islanders live in Lovell Village close to the headland between Plantain and Britannia Bays.

The wreck of the *Antilles*, a 20,000 ton French liner lies off l'Ansecoy Bay on the northern coast. It is possible to take a day charter to Mustique and walk around the island in a couple of hours whilst rubbing shoulders with the rich. Visitors can even rent a scooter and be really lazy. While villas may appear expensive to rent through the Mustique Company, they are affordable if a group of friends or family get together to share the cost.

The only hotel on the island is the luxurious Cotton House Hotel, a spacious eighteenth century great house, which has been superbly converted for its present use.

The Firefly Guesthouse is a private house overlooking Britannia Bay and offers rooms with breakfast for those want to enjoy the Mustique life style at very reasonable cost in charming surroundings. The Firefly was the first house built on the island.

Basil's Bar and Raft Restaurant on Britannia Bay, serves fresh seafood, especially lobster and shrimp, and local specialities. A great atmosphere where visitors are likely to see the rich and famous relaxing and enjoying the good food and fine wines. There is a weekly barbecue and jump up. ☎ 458-4621.

**Balliceaux** and **Battowia** are two small islands off Mustique. Balliceaux, a corruption of the French 'belles oiseaux' meaning beautiful birds, was the island where the Caribs were sent in 1797 after the Carib War, prior to their transportation to Honduras.

# CANOUAN

The island is named after the Carib word for 'turtle', because so many of these sea creatures once came ashore here to lay their eggs. Today, these beaches play host to holidaymakers who looking to escape from reality. The island is small and has a population of about 740. Inland there are rolling hills where one can stroll without seeing another soul, except perhaps for a young boy tending the family's herd of goats. There used to be a large gun mounted on the summit of Fort Caribe Hill. The old stone early nineteenth century Anglican Church, sits on a hill at the north of the island looking out to sea. The church and the village surrounding it were abandoned after being badly damaged by a hurricane in 1921. The townsfolk relocated to Charlestown in the south of Canouan.

There is an airport towards the southern tip of the island which has night landing facilities, and Air Martinique run scheduled flights from St. Vincent. Mustique Airways and SVG Air also provide regular charter services. Visitors planning to fly into Canouan should try to schedule it during the daytime if possible, because the views of the area across the islands is not one easily forgotten. Visitors can sail their own vessel to the island, or catch the *MV Snapper*, which leaves Kingstown on Mondays, Thursdays and Saturdays at 10.30am and arrives in Canouan about four-and-a-half hours later.

## Eating out on Canouan

Anchor Inn $$
Grand Bay
☎ 458-8568
West Indian and seafood

Canouan Beach Hotel $$
☎ 458-8888
West Indian and seafood

Crystal Sands Beach Hotel $$
☎ 458-8309
West Indian and international

Tamarind Beach Hotel $-$$
☎ 458-8753
West Indian and seafood

Villa Le Bijou $$
☎ 458-8025
Seafood and creole specialities

## Mayreau

A small, privately-owned island covering about one square mile, with a population of about 180. The island is reached only by boat and is a thirty-minute trip from Union Island. Even the mail boat has to be met in the bay by smaller craft which take on board supplies for the island. The larger cruise ships also transfer their passengers into smaller boats to be ferried ashore. It has several white sand beaches, one resort hotel on the sweeping Salt Whistle Bay, and Denis' Hideaway, a guest house and restaurant, which serves excellent seafood and West Indian specialities. ☎ 458-8594.
There are no roads, and electricity is provided by generators.

## Tobago Cays

The Tobago Cays are located south of Canouan and east of Mayreau, and offer world class diving. The Cays largely consist of five small islands — Petit Rameau, Petit Bateau, Jamesby, Baradal and Petit Tobac. The islands are noted for their serrated coastlines which create hundreds of tiny coves, bays and inlets to explore and enjoy. The islands are also protected by a ring of coral reefs — World's End Reef and Horseshoe Reef — and can only be reached by boat. Horseshoe Reef is a stunning wall dive with visibility to 120ft (36m). The colours of the coral-encrusted wall are quite spectacular and divers will encounter myriad tropical fish as they descend beneath the surface. Visitors are assured of the luxury of their own near-deserted tropical island. The area of the Tobago Cays are protected as a National Marine Park and fishing is strictly prohibited.

## Palm Island

Another tiny, beautiful privately-owned island with a resort consisting of twenty-four stone cottages all facing the beautiful white sands of Casuarina Beach. There is an open air restaurant and a host of watersports are available. The island really does boast some of the most beautiful beaches in the Caribbean — if not the world — including Coral Bay, Tamarind Beach, Coral Cove and Secret Beach. The island used to be called Prune Island, although nobody knows why, and the name was changed when it was acquired on lease in 1966 by John Caldwell, who with his wife Mary, sailed around the world in their yacht *Outward Bound* which they built themselves. Together they planted hundreds if not thousands, of palm trees on Palm Island and the other Grenadines, and single-handedly eradicated every mosquito on the island. Snorkelling safaris are offered and there is even a jogging trail! Access by air is via Union Island from where passengers are transferred by boat on the one mile journey to Palm.

## Petit St. Vincent

This island, often referred to as simply PSV, is the most southerly of the Grenadine islands which fall under the jurisdiction of St. Vincent. It used to be owned by Lilly Bethel, who came from Petit Martinique, and her sons ran a fleet of trading schooners between the islands. In the 1960s she sold to the present resident owner Haze Richardson, who has lovingly carved out this luxurious resort into the glorious sanctuary it is today.
The tiny island is one large 113-acre luxury resort with rolling hills and woodland, surrounded by stunning

Above: Tiny islands of the Tobago Cays dotted like emeralds in the azure sea.
Below: Dazzling white sandy beach on tiny Palm Island.
Opposite: Glorious sunset over Salt Whistle Bay in the Grenadines.

white beaches, turquoise waters and reefs offshore. Twenty-two guest cottages, each with their own private patio nestle on the shore and hillsides affording visitors the ultimate in privacy and comfort. Breakfast and room service is delivered to the cottages by charming staff who ply the island in the hotel's vehicles. There is a restaurant and bar, boutique, tennis and boats for charters and trips.

The island is a popular venue with yacht charters, although it is necessary to make reservations to eat in the restaurant in advance.

## Union Island

Approaching the island by sea from the south, there appears to be three sets of hills. The most spectacular is the towering central hill known as The Pinnacle, which rises over 900ft (274m) above sea level. The sides are so steep that it has often been compared to the spire of a cathedral. On the western side of the island there are a series of three hills — Mount Parnassus, Mount Tabor and Mount Olympus which run from south to north. Fort Hill was named because of the fort which used to protect the harbour and sea approaches and dominates the eastern side of the island. The approach by boat from Tobago Cays is also extremely spectacular. The *MV Snapper* calls at Union Island on Mondays, Thursdays and Saturdays. There are regular scheduled services with LIAT and Air Martinique, and Mustique Airways and SVG Air offer charter services. It is a busy airport because apart from bringing passengers to stay on Union Island, it also ferries in many others who are catching boat connections to neighbouring islands, or going cruising.

The island boasts fabulous beaches and is a favourite watering hole for yachts cruising through the Grenadines and eastern Caribbean. Clifton is the main town and port, and the waterfront has a number of charming small inns. It is linked with Ashton, the island's other small town, by a coast road which offers stunning views out to sea over the coral shelf towards Carriacou.

The tourist information bureau is on the left as you disembark from the ferry, and the Post Office and Anchorage Hotel is situated on the right. The small clinic is along the bay south of the tourist office.

The Anchorage Yacht Club is between the airstrip and the sea, and can accommodate guests who want to fly or sail in. The Sunny Grenadines is also on the waterfront in lush tropical gardens and is a yacht charter centre. The island has several fine beaches with safe swimming and excellent scuba and snorkelling offshore. Dive Anchorage offers diving tuition and trips, and can arrange watersports.

### Eating out on Union Island

**Anchorage Yacht Club** $$-$$$
☎ 458-8221
French and creole specialities

**Clifton Beach Hotel** $$
☎ 458-8235
West Indian specialities

**Eagle's Nest** $
☎ 458-8319
Snacks and local specialities

**Lambi's** $-$$
☎ 458-8549
Seafood

**Sunny Grenadines** $$
☎ 458-8327
Seafood and international

**T & N** $-$$
☎ 458-8207
West Indian specialities and seafood

# St. Vincent Fact File

## Arrival, Entry Requirements and Customs

British, American and Canadian citizens staying for less than six months, do not need a passport provided they have proof of citizenship, such as a birth certificate. Visitors from the United States and Canada may enter on an ID card but must have a valid return ticket. It is, however, a good idea to travel with your passport, and citizens from all other countries require one. Visas are not required.

Visitors may be asked to pay a deposit on certain personal items such as radios and electrical goods, which is refunded on departure providing they are still in your possession.

## Accommodation

Prices, unless clearly stated, do not usually include the seven per cent Government tax and there may also be a ten per cent service charge. In the information provided, the abbreviated terms stand for the following:-

CP: *Continental Plan* (bed and breakfast)
MAP: *Modified American Plan* (breakfast & dinner included)
EP: *European Plan* (bed only, no meals)
AP: *American Plan* (all meals included)

$ Inexpensive accommodation
$$ Moderate
$$$ Luxury

### St. Vincent

**Argyle Nature Resort** $-$$ CP
☎ 458-0992
A small six-bedroom resort overlooking Argyle beach with pool, small restaurant and beautifully-furnished rooms. Facilities for windsurfing and horse riding.

**Beachcombers Hotel** $ CP
Villa Beach
☎ 458-4283
Attractive terraced villas and self-catering en-suite rooms set in tropical gardens which lead down to the beach. Waterside bar and restaurant.

**Brownes Hotel** $ EP
Villa Beach
☎ 457-4000
Twenty-five rooms. Under new management being completely refurbished. Due to re-open 1996.

**Cobblestone Inn** $ CP
Kingstown
☎ 456-1937
Nineteen rooms. This historic inn overlooking the harbour, was built in 1814 as a sugar warehouse. It has been attractively converted and restored and all rooms have en-suite facilities. It retains many charming features such as the original cobblestone walkways and arches. Two restaurants, two bars. A five-minute drive to the beaches.

**Coconut Beach Hotel** $ EP
Indian Bay
☎ 457-4900
Ten rooms. The hotel is situated right on the beach and only ten minutes from town. All rooms have en-suite facilities. It has a water's edge restaurant and bar.

**Emerald Valley Resort and Casino** $ EP
☎ 456-7140.
Twelve cottages set in twelve acres of lush, tropical gardens in the valley overlooking the river. This hotel centres around the casino, poolside restaurant, bar and unique nine-hole golf course. There is often live music and barbecues.

**Grand View Beach Hotel** $$-$$$ EP
Villa Point,
☎ 458-4811
This twenty bedroom family-run hotel is set in eight acres of landscaped gardens with wonderful views of the Grenadines. The large en-suite rooms are attractively furnished, Bar, pool with swim-up bar.

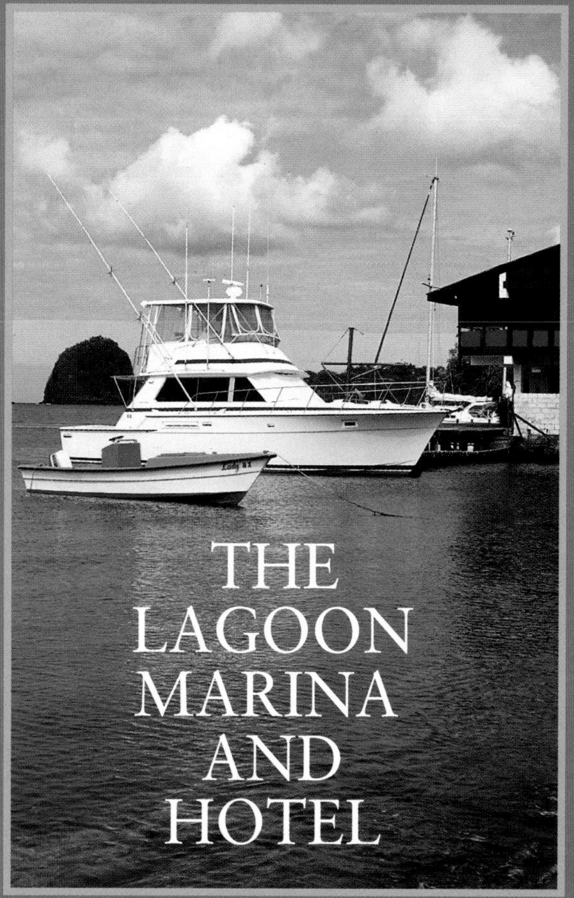

- Nineteen first-class rooms with private balcony overlooking the bay
- Excellent restaurant, relaxed bar and exotic pool deck
- Business lunches and conferences
- Fully-equipped marina including fuel, water, electricity, laundry and showers

***For excellent service in a charming and friendly environment***

PO BOX 133
ST. VINCENT AND
THE GRENADINES
TEL: (809) 458-4308
FAX: (809) 457-4716

**Haddon Hotel** $ EP
Kingstown
☎ 456-1897
This friendly seventeen-room hotel is close to downtown Kingstown, only five minutes from the airport and ten minutes from the beach. It offers ten executive self-contained suites, and its restaurant is noted for specialising in local cuisine. Self-drive cars and tennis is available.

**Heron Hotel** $ CP
Bay Street
Kingstown
☎ 457-1631
Fifteen rooms. A comfortable and friendly bed and breakfast hotel with en-suite facilities, close to the centre of town, and only a short drive to the beaches. There is a friendly bar and restaurant specialising in local dishes.

**Indian Bay Beach Hotel** $ CP, EP, MAP
Indian Bay Beach
☎ 458-4001
Thirteen bedrooms. Situated by the white sands of Indian Bay, the hotel has a restaurant that specialises in seafood and local cuisine. There is also a bar. Watersports are available nearby, and there is wonderful snorkelling in the underwater gardens offshore.

**Lagoon Hotel and Marina** $-$$ EP
Blue Lagoon
☎ 458-4308.
A fine hotel with nineteen en-suite rooms nestling beside the Caribbean Sailing Yachts marina. It has a restaurant and bar and two-tiered swimming pool. Facilities include snorkelling, windsurfing and daily skippered sailing trips to Bequia and Mustique. It also has conference facilities.

**Mariners Inn** $$ CP
Villa Beach
☎ 458-4287
Twenty-one rooms. Nestling between palm trees at the water's edge, this colonial-style inn has charming rooms, some with four-poster beds, and an open-air restaurant and bar.

**New Montrose Apartment Hotel** $-$$ CP
New Montrose, Kingstown
☎ 457 0172/456 1553
Twenty unit apartment hotel which includes executive suites, studios and one- and two-bedroom apartments. All havae air-conditoning, telephone, television and full bathroom. Shopping prior to guests arrival is available.

**Petit Byahaut** $$-$$$ AP
Petit Byahaut Bay
☎ 457-7008
Set in a fifty-acre valley which runs from the beach and only accessible by boat. Seven luxury permanent tents provide romantic accommodation. Great base for hiking, diving, fishing, nature watching or just getting away from it all.

**Sunset Shores Hotel** $$ EP
Villa Beach
☎ 458-4411
This beachfront hotel has thirty-two en-suite rooms, many with their own private patios. The courtyard, set in lush, tropical gardens, includes a covered bar and pool. The restaurant specialises in seafood prepared in exotic and tasty sauces. Watersports and snorkelling are available, and the hotel also has excellent conference facilities.

**Villa Lodge Hotel** $$ EP
Villa Point
☎ 458-4641.
The ten bedroom hotel is set in wonderful tropical gardens on the hillside overlooking Indian Bay. The restaurant is noted for seafood and barbecued steaks, and there is a cocktail bar and luxurious pool. There is a barbecue with live music on Saturday nights. The beach is nearby and water-sports and snorkelling are available.

**Young Island Resort** $$$ AP
Young Island
☎ 458-4826.
A thirty-five-acre privately-owned island. There are 29 cottages all with sea views set amidst the palm trees. Three restaurants, two bars, watersports, snorkelling, scuba and floodlit tennis. The resort has its own vessels, including two yachts, which are available to guests.

## The Grenadines

### Bequia

**Bequia Beach Club** $-$$ MAP
Friendship Bay
☎ 458-3248
Ten terraced bungalows, all furnished to a high standard, form their own little village and are close to the beach. There is daily maid service. There is a bar and restaurant, and facilities on offer include diving school with snorkelling and scuba, surfing, sailing and fishing, and island tours.

**Blue Tropic Hotel** $ CP
Friendship Bay
☎ 458-3573
A new apartment hotel — all ten rooms have private balconies with magnificent sea views — is set on a small hill overlooking the bay yet only a minute's walk from the beach. The hotel is noted for its Flame Tree garden restaurant and also has a friendly bar. Free use of bicycles for exploring.

**Creole Garden Hotel** $ MAP
Lower Bay
☎ 458-3154
Four rooms. The hotel stands at the end of the bay with great harbour and sea views. New studio apartments have their own private terrace and garden area. There is a bar and restaurant.

**De Reef Apartments** $-$$ EP
Lower Bay
☎ 458-3447
These five new, well-equipped, self-contained apartments are set in their own gardens and are just a few yards from the beach. There is a beach bar and waterside restaurant that specialises in sea food seven days a week. Sunday lunches at De Reef are an enjoyable occasion.

**Fairmont Apartments** $-$$ CP
Belmont
☎ 458-4037
Three well-equipped apartments with maid service, in a delightful garden setting in Belmont overlooking Admiralty Bay. The terraced apartments, set well back off the road, have large balconies and are surrounded by trees.

**Frangipani** $ EP
Port Elizabeth
☎ 458-3255
Sixteen rooms. A charming, small hotel set in colourful gardens and with fabulous views over Admiralty Bay. It is noted for its lively Thursday night barbecue and jump-up. The main house is built in classic West Indian Gingerbread-style, and there is also accommodation in the attractive wood and stone cottages set around the garden. There is an open-air bar and restaurant noted for fresh seafood and local cuisine. Facilities include boat trips, diving, snorkelling, scuba, organised hikes, guided tours, watersports and tennis. The hotel has its own small boutique.

**Friendship Bay Hotel** $$ CP
Friendship
☎ 458-3222
Twenty-seven en-suite rooms. A lively, comfortable hotel beside a long stretch of sandy beach. It is noted for its well-stocked bar and Spicy 'n Herby Restaurant which serves an interesting variety of Caribbean and creole dishes with hints of Swedish and Oriental cuisine. There are daily specials. There is lots of live music and the hotel is renowned for its regular Saturday night jump-ups. There is also a beach bar, tennis, volleyball court, diving and snorkelling, sailing, windsurfing and water skiing. Yacht charters, boat trips and island tours can also be arranged.

**Gingerbread Apartments** $ EP
Admiralty Bay
☎ 458-3800
Three apartments on Admiralty Bay and only a short walk from Port Elizabeth. The verandah, hanging balcony and eaves are a mass of gingerbread ornamentation. There is a restaurant and bar, as well as an open air cafe and store. Facilities are available for tennis, snorkelling, scuba and sunfish.

**Hibiscus Apartments** $ EP
Union Vale
☎ 458-3316
The four self-contained apartments are conveniently situated close to Port Elizabeth. The beaches at Admiralty Bay on the west coast and Spring Bay on the east coast are all about a ten-minute walk away.

**Julie's Guest House** $ AP
Port Elizabeth
☎ 458-3304
A delightful guest house with twenty rooms offering very friendly service. All rooms have their own balcony with glorious views. It has a dining room specialising in local dishes and bar, and it holds barbecues and beach picnics to the accompaniment of steel bands. Watersports, boat trips and island tours can be arranged.

**Keegan's Guest House** $ AP
Lower Bay
☎ 458-3530
Eleven rooms and two apartments. The guest house is almost on the white sand beach and has a restaurant and bar.

**The Old Fig Tree Guest House** $ EP
Admiralty Bay
☎ 458-3201
On the beach and close to the jetty. Six rooms. Light meals on request.

**Old Fort Country Inn** $$ EP
Mount Pleasant
☎ 458-3440
This former estate house built on top of the hill 450ft above sea level, has been curiously rebuilt to resemble a fortified medieval block house. The six en-suite rooms are large and comfortable, and the house is set in magnificent gardens. There is a restaurant and open air bar, and boat trips and island tours can be arranged.

**Plantation House Hotel** $$-$$$ AP, EP
Belmont
☎ 458-3425
An excellent resort which has recently been extended and upgraded. Set in over ten acres of tropical gardens there are twenty-seven beautifully furnished and appointed cottages all with verandahs and sea views, and thirteen garden cottages, as well as large rooms in the colonial-style main building. The main restaurant offers the best dining on the island. The European chef grows many of his own vegetables and herbs. The hotel is also the home of Dive Bequia, which operates from headquarters by the beach. Other facilities include boutique, tennis, pool, water-skiing, windsurfing and sailing.

**Spring on Bequia** $$-$$$ EP, MAP
Spring
☎ 458-3414
A delightful, small hotel set in the grounds of the historic Spring Plantation established more than 250 years ago. Some of the ten guest rooms are built on the foundations of the original great house. There is an open-air bar and restaurant, freshwater pool, tennis and snorkelling.

**Village Apartments** $ EP
Lower Bay
☎ 456-4960
The eight self-contained apartments overlook Admiralty Bay and are only a short walk from the beach. Snorkelling, scuba, sailing and yacht charters can be arranged, as well as island tours.

**Bequia Villa Rentals** (☎ 458-3393), and **Friendship Bay Villa Rentals** (☎ 458-3222) offer a large number of villas and apartments for holiday lets.

## Canouan

**Anchor Inn Guest House** $ MAP
☎ 458-856
Four rooms

**Canouan Beach Hotel** $$-$$$ AP
☎ 458-8888
Forty-three rooms. This resort hotel is right beside the white sandy beach set in tropical flower gardens, with lush hillsides behind. Most of the comfortably-furnished rooms have ocean views. There is a bar and restaurant, and facilities include tennis and table tennis, volleyball, watersports, scuba, snorkelling and catamaran trips.

**Crystal Sands Beach Hotel** $-$$ CP, EP
☎ 458-8309
Five attractively furnished cottages with verandahs just feet from the beach. There is a restaurant and bar and facilities include watersports, snorkelling, scuba, sailing, fishing and sightseeing trips.

**Tamarind Beach Hotel** $$-$$$ AP
☎ 458-8753
A recently-built luxury hotel with forty-eight rooms. Facilities include two restaurants, bar, beach bar, watersports and conference facilities.

**Villa Le Bijou** $$ MAP
☎ 458-8025
A small ten room guest house on the hill with beautiful views of the other Grenadine islands, and only five minutes from the beach.

## Mayreau

**Dennis' Hideaway** $ EP
☎ 458-8594
A comfortable, very friendly little guesthouse with restaurant. Three rooms.

**Salt Whistle Bay** $$-$$$
☎ Boatphone 493-9609
Luxury twenty-seven room hotel on the beach with delightfully furnished, en-suite rooms and bungalows. There is an open-air restaurant and bar, and facilities include watersports, snorkelling, scuba, volleyball and table tennis, and fishing and sailing trips can be arranged.

## Mustique

**Cotton House** $$-$$$
☎ 456-4777
Twenty four rooms. A delightful eighteenth century stone and coral building surrounded by guest cottages. The main building was originally a cotton store house which has been converted into the luxury hotel it is today. There is a restaurant and bar, and facilities include swimming pool, tennis, horseback riding and watersports. Boat trips and island tours can be arranged.

**Firefly House** $$ CP
☎ 456-3414
An unusual and delightful private villa built on the side of a hill overlooking Britannia Bay. The Firefly provides privacy and seclusion in a unique setting. The rooms have views of the bay instead of walls! Four elegantly-decorated room with private bathrooms and refrigerators are comfortable and relaxing. Picnic equipment is provided. It is two minutes from deserted beaches.

**Mustique Company Villas**
☎ 458-4621.
Arrange villa rentals on the island for small or large parties.

# THE FIREFLY GUEST HOUSE
# MUSTIQUE ISLAND

**PO Box 349, Mustique,**
**St. Vincent and the Grenadines**
**Telephone: 809 456 3414**
**Fax: 809 456 3514**

ɔf the Caribbean's loveliest
:houses is hidden on a hillside
st lush foliage overlooking
ique's exquisite Britannia Bay.
harming rooms all have private
ooms, paddle fans, air
itioning and spectacular views
the bay and Grenadine islands
nd. Although the island enjoys
utation as being a playground
e rich and famous, everybody
lcome at this charming,
nably-priced villa. The Firefly
thin easy walking distance of
stretches of deserted white
y beaches, watersports facilities
Basil's Bar and Restaurant.

This modern apartment complex offers luxurious accommodation at competitive rates. Facilities include air-conditioning, telephone, television, kitchenette, full bathroom, private balcony and shopping requirements prior to guests arrival.

BOX 215, KINGSTOWN, ST. VINCENT AND THE GRENADINES, WEST INDIES
TELEPHONE: (809) 457-0172 • 456-1635 • 456-1553 FAX: (809) 457-1233

## Palm Island (Prune Island)

**Palm Island Beach Club** $$-$$$ AP
☎ 458-8824
Guests can take their pick from five beaches on this 130-acre private island. Excellent accommodation in the beach club or in the surrounding villas. All twenty-four rooms have en-suite facilities and patio, and the restaurant is noted for its seafood dishes, especially lobster, and creole cuisine. Barbecues are held regularly. Facilities include tennis, fitness centre, watersports, scuba, snorkelling, fishing, sailing and cruising.

## Petit St. Vincent

**Petit St. Vincent Resort** $$$ AP
☎ 458-8801
A 113-acre private island resort surrounded by fabulous sandy beaches. The island is four miles from Union Island which has the nearest airstrip. Luxury accommodation in twenty-two spacious cottages set among the tropical gardens. The restaurant has a deservedly high reputation, and there is a piano bar. Facilities include shop, floodlit tennis, badminton, croquet, watersports, scuba, snorkelling, sailing, deep sea and reef fishing and diving. Self drive vehicles on the island and boats are also available.

## Union Island

**Anchorage Yacht Club** $$-$$$ CP, MAP
Clifton
☎ 458-8221
A splendid resort with ten excellent rooms or villas with fabulous views of the neighbouring Grenadines. The club, with its own airstrip, is based on the water's edge with excellent facilities for visiting yachts The restaurant is noted for its French and speciality local dishes. There is also a lively terrace bar, much frequented by visiting yachtsmen, and the club is noted for its steel band jump-ups. It also has its own boutiques, and offers mini-cruises, sport and line fishing and diving.

**Cays Apartments** $-$$ EP
Richmond Bay
☎ 456-2221
Five apartments

**Clifton Beach Hotel** $$-$$$ MAP
Clifton
☎ 458-8235
Twenty-five rooms. Stay in the hotel, guest house, or one of the apartments and cottages all conveniently close to the sea and the superb beach. There is a waterside restaurant specialising in local cuisine, although some rooms have kitchenettes for self catering. Guests can enjoy a snack on the terrace overlooking the jetty, or a drink in the carousel-shaped bar. Watersports, snorkelling, and shopping are available nearby.

**Lambi's Guest House** $ EP
Clifton
☎ 458-8549
A lively place during the season with a steel band entertaining dinner guests in the restaurant. The guest house has fourteen double rooms, its own dinghy dock, and minimarket

**Sunny Grenadines** $ CP, MAP
Clifton
☎ 458-8327
Fourteen rooms. This charming, comfortable small hotel is on the beach at Clifton Harbour. The restaurant specialises in seafood and local cuisine. Facilities include watersports, scuba diving, snorkelling, sailing, cruising and island tours. It has a conference room.

## Airlines

**Air Carriacou**
☎ 444-2898

**Air Martinique**,
St. Vincent ☎ 458-4528,
Union Island ☎ 458-8826.

**BWIA International**
In the USA 1-800-538-2942
In the UK 0171-839-9333

**British Airways**
☎ 457-1821

**Carib Express**
☎ 1-800-744-3333 from the Windward Islands
☎ 809-431-9200 from other locations

**LIAT**, Kingstown ☎ 457-1821
E.T. Joshua Airport ☎ 458-4841
Union Island Airport ☎ 458-8230

**Mustique Airways**
☎ 458-4380

**SVG Air**
☎ 456-5610

## Banks

Banks are open Monday to Friday from 8am to 3pm, and to 5pm on Fridays. There are banking facilities at E.T. Joshua Airport from Monday to Saturday between 7am and 5pm, with longer hours over Christmas, Easter and Carnival.
There are branches of the following banks available on St. Vincent.

**Barclays Bank**
Halifax Street, Kingstown
☎ 456-1706
Bequia ☎ 458-3215

**Canadian Imperial Bank of Commerce**
Halifax Street, Kingstown
☎ 457-1587

**Caribbean Banking Corporation**
South River Road, Kingstown
☎ 456-1501

**First St. Vincent Bank**
Granby Street, Kingstown
☎ 456-1873

**National Commercial Bank of St. Vincent**
Grenville Street, Kingstown
☎ 457-1844
Also at Halifax Street, Kingstown, E.T. Joshua Airport, and on Bequia and Union Island.

**St. Vincent Cooperative Bank**
Middle Street, Kingstown
☎ 456-1894

**Scotia Bank** (Bank of Nova Scotia)
Halifax Street, Kingstown
☎ 457-1601

## Camping

There are no camping facilities on St. Vincent.

## Car Hire

Hire car rates range from US$300 to 400 a week depending on the type of vehicle and the rental company. Average daily rates are around US$65 exclusive of insurance which costs an additional US$15-20 per day.
A temporary St. Vincent driving licence is required, and can be obtained on production of a current driving licence or valid international driving licence. Licences are issued for a fee of EC$40 at the airport, the police station in Bay Street, the motor licensing authority in Halifax Street (open Monday to Friday 9am to 3pm), or the car hire office.

**Avis Rent-a-Car**
Amos Vale
☎ 458-5610

**David's Auto Clinic**
Upper Sion Hill, Kingstown
☎ 456-4026

**Hertz**, Grenville Street, Kingstown
☎ 456-1743

**Kim's Rentals**
Grenville Street, Kingstown
☎ 456-1884

**Star Garage**
Grenville Street, Kingstown
☎ 456-1743

**Sunshine Auto Rentals**, Amos Vale
☎ 456-5380

**UNICO Auto Rentals**, Amos Vale
☎ 456-5744

Scooters can be rented, together with crash helmets, from:
**J G Agencies**
☎ 456-1409

**Sailors Cycle Centre**
☎ 457-1712

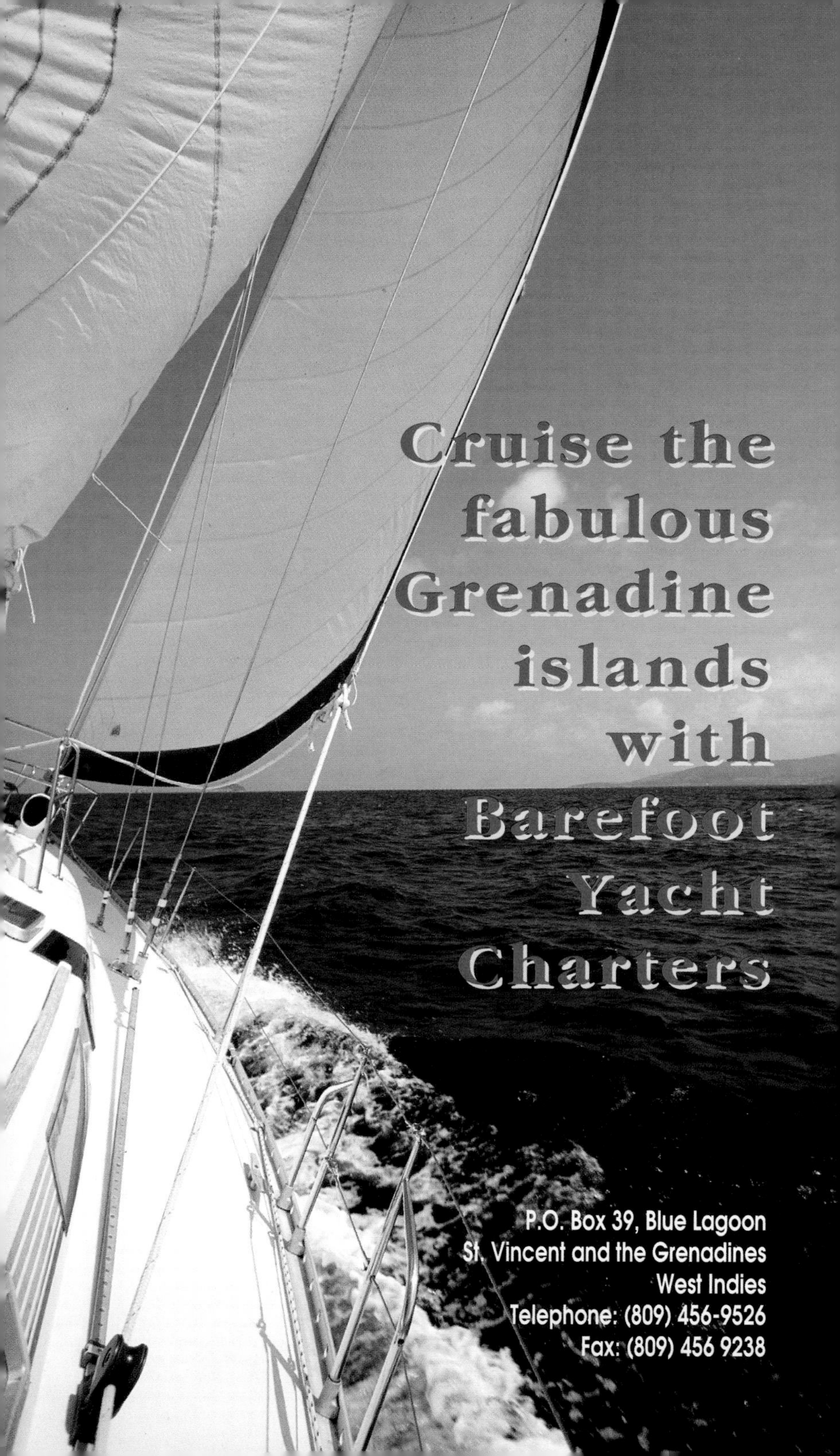
Cruise the fabulous Grenadine islands with Barefoot Yacht Charters
P.O. Box 39, Blue Lagoon
St. Vincent and the Grenadines
West Indies
Telephone: (809) 456-9526
Fax: (809) 456 9238

## Churches

The following denominations are represented:
Roman Catholic, Anglican, Episcopal, Methodist, Salvation Army, Baha'i Faith.

## Departure Tax

There is a departure tax of EC$20 for all passengers leaving the island.

## Embassies and Consulates

**British High Commission**
Grenville Street
Kingstown
☎ 457-1701

**Consulate of the Netherlands**
St. Clair House
Melville Street
Kingstown
☎ 457-2677

**French Consulate**
Middle Street
Kingstown
☎ 456-1615

**Embassy of Venezuela**
Granby Street
Kingstown
☎ 456-1374

## Emergency Telephone Numbers

For police, fire and ambulance
☎ 999
Coastguard ☎ 457-1211/4578

## Gambling

Emerald Valley Casino
☎ 456-7140

## Hospitals

There is a general hospital in Kingstown off the Leeward Highway (☎ 456-1185), with x-ray facilities, dental and eye clinics.
There are facilities at Georgetown on the east coast (☎ 458-6652), and Chateaubelair on the west coast. There is also an infants' hospital at Mount Bentinck in Georgetown. (☎ 458-6244).
There are also a number of health clinics on the islands including:

**The Bayside Medical Clinic**
Lower Bay Street, Kingstown
☎ 456-1127

**Botanic Clinic**
New Montrose
☎ 457-9781

**Campden Park Clinic**
Campden Park
☎ 456-1640

**Clare Valley Clinic**
Clare Valley
☎ 457-8390

**Medical Associates Clinic**
Middle Street, Kingstown
☎ 457-2598

**Rampersaud Clinic**
Grenville Street, Kingstown
☎ 457-1873

**Regisford Clinic**
Tyrell Street, Kingstown
☎ 457-2991

**Union Island Health Centre**
☎ 458-8339.
There is a small casualty hospital in Port Elizabeth, Bequia, and clinics on Mustique and Union Island.

## Media

There is a weekly newspaper and the Government runs a free public library system. There is also the free and

useful tourist publication *Discover St. Vincent and the Grenadines* which provides information on the island and about what's on. There is also *Discover Bequia* on Bequia.
The island has two television stations and one radio station broadcasting on AM 705Khz.

## Nightlife

Most people get up very early in St. Vincent and go to bed early, so there are few night clubs. Most hotels provide some evening entertainment with steel bands, local folk troupes and dancing. There are also beach barbecues and some notable regular jump-ups at one or two hotels. In St. Vincent the recommended nightspots include the Aquatic Club, The Attic in Melville Street, Spotlight Stadium, Philos and the Touch Entertainment Centre.

On Bequia and the other Grenadines, most of the evening entertainment is provided by the hotels, but on Bequia try Crescent Beach or Harpoon Saloon. On Mustique, pop into Basil's Bar for lively entertainment amidst an enchanting waterside setting.

## Pharmacies

Visitors taking drugs and medicines prescribed by a doctor should bring enough to last throughout their stay.
There are a number of pharmacies in Kingstown including:

**Davis Drug Mart**
Corner of Tyrrell and McCoy Streets
☎ 456-1174

**Deane's Pharmacy**
Middle Street
☎ 456-2877

**Gaymes Pharmacy**
Grenville Street
☎ 456-1861

**Grant T Geddes Pharmacy**
Middle Street
☎ 456-1325

**Medix Pharmacy**
Grenville Street
☎ 456-2989

**Pharmco**
Tyrrell Street
☎ 456-1797

**Reliance Pharmacy**
Halifax Street
☎ 456-1734

**Royal Pharmacy**
Grenville Street
☎ 456-1817

**Thomas Matthew Pharmaceuticals**
Grenville Street
☎ 456-2133.

There is also the
**Mespo Pharmacy** in Mesopotamia
☎ 458-1743

**Bequia Pharmacy**
Port Elizabeth, Bequia
☎ 458-3296

## Police

The police headquarters are in Upper Bay Street, Kingstown
☎ 457-1211

## Ports

The main port is Kingstown although there are yacht facilities and jetties around St. Vincent and throughout the Grenadines. There is a marina in Bequia with repair facilities.

## Post Offices

Post Office hours are 8.30am to 3pm Monday to Friday and Saturday 8.30am to 11.30am. The General Post Office is in Halifax Street, Kingstown, and there are sub post offices in all towns and villages.

## Public Holidays/Festivals

(check locally to confirm times and dates)

| | |
|---|---|
| **1 January** | New Year's Day |
| **22 January** | St. Vincent and the Grenadines Day |
| **March** | National Music Festival |
| April | Good Friday |
| | Easter Monday |
| | Easter Regatta — Bequia |
| **1 May** | Labour Day |
| **June** | Whit Monday |
| **July** | Carnival |
| | Caricom Day |
| **August** | August Bank Holiday |
| | Canouan Regatta |
| **September** | National Dance Festival |
| **October** | National Drama Festival |
| **27 October** | Independence Day |
| **25 December** | Christmas Day |
| **26 December** | Boxing Day |
| 31 December | New Year's Eve |

## Service Charges and Taxes

There is a Government tax of eight per cent on all hotel and restaurant bills, and a service charge of ten per cent is usually added. Menus and tariffs sometimes include these charges so check to ensure they have not been added twice. In shops, the price on the label is what you pay. When buying in markets and from street vendors, try haggling over the price.

## Shopping

Shops are usually open Monday to Friday from 8am and 12noon and 1pm to 4pm and between 8am to around 12noon on Saturday. There is an increasing trend for larger stores not to

close over lunch, and to remain open later in the evening. There is a good range of goods to choose from for souvenirs and gifts, including locally-made handicrafts, batik wear and goods, leather goods, wood carvings and paintings by island artists. Many of the T-shirts sold are hand painted, so don't be too dismissive. There are also several shops selling duty-free goods such as jewellery, watches, perfumes, crystal glass, figurines and china. Noah's Arkade on Bay Street has gifts and several books about the island and its history, culture and folklore. The market is also a good source for interesting gifts, especially spices and products such as jams, jellies and syrups made from them.

## Sightseeing

Sightseeing and island tours by land or sea can be organised through hotels, tour representatives or one of the many specialist tour companies on the island (see tour operators).
Many companies also offer boat trips to secluded beaches inaccessible by road or to other islands.
These include:

**Anchorage Yacht Club**
Union Island
☎ 458-8221

**Baleine Tours**
☎ 457-4089

**Dive St. Vincent**
☎ 457-4714

**Dennis' Hideaway**
☎ 458-8594

**Grand View Beach Hotel**
☎ 458-4811

**Grenadines Dive**
Union Island ☎ 458-8138

**Sea Breeze**
☎ 458-4969

**Dive Canouan**
☎ 458-8648

## Sport

### Cycling

Çycling is a good way to get around especially on the Grenadines where there is a lot less motor traffic. On St. Vincent care needs to be exercised when cycling on busy roads. Bikes can be hired from the Sailors Cycle Centre on St. Vincent ☎ 457-1712, and from the Lighthouse on Bequia ☎ 458-3084.

### Fitness Gyms/Exercise Centres

**Grand View Hotel**
Health Club and Sauna

**Beachcombers**
Recently-opened owner managed modern spa with steam room, sauna, plunge pool and gym.
Massages including divine aroma-theraphy sessions using luxurious oils and treatments, reflexology, facials.

### Hiking

All the islands offer great hiking and have many official trails. Some hikes require a great deal of physical fitness so check first. It is also advisable to use the services of a guide on some of the longer hikes into the interior. Guides are inexpensive, very knowledgeable and they work hard to ensure visitors get the most out of their trip. When walking inland, it is a good idea to wear long trousers and carry a waterproof top and light sweater, and sturdy footwear is essential. Wear a hat if not used to being out in the sun, use sun screen and insect repellent, and carry adequate drinking supplies, if water is not available along the way.

### Horseback Riding

Cotton House Hotel, Mustique.

## Scuba Diving

The waters around St. Vincent offer world-class diving, and also boast a number of species of fish not often found elsewhere. These include high hats, jack knife fish and spotted drums, and you will also see sea horses, blennys, angler fish and many others. The diving off the Grenadines is perhaps even better than off St. Vincent. Bequia and the Tobago Cays in particular, offer spectacular diving.

**Dive Centres include**:

**Bequia Dive Resort**
Friendship Bay, Bequia
☎ 458-3249

**Dive Anchorage**
Anchorage Yacht Club, Union Island
☎ 458-8221

**Dive St. Vincent**
Young Island Dock
☎ 457-4714

**Dive Bequia**
Belmont Bequia
☎ 458-3504

**Dive Canouan**
Canouan
☎ 458-8648

**Dive Paradise**
Bequia
☎ 458-3563

**Grenadine Dives**
Union Island
☎ 458-8138

**Petit Byahaut**
St. Vincent
☎ 458-7008

**St. Vincent Dive Experience**
Blue Lagoon
☎ 456-9741

**Sunsports**
Port Elizabeth, Bequia
☎ 458-3577

## Squash

Cecil Cyrus Squash Complex, Grand View Beach Hotel, and Prospect Racquet Club.

## Tennis

Many resorts and large hotels have their own tennis courts which are often floodlit.
**St. Vincent**: Grand View Beach Hotel, Kingstown Tennis Club, Prospect Racquet Club, and Young Island
**Bequia**: Friendship Bay Hotel, Plantation House, Spring on Bequia and Sunsports
**Canouan**: Canouan Beach Club
**Mustique**: Cotton House Hotel
**Palm Island**: Palm Island Beach Club
**Petit St. Vincent**: Petit St. Vincent Resort

# Tourist Information offices

**St. Vincent**
Bay Street
Kingstown
☎ 456-2610
Open: Monday to Friday: 8am to 12noon and 1pm to 4.15pm.

E.T. Joshua Airport
☎ 458-4685
Open: Monday to Friday: 8am to 12noon and 1pm to 4.15pm.

**Bequia**
Tourist Bureau
Port Elizabeth
☎ 458-3286
Open: Sunday to Friday: 9am to 12.30pm and 1.30pm to 4pm.
Saturday: 9am to 12.30pm.

**Union Island**
Tourist Bureau
☎ 458-8350
Open daily: 8am to 12noon and 1pm to 4pm.

# Dolphin Watching around St. Vincent

Dolphins have a mysterious affinity with man which is reputed to come from a theory that somewhere in evolution man took to the water and swam with them. Whatever the reality between fact and myth, visitors to the Windward Islands are virtually guaranteed sightings of these playful mammals during a boat trip around the coastline of these enchanting islands.

One of the most reputable companies to travel with is Sea Breeze Yacht Charters based on St. Vincent close to Kingstown. Owner/manager Hal Daize skippers regular trips from Kingstown up the coast to the spectacular Falls of Baleine close to the north of the island. On most trips he will stop the boat halfway through the journey requesting that all passengers sit quietly and wait patiently for a few minutes. The boat is invariably surrounded by dolphins offering visitors an unrivalled opportunity to watch them play in the sparkling waters. Hal has been hosting these trips for many years and has developed a close relationship with the dolphins. He is insistent that visitors do not point at them, as this can resemble a fisherman's harpoon and scare them away. His gentle and reassuring ways certainly encourage the dolphins, as well as pilot whales, to swim very close to the boat seemingly without any fear or anxiety.

There are numerous recorded cases of dolphins and their close, but mysterious interest in man, and many stories of them rescuing injured or stranded people.

When hundreds died in the floods in Bangladesh in the late 1980s, the damage was devasting. At the height of the disaster, a dolphin swam into shore carrying something in its mouth. It turned out to be a small child who was alive and unhurt.

A group of Japanese fishermen were marooned about thirty miles out at sea when their vessel sank. Six of the crew drowned, but the survivors attempted to swim to shore. After many hours, tired and exhausted, they began to call for help. Two dolphins appeared and started nudging the men. They allowed the four survivors to climb on their backs — two per dolphin — and swam them all the way to the shore.

The strangest story is perhaps the dolphin who swam up to a Soviet fishing boat in the waters around northern Japan in the early eighties. It tried more than once to jump aboard the boat, but failed. The sailors eventually hauled it up onto the boat to find that it was badly injured. The ship's doctor stitched up the wound, after which the dolphin was returned to the sea. It was greeted with huge enthusiasm by its companions who performed with a spectacle of marine acrobatics before swimming off.

Hal, who is extremely knowledgeable on his subject can regail his guests with many fascinating stories of these graceful creatures, as well as other marine life which live in the Caribbean waters. It is a not-to-be missed, enjoyable and unforgettable day out. Telephone: (809) 458-4969

**Barbados**
Grantley Adams International Airport
Arrivals hall
☎ 809-428-0961
Open daily: 1pm until the last flight to St. Vincent has boarded.

## Tourist Offices Abroad

**United Kingdom**
10 Kensington Court
London W8 5DL
☎ 0171-937-6570
Fax: 0171-937-3611

**United States of America**
801 Second Avenue
21st Floor
New York, NY 10017
☎ 1-800-729-1726
Fax: 212-949-5946

*Also at:*
6505 Cove Creek Place
Dallas, Texas
TX 75240
☎ 214-239-6451
Fax: 214-239-1002

**Canada**
32 Park Road
Toronto, Ontario
M4W 2N4
☎ 416-924-5796
Fax: 416-924-5844

**Germany**
Wurmbergstrasse 26
D-7032 Sindelfingen
☎ 70-3180-6260
Fax: 70-31-8050

## Tour Operators

There are many tour operators on the island which offer various trips and excursions or will tailor an itinerary to suit specific requirements. Many tours sound the same, so ensure you are getting good value for moneyl.

**Main operators in St. Vincent are:**

**W J Abbott**
Upper Bay Street, Kingstown
☎ 456-1511

**Baleine Tours**
Villa Beach
☎ 457-4089

**Barefoot Holidays**
Blue Lagoon
☎ 456-9334

**Caribbean Travel Services**
Granby Street, Kingstown
☎ 457-1841

**Emerald Travel & Tours**
Halifax Street, Kingstown
☎ 457-1996

**Global Travel Service**
White Chapel, Kingstown
☎ 456-1601

**Grenadines Travel Company**
Amos Vale
☎ 458-4818

**Sam's Taxi Tours**
☎ 458-4338
☎ 458-3686

**Paradise Tours**
PO Box 280, Kingstown
☎ 458-5545

**Travel World**
Bay Street, Kingstown
☎ 456-2600

**Universal Travel**
Bay Street, Kingstown
☎ 457-2779

### *On Bequia*

**Grenadines Travel**
Port Elizabeth
☎ 458-3795

### *Union Island*

**Eagles Travel**
Clifton, ☎ 458-8179

## Weddings

Visitors planning to marry on St. Vincent must file an application for either a church or civil wedding along with the appropriate fee to the Ministry of Justice, and a special Governor General's licence is required. The licence is valid for three months.

- Visitors must have been resident on the island for three working days before applying for a marriage licence.
- produce their passport and birth certificates.

Most denominations of church weddings can be arranged in advance, and registrars usually charge a fee plus travel costs. Valentine's Day is a very popular day for weddings, and registrars are usually very busy rushing around conducting marriage after marriage. The Registry is open Monday to Friday between 9am and noon and 1pm and 3pm, and on Saturday between 9am and 11am.

## Yacht Charter and Private Moorings

There is a good selection of vessels and crews for charter for sailing, sightseeing, fishing and diving.

**Companies offering yacht charters are**:

*St. Vincent*:
Barefoot Yacht Charters
Blue Lagoon, St. Vincent
☎ 456-9526

Lagoon Marina and Hotel
☎ 458-4308

Both offer bareboat and crewed charters.

*Bequia*:
Frangipani Yacht Services
☎ 458-3244

*Union Island*:
Anchorage Yacht Club
☎ 458-8221

# Martinique

FF229062

As the aircraft wings dip down to reveal the island of Martinique, one has an immediate sense of this island being somewhere very special. Although Martinique is in the Caribbean, it is in every sense part of France. French is spoken, there are skyscrapers and motorways, huge, busy modern ports and luxury hotels and marinas.

Martinique is a Région of France, and as much a part of the country as Normandy or Brittany — even though it is 4,400 miles (7,100km) away across the seas. The French have poured money into it which explains its high-rise buildings, modern highways and infrastructure. However, the essence of the Caribbean is very much in evidence with its lush vegetation, mountainous interior and spectacular beaches.

For those who love France but want to experience everything the Caribbean has to offer, this is the perfect destination. Visitors can sunbathe on stunning beaches, swim or dive in warm tropical crystal-clear waters, explore the tropical rainforests and Mount Pelée, enjoy chic shopping — and of course, dine in true French style on some of the best food and drink in the Caribbean.

Martinique is the largest of the Windward Islands, sandwiched between English-speaking St. Lucia 16 miles (25km) to the south and Dominica, 22 miles (35 km) to the north. It is 1,965 miles (3,144km) from New York, 1,470 miles (2352km) from Miami, and 4,261 miles (6,817km) from Paris.

The island covers 421 sq miles (1,091 sqkm) and is almost 50 miles (80km) from north to south and 22 miles (35km) at its widest. The population is around 359,570, and about a third live in the capital of Fort-de-France.

The island is mountainous volcanic rock, much of it 3,000ft (900m) above sea level. There are three main mountain ranges. Mount Pelée in the far north, is the highest point at 4,583ft (1,397m). It is a dormant volcano which last erupted on 8 May 1902 when lava flows destroyed the town of Saint-Pierre on the west coast causing the loss of more than 30,000 lives. The Carbet Mountains, dominated by Lacroix Peak 3,923ft (1,196m) occupy much of the interior north of the capital, while Mount Vauclin, 1,654ft (504m) is the highest point in the range covering most of the south.

The mountainous north and south are separated by the Lamentin Plain which is the Lézarde River basin, and together with the narrow coastal plains comprise the only flat land on Martinique. There are many short fast-flowing rivers running down the mountain sides in all directions to the sea, and the deeply-indented coastline means that no part of the island is more than 7 miles (11km) from the sea. In the north and north-west there are steep cliffs while the central-western and south-western coast is dominated by two bays, home of Fort-de-France, and to the south Le Marin. Along the eastern coast there are scores of coves and inlets with coral reefs offshore.

## Getting there

**By air**: There are regular scheduled air services from North America and France to Martinique's international airport at Lamentin. There are direct flights from New York's JFK Airport every Saturday on North American Airlines, and regular flights on American Airlines from New York, Newark and other US cities via their Caribbean hub at San Juan on Puerto Rica. There is also a Sunday flight from Miami on Air France.

Air Martinique flies to and from St. Maarten, Antigua, Dominica, St. Lucia, Barbados, St. Vincent,

Mustique, Union Island and Canouan. There are also frequent daily flights to and from Guadeloupe on Réseau Aérien Francais des Caraibes, a French Caribbean airline consortium which includes Air Martinique, Air Guadeloupe and Air France. LIAT also flies between Martinique and Anguilla, Antigua, Barbados, Caracas, Dominica, Grenada, Guadeloupe, Guyana, Montserrat, Nevis, Port of Spain, San Juan, St. Kitts, St. Lucia, St. Maarten, St. Thomas, St. Vincent, Tortola and Union Island.

**By sea**: The main port is Fort-de-France, and the island is serviced year-round by *Emeraude Express*, a high speed catamaran from Guadeloupe and Dominica.

**By cruise ship**: The new Pointe Simon Cruise Terminal is on the waterfront in the heart of the city and can accommodate a maximum of one large and two smaller cruise ships. Martinique attracts well over 400,000 visitors aboard almost 500 cruise ships a year.

## Getting Around

Lamentin International Airport is 9km (5.5 miles) from Fort-de-France, 20km (12.5 miles) from Trois Islets and 40km (25 miles) from Le Marin.

The island has some of the best roads in the Caribbean and one of the highest densities of motor traffic so jams in and around Fort-de-France during the rush hours are common.

Hiring a car offers the best way of exploring the island at leisure.

**Taxis**: Martinique has over 200 taxis which are mostly luxury Mercedes-Benz. There are taxi ranks at Lamentin Airport, in Fort-de-France and outside most large hotels. They are reasonably-priced and a good way of travelling around. Typical taxi fares from the airport to the Pointe du Bout hotels are between 150-200FF, and from the airport to the centre of Fort-de-France 70-80FF. There is a forty per cent surcharge between 8pm and 6am.

**Public transport and collective taxis**: Public buses are inexpensive and there is a good service in and around Fort-de-France. Most public transport, however, is provided by eight- seat shared taxis which carry the sign 'TC'. There are about 400 on the island and they run from early morning until around 6pm. The main bus terminal is in Fort-de-France at Pointe Simon near the cruise ship berth. Travel by TC is cheap and offers a good way of meeting the islanders who will chat along, often having to shout to be heard over the non-stop music that accompanies every journey. Typical fares are usually: Fort-de-France to Trois Ilets — 17FF, to Diamant 19FF, to Sainte-Anne 39FF, to Saint Pierre 18FF and to Grand Rivière 40FF.

**By boat**: There are daily ferries from Fort-de-France to Pointe du Bout which run from early in the morning until after midnight; and to the beaches of Anse Mitan, Anse-à-l'Ane, and Grand Anse d'Arlet from early morning to late afternoon, The ferries, known locally as *vedettes,* sail to and from the Quai d'Esnambuc in Fort-de-France. A round trip adult ticket from Fort-de-France to Pointe du Bout or Anse Mitan is around 24FF.

## Beaches

The beaches south of Fort-de-France have white sand, while those to the north have grey sand. The best beaches in the south are: Plage des Salines with several miles of golden sand, Sainte-Anne, Cap Chevalier, Anse Michel, L'Anse Grosse Roche, Plage de Macabou, Le Diamant and Anses d'Arlets. In the north the best beaches include Anse Céron, Anse Turin and Plage Carbet. There are no nudist beaches on the island, although many hotels allow topless bathing.

Martinique
Grand Rivière
Macouba
Basse-Pointe
Leyritz Plantation
Great House
Lorrain
Marigot
Montagne
Pelée
Le Prêcheur
MacIntoch
Plantation
Le Morne Rouge
Sainte-Marie
Caravelle Peninsula
Chateau Dubuc
St James
Distillery
La Trinité
Fond St Jacques
(Museum du
Père Labat)
St. Pierre
Museum of
Volcanology
St Pierre Historical
Museum
Le Carbet
Amazona Zoo
du Carbet
Paul Gauguin
Museum
Fond St Denis
Gros-
Morne
Pitons
du Carbet
Le Robert
Bellefontaine
Balata-
Tourtet
St Joseph
Case-Pilote
Le Francois
Rhum Clement
Domain Acajou
Schœlcher
Le Lamentin
Aquarium
Rhum Dhillon
Distillery
Botanical Gardens
Biblioteque
Schoelcher
Fort-de-France
Airport
Ducos
Baiè de Fort de France
Le Saint Esprit
Museum of
Popular Arts
Le Vauc
Anse-à-l'Ane
Les Trois-
Ilets
Museum of
Seashell Art
Parcs de
Floralies
Domaine
de la
Pagerie
Riviere
-Salee
La Mauny
Distillery
Grand Anse
Rivière-
Pilote
LesAnses-D'Arlets
Le Diamant
Ste-Luce
Le Marin
Rocher du
Diamant
Ste-Anne
N
W
E
S
Grand Anses
des Salines

Above: The Bibliothèque Schoelcher is the city's most spectacular building.

## Fort-de-France

Fort-de-France, formerly called Fort Royal, is the island capital and administrative and cultural centre, with a downtown area surrounded by ever expanding suburbs.

Begin a tour of the island by visiting the **Tourist Office** on the Boulevard Alfasa which is on the waterfront in the centre of town. It has English-speaking staff and is open from 7.30am to 12.30pm and 2.30pm to 5.30pm weekdays. It closes at 5pm on Fridays and is open from 8am to 12noon on Saturdays. There is also a tourist information desk at Lamentin Airport to meet arriving flights.

Fort-de-France is a charming city which successfully combines both its Caribbean and French heritage. It is home to more than 100,000 people — a third of the island's population, and with its busy port and cruise ship terminal, it is a bustling centre by day, but is generally quiet at night.

The heart of the city is best explored on foot and there are several fine old buildings to visit. There are car parking places along the waterfront, or in one of the car parks located either side of the tourist office.

Many of the streets are narrow and are lined with shops, restaurants and cafes. Many buildings have overhanging wrought-iron balconies which almost touch each other across the road.

From the tourist office head east along Boulevard Alfassa past La Savane Park (Savannah Park) on the left. This leads to **Fort Saint Louis**, a reminder of the island's turbulent history, when it was constantly fought over by the French and British. The fort was built by some of the first colonists in the late 1630s, about two years after D'Esnambuc landed on Martinique and claimed it for the French crown.

The first fort was a simple wooden structure, but in 1640 Governor De Baas ordered the construction of a major fortification with a moat, high walls and twenty-six cannon, to protect the harbour. In 1674 it was put to the test when a Dutch military force attacked continuously for three days without success. The Dutch suffered massive losses and left, and a town was quickly established near the fort. In January 1762, the fort was captured by the English who renamed it Fort Edward, but it was returned to the French a year later in the Treaty of Paris and became Fort Royal again. At the beginning of the twentieth century, a small zoo was established in the grounds, but because of its strategic importance, it was assigned to the navy during the World War II, and since then has been the headquarters of the Captain of the Fleet Commanding the Antilles Guyane Navy.

You can then walk through the 12.5 acre (5 hectare) La Savane gardens to join rue de la Liberté, which runs inland from the tourist office. **La Savane** is the city's central park and offers a quiet interlude from the traffic and shops. It is noted for its huge traveller's palms, many more than 100ft tall. There are two war memorials of Pierre Belain d'Esnambuc, the French nobleman who claimed the island for France in 1635, and of Marie Josèphe Rose Tascher de la Pagerie, who was born on her father's plantation at Trois Ilets across the bay, and later became Napoléon's Empress Josephine. There are usually a few handicraft stalls to browse around.

Back in rue de la Liberté, on the corner with rue Victor Hugo, is the **Musée Départemental** with a fascinating collection of pre-Columbian exhibits. The museum occupies the late nineteenth century building which used to house the Military Command. It has more than 2,000 exhibits tracing the history of the Arawak and Carib peoples on the island before the arrival of Christopher Columbus. The Amerindians craftsmanship, especially in pottery, is evident from the finely engraved and painted cups, vases and other ornaments. It is open Monday to Saturday 9am to 1pm and 2pm to 5pm. There is an admission charge. ☎ 71.57.05

Continue along the road until you reach the **Bibliothèque Schoelcher** on the corner of rue Perrinon and rue de la Liberté. It is the city's most spectacular building and an architectural masterpiece. It is even more impressive when one considers that it was built for the Paris Exposition of 1889, then dismantled mosaic by mosaic and shipped to Martinique to be re-built on the site of the old Hotel du Petit Government where Empress Josephine used to live. The Romanesque-Byzantine building was named after Victor Schoelcher, the French abolitionist whose campaigning helped end slavery on the island. After Emancipation he played a major role in helping educate the black population, and in 1883 donated his library of more than 10,000 volumes to the island. The library was designed by architect Henri Pick who was also the creator of the Cathedral of Saint Louis. The library, now a registered historic monument of France, is open from 8.30am to12.20pm and 2pm to 6pm on Monday, Tuesday and Thursday, 8am and 1pm Wednesday and Friday, and 8.30am and 12noon on Saturday.

The **police headquarters** is behind the library on rue Schoelcher, and the Prefecture is across the road from the library where the rue de la Liberté runs into rue Félix Eboué after it crosses rue Victor Sévère.

The route leads left from the library into rue Perrinon. Cross over rue Schoelcher to visit the colonial-style Palais de Justice with its statue of

Victor Schoelcher. Then retrace your steps to rue Schoelcher and turn right for four blocks to visit the **Cathedral of Saint Louis** built in 1895 with a Roman-style bell tower. It is noted for its stained glass windows, massive organ and interesting plaques. Many of the island's Governors are buried in the chancel. It is believed to be the sixth church on the site.

Turn right into rue Blénac to visit the **main market**, sandwiched between rue Isambert and rue Suchet. The covered market is in rue Isambert, and the open-air market is held in boulevard Général de Gaulle. Continue to Boulevard Allègre and turn right along the waterfront to visit the new fish market at Rivière Madame. Across Place José Marti is the **Botanical Gardens** and the **Exotarium**, a museum of island geology and botany. ☎ 70.68.41. It is open Monday to Saturday 9am to 12.30pm and 2.30 to 5.50pm. There are also a number of craft workshops in the gardens.

Take Boulevard Général de Gaulle on the way back into town and then turn into rue de la République. On the corner is the new **City Hall** with the old one, which has been converted into a theatre, next door.

Azimut offers a number of reasonably-priced conducted walking tours of the capital. ☎ 60.16.59

The **aquarium** on boulevard de la Maine is on the road to Saint Pierre, and devoted to Caribbean marine flora and fauna. It houses more than 2,000 fish, making it the largest aquarium in the Caribbean and one of the largest in Europe ☎ 71.57.05.

The **Aquaterrarium** is a fascinating 59ft (18m) cross section of a tropical river showing the diversity of life which co-exists within its waters. It is open daily from 9am to 7pm. There is an admission charge.

The **Rhum Dillon Distillery** is on the outskirts of Fort-de-France on the old Lamentin Road. There are guided tours of the 200-year-old distillery with its old steam engine, and free tastings. It is open Monday to Friday between 9am and 4pm, and on Saturday by appointment.

## Eating out

A phrase book might be useful in negotiating your way round a French menu, and the following might help in understanding some of the Creole terms.

*Accras* — small fish or vegetable fritters, also called 'marinades'

*Blaff* — a method of cooking fish or shellfish in stock

*Blanc Manger* — coconut custard

*Calalou* — soup made from Dasheen with pork or crab

*Chatrou* — octopus

*Chiquetaille de Morue* — shredded and grilled cod served with vinaigrette

*Cirique* — succulent small sea crabs (also called *etrille)*

*Colombo* — meat cooked in a spicy, hot sauce similar to curry

*Crabes farcis* — delicious crab stuffing

*Dife* — very piquant

*Féroce* — a fiery avocado and salt cod salad with manioc flour and hot pepper

*Giraumon* — pumpkin

*Manicou* — a small opossum and an island speciality

*Maracudja* — passion fruit

*Ouassou* — crayfish

*Oursins* — sea urchins

*Pate en pot* — mutton or lamb soup with capers in white wine

*Patate Douce* — sweet potato

*Pisquette* — small fish fried or used in casseroles

*Pistache* — peanuts

*Soudons* — clams

*Titiri* — white bait, deep fried or casseroled

*Z'habitant* — large crayfish

Above: The bustling harbour front in Fort-de-France
Below: Colourful façade of one of the many old buildings in Fort-de-France.

## Eating out in and around Fort-de-France

**L'Arrosoir** $-$$
in the Euromarket
☎ 75.35.54
French cuisine. Open Monday to Friday 8am to 6pm, and Saturday 8am to 4pm.

**La Belle Epoque** $$
Route de Didier
☎ 64.67.24
French cuisine. Open daily including Sunday afternoon.

**Le Bistrot de la Marne** $$
Le Squash Hotel
Boulevard de la Marne
☎ 63.00.01
French and creole, open daily.

**Le Blénac** $-$$
Rue Blénac
☎ 70.18.41.
French and creole, open daily except Sunday evening.

**La Bodega** $$
Rue Ernest Déporge
☎ 60.48.48). Open every evening except Sunday.

**La Case** $$
Rue Ernest Déporge
☎ 63.04.00
French, creole and Italian, open daily except Sunday.

**La Cave du Roi** $
Rue Garnier Pagès
☎ 60.22.63
Créperie and salad bar, open daily.

**Le Chandlier** $$
La Véranda
Cluny
☎ 70.20.32
Oriental, open daily except Sunday evening.

**Chez Gaston** $$
Rue Félix Eboué
☎ 73.53.52
French, open daily 8am to 2am.

**El Chico** $-$$
Rue Garnier Pagès
☎ 72.48.92
Creole open Monday to Saturday from noon.

**Le Chinatown** $$
Rue Victor Hugo
☎ 71.82.62
Chinese, open Monday to Friday lunch.

**Citron Vert** $$
Route de Cluny
☎ 63.12.43
French and creole cuisine

**La Crèperie** $
Rue Garnier Pagès
☎ 60.62.09
Créperie and salad bar, open Monday to Saturday.

**Le Coq Hardi** $$
Rue Martin Luther King
☎ 71.59.64
Steakhouse, open Monday to Saturday.

**Le Couscoussier** $$
Rue Perrinon
☎ 60.06.42
North African, open for lunch and dinner Monday to Friday.

**Le Crew** $
Rue Ernest Déporge
☎ 73.04.14
French

**Espace Creole** $$
Rue Voltaire
Terres Sainville
☎ 70.05.95
Creole, open Monday to Saturday 11am to 10pm.

**Au Fin Palais** $$
Rue Moreau de Jones
☎ 71.34.11
French, open Monday to Saturday.

**La Fontaine** $$-$$$ **
Route de Balata
☎ 64.28.78
French and creole, open daily except Sunday evening.

**La Grand Voille** $$
Pointe Simon
☎ 70.29.29
French, open Monday to Saturday.

**Grill le Strike** $$
Pont de Californie
☎ 50.16.37
French grill, open daily.

**Le Josephine** $$-$$$
Hotel Impératrice
Rue de la Liberté
☎ 63.06.82
Creole and seafood, open daily except Saturday.

**Le King Creol** $$
Ave des Caraibes
☎ 70.19.18
Creole and seafood, open Monday to Friday and lunch only on Saturday.

**Le Lotus D'Asie** $$
Boulevard de la Marne
☎ 71.62.96
Vietnamese, open daily.

**Le Madiana** $$
Madiana Plage
☎ 61.06.99
French and seafood, open daily.

**Le Mareyeur** $$
Pointe des Nègres
☎ 61.74.70
Creole and seafood, open Monday to Friday and Saturday evening.

**Marie Sainte** $$
Rue Victor Hugo
☎ 70.00.30
Creole and seafood, open Monday to Saturday.

**Le Millesime** $$
Rue de Vieux Chemin
☎ 60.50.50
French and creole, open daily.

**La Mouina** $$-$$$ **
Route de Redoute
☎ 79.34.57
French and creole, open daily except Sunday.

**La Muraille** $$
Rue Martin Luther King
☎ 63.47.96
Chinese, open daily except Sunday evening.

**Le Nectar** $$
Corner rue Voltaire and Vieux Chemin
☎ 60.47.61
French, open Monday to Saturday

**Le New Peking** $$
Route de Schoelcher
☎ 61.64.46
Chinese, open daily except Monday lunch and Sunday evening.

**La Paille Dorée** $$
Ave Frantz Fanon
Bellevue
☎ 61.34.11
Open daily except Sunday evening.

**Le Papagayo** $-$$
Point de Didier
☎ 72.62.62
French, Italian and ice creams, open daily except Sunday lunch and Monday evening.

**La Parilla Grill** $$
Route de Schoelcher
☎ 73.82.90
Steakhouse, open Monday to Saturday

**El Raco** $$
Rue Lazare Carnot
☎ 73.29.16
French, open daily except Monday and Saturday lunch and Sunday dinner.

**Le Ramsis** $-$$
Rue Blénac
☎ 70.47.78
Oriental and Lebanese cuisine.

**Restaurant du Squash Hotel** $$-$$$
Boulevard de la Marne
☎ 63.00.01
French and international, open daily.

**Le Salambo** $$
Patio de Cluny
☎ 60.47.40
Tunisian, open Wednesday to Saturday.

**Le Second Souffle** $-$$
Rue Blénac
☎ 63.44.11
Vegetarian, open for lunch Monday to Friday.

**Las Tapas de Sevillas** $$
Rue Garnier Pagès
☎ 63.71.23
Spanish cuisine

**La Terrasse du Port** $$
Passage de l'Hydrobase
☎ 60.25.67
French, open Monday to Friday.

**Le Victor Hugo** $$
Rue Victor Hugo
☎ 63.61.08
French and creole, open daily except Sunday lunch.

**La Vielle Chaumiere** $$
Rue Ernest Déproge
☎ 63.70.60
French, open Monday to Saturday.

**Le Vieux Milan** $$
Ave des Caraibes
☎ 60.35.31
Italian, open Monday to Friday, closed at weekends.

**Le Xuandre** $$
Pointe des Négres
☎ 61.54.70
Vietnamese cuisine, open Tuesday to Saturday evenings and all day Sunday.

**La Plantation** $$-$$$
☎ 50.16.08
French and creole, closed Saturday afternoon and Sunday.

**Le Ti-Bo** $$
Place d'Armes
☎ 51.43.09
closed Sunday.

**Le Verger** $$-$$$
Place de l'Armes
☎ 51.43.02
French, open Monday to Saturday, closed Sunday.

## The Northern Tour

The drive north along the coast to the old capital of **Sainte Pierre** takes about one hour, but plan to spend longer as there are several points of interest along the way, and the return part of the journey is inland through the tropical rainforests.

The first town is **Schoelcher**, which was known as Case-Navire until 1889 when the inhabitants renamed it in commemoration of the abolitionist. It is now a suburb of Fort-de-France and houses the university campus.

There are many small fishing villages along the leeward coast including **Case-Pilote** which is one of the oldest settlements on the island. It is believed to have got its name from a Carib chief called Pilote, who had his 'carbet' in the cove. The rococo church dates back to the seventeenth century, and is the oldest on the island.

**Bellefontaine** is another delightful fishing village perched on the cliffs. There is a strange boat-shaped house on the hill on the right side on leaving the village. Visitors can also watch the fishermen casting their special 'senne' nets.

Inland is **Morne-Vert**, known locally as 'Swiss Canton' because it nestles among the Carbet peaks at 1,200ft (365m).

**Carbet** is reputed to be where Columbus landed on 15 June 1502, and it was the home and living studio of Gauguin for several months in 1887. The **Paul Gauguin Museum and Memorial Art Centre** is situated in the hills just above the village and is worth a visit. Built in 1979, it is close to the site where the famous French painter lived and worked for five months with his friend Charles Laval. There are exhibits of letters written by the artist to his wife, other mementoes and photographic reproductions of his

most famous works. The paintings include work inspired by island life such as *The Mango Harvest*, *Life in Saint Pierre*, *Tropical Vegetation*, *The Beach* and *The Raisinier Tree*. There are also tributes from many island artists who have contributed original works for a permanent exhibition, as well as a display of Martiniquais costumes and head-dress. The museum (☎ 78.22.66) is open daily from 10am to 5pm, and there is a small admission charge. On the Place de la Mairie is the **Gallerie D'Histoire et de la Mer** (☎ 78.03.72) which traces the area's history on land and sea. It is open daily from 9am to 12noon and 3pm to 6pm.

It is worth visiting the renovated **Amazona Zoo du Carbet** (☎ 78.00.64) which features seventy species of animals from the Caribbean, Amazon and Africa. Founded in 1981 by B. Prevoteau, it is open daily between 9am and 6pm. There is an admission charge.

The nearby **Valley of the Butterflies** is a recent attraction at Carbet's **Botanical Gardens**, situated within the ruins of one of the earliest seventeenth century plantations on Martinique. (☎ 78.19.19). After the wonders of the butterfly world, visitors can enjoy a drink and snack at Le Poids du Roy before visiting the **Distillerie Bally** (☎ 78.08.94). It is open from Monday to Friday 8am to 4.30pm, Saturday from 9am to 3.15pm, and Sunday from 9am to 12noon. The house dates from 1776, and the distillery produces the famous Thum de la Plantation Lajus. There is an admission charge.

Saint Pierre, used to be known as 'the Paris of the West Indies' until 8 May 1902 when Mount Pelée erupted and within three minutes, the town and 30,000 citizens perished. It was the island's economic and cultural capital, and had a larger population than the capital Fort-de-France. Saint Pierre was the site where Belain d'Esnambuc landed in 1635 from the Capitaine Drouault to colonise the island. His ship anchored at the mouth of the river he subsequently named Roxelane, and his crew set about building a wooden stockade. The settlement prospered for more than 260 years and the bay was invariably filled with merchant ships from both sides of the Atlantic.

There is a small, but fasciating **Museum of Volcanology** which graphically depicts the story of the eruption and the ensuing tragedy. The museum was founded in 1932 by American volcanologist Frank Perret on an old gun battery site overlooking the bay. There are photographs and paintings of the town before the eruption, as well as objects excavated from the ruins including twisted musical instruments, petrified food and melted glass objects.

The volcano had started to rumble a few days before it erupted and molten mud had slid down the mountain engulfing a small factory. About 1,000 of the townspeople left for Fort-de-France but most were persuaded to stay by officials who were reluctant to postpone an impending election. The eruption started at 7.45am when the sky darkened and Pelée's rumblings could be heard miles away. Suddenly the volcano exploded and a deadly cloud of gas and thousands of tons of hot lava and ash roared down the mountain blanketing the town. The heat was so intense that even ships in the bay caught fire. By two minutes past eight, three minutes after the eruption, all the inhabitants but one were dead. Cyparis was the only person to survive. A few days before the disaster he was arrested for being drunk and sent to prison but he escaped from his cell. He was caught a second time for drunk and disorderly behaviour and was locked away in the jail's deepest dungeon. It was this that

Above: Cannon overlook the bay of Saint Pierre.
Below: The Jardin de Balata is home to exquisite flowering plants and trees.

saved his life because the red-hot lava and ashes could not reach him. The volcano continued to spew lava and ash for several months. The museum is open daily between 9am and 12.30pm and 3pm and 5pm. There is a small admission charge.

Visitors can walk through the northern part of town, where a living museum to the devastation has been preserved. The ruined theatre and the dungeon that held Cybaris, the shells of the old warehouses that stood alongside the old city walls and the destroyed streets still stand today.

There is also the **Saint Pierre Historical Museum** in rue Victor Hugo, which traces the history of the town. It is open from Monday to Saturday from 9.30am to 5pm. There is a small admission charge.

In 1990 the town was declared a Ville d'Art et d'Histoire.

One way to see Saint Pierre is by the **Cyparis Express**, a small train which offers one-hour tours during the week, and half-hour tours at weekends.

A new and exciting way of exploring the coastline is by **submarine**, and a fifty-seat submarine now operates from Saint Pierre offering trips to explore the many offshore shipwrecks.

The distillery at Depaz is worth visiting. The **Plantation de la Montagne Pelée** has been producing rum from sugar cane for 400 years, and the quality of the rum is largely attributed to the fertile volcanic soil and the pure mountain spring water. The old mill has been converted into a restaurant. It is open Monday to Friday from 8am to 4pm and on Saturday from 8am to 12noon (☎ 78.13.14).

The community of **Le Prêcheur** is the last village along the northern Caribbean coast and is known for its lovely sandy beaches, inland volcanic hot springs and the Tomb of the Carib Indians. According to legend, a group of Carib fishermen returned to their village to find it had been destroyed by settlers. The men were so grief-stricken that they all committed suicide. There are Carib carvings on the rocks in the area.

The main coastal road ends at Le Prêcheur but many hikes begin here. It is about a one-and-a-half hour walk to the hot springs, and about the same to Grand Rivière on the Atlantic coast.

From Le Prêcheur one has to return to Saint Pierre and head inland for Le Morne Rouge and the spectacular return journey to Fort-de-France through the mountains and the tropical rainforest.

**Le Morne Rouge**, is a small town that enjoys a cooler climate because of its altitude. It is also the home of the **MacIntosh Plantation**, famous for its cultivation of anthuriums which are exported worldwide. The gardens are open Monday to Saturday from 9am to 4.30pm. The town is also famous for its bottled mineral water and pineapple jam.

On the northern outskirts of the village there is a narrow and twisting side road on the left leading to the lower slopes of **Mount Pelée** as far as Aileron, from where the journey must continue on foot. Allow at least seven hours to reach the summit and return, and longer if for anybody who is not particularly fit. Remember to take plenty of water and carry a waterproof jacket and sweater because it can be chilly at higher altitudes.

The **Route de La Trace** is nearby and leads on an unforgettable drive through the rainforest. La Trace was originally a path cut by the Jesuits to connect Fort-de-France and Saint Pierre. It is now a main road with numerous signs indicating points of interest along the way. There are many banana and pineapple plantations in the area, as well as avocado groves, sugar cane fields, and some charming old inns to visit, such as Leyritz and Habitation Lagrange.

There is a short detour to **Fonds Saint Denis**, another small community of less than 1,000 people, whose carefully tended flower gardens are a treat. The village is close to the heart of the volcanic region and scientists constantly monitor activity at the Seismographic Station on the summit of Morne-des-Cadets.

The **Jardin de Balata** (☎ 64.48.73) is on the Route de la Trace, and is one of the most beautiful of the many flower gardens on the island. Lying between Fort-de-France and Le Morne Rouge, it not only offers the chance to visit spectacular **botanical gardens**, but provides dramatic views of the Carbet peaks to the north and the bay of Fort-de-France to the south. The gardens are the result of over twenty years collecting and work under the direction of Jean-Philippe Thoze. It is also a haven for wildlife, including hummingbirds. There is also a traditional Creole house with antique furnishings, prints and displays. The gardens are open daily from 9am to 5pm, with tickets on sale until 4pm. There is an admission charge.

Close by is the **Sacré-Coeur de Balata**, built in 1924, and a replica of the famous basilica which dominates the Montmartre skyline in Paris. From the church there are excellent views over Fort-de-France and its sweeping bay.

## Eating out in the north

**Carbet**
**Le Grain d'Or** $-$$
☎ 78.06.91
French and creole, open daily.

**L'Imprevu** $$
☎ 78.01.02
French and creole, closed Sunday and Monday evenings.

**O-Ra-La-Lanme** $-$$
☎ 78.08.48
French and creole, open daily.

**Le Marouba Club** $-$$
☎ 78.00.21
Buffet to full à la carte French, open daily for lunch and dinner.

**Le Trou Crabe** $$
☎ 78.04.34
French and creole, open daily.

**Case-Pilote**
Celeste's Village $$
☎ 78.85.13
Creole and exotic French, open daily.

**Le Maniba** $$
Maniba
☎ 78.73.89
French and creole, open Tuesday to Saturday.

**Le Varet** $$
☎ 78.80.56
French and creole, open 12noon to 7pm daily.

**Fonds Saint-Denis**
Auberge du Mont Béni $-$$
☎ 55.82.42
French and creole, open daily.

**Le Morne Rouge**
L'Auberge de la Montagne Pelée $$
Route de l'Aileron
☎ 52.32.09
French and creole, open daily from 12noon.

**Precheur**
La Belle Capresse $-$$
☎ 52.96.23
French and creole, open daily for lunch except Wednesday.

**Chez Ginette** $-$$
☎ 52.90.28
French and creole, open daily except Thursday.

**L'Etoile du Nord** $$
Anse Bellevue
☎ 52.96.96
French and creole, open daily.

**Mélodie** $-$$
☎ 52.90.31
French and creole, open daily 10am to 10pm.

**Relais Prechotain** $-$$
☎ 52.92.98
Martinique specialities, open daily for lunch and dinner by reservation.

**Saint Pierre**
Le Cargo Bleu $$
Rue Victor Hugo
☎ 78.26.60
French, open daily

**Le Cyparis Station** $-$$
Rue Saint Louis
☎ 78.36.73
French, creole and seafood, open daily.

**La Factorie** $-$$
☎ 78.12.53
Creole, open daily for lunch except Saturday, dinner reservations required.

**Le Fromager** $-$$
Route Fonds Saint Denis
☎ 78.19.07
Creole, open daily.

**Chez Hugo** $
Place Bertin
☎ 78.11.00
Snacks, open daily.

**La Nouvelle Vague** $-$$
☎ 78.14.34
French

**Schoelcher**
**Pomme Canelle** $$
Hotel a l'Anse Colas
☎ 61.28.18
French and creole, open daily.

**Hotel Casino Batelière** $$
☎ 61.49.49
French and creole, nightly live entertainment.

**Le Foulard** $-$$
☎ 61.15.72
French and creole, open daily except Sunday.

## Eastern Coast Tour

From Fort-de-France take the N4 out of Fort-de-France to **Saint Joseph** which is set amidst verdant tropical vegetation. At **Coeur Bouliki** there is a charming picnic area along the banks of the Rivière Blanche.

At **Gros Morne** one can visit the fruit processing plant that produces jams, jellies and juice, and the tourist information office has details about the many hikes in the area. Continue to **La Trinité** and the 8-mile (13km) long **Caravelle Peninsula** to the ruins of **Chateau Dubuc**. It was Louis-Francois Dubuc who was responsible for preventing the spread of the French Revolution to Martinique, and Aimée Dubuc de Rivery earned her place in history when she was captured by pirates while returning from finishing school in Nantes. She was sold into slavery and given as a gift to the Sultan of Constantinople, and became Sultana Validé, mother of Sultan Mahmoud II. The first record of the Chateau appears on a Martinique map dated 1773. Pierre Dubuc had landed on the Caravelle in 1657, the year of the last major battle between the new settlers and the Carib Indians. The following year, the settlers divided up the island between themselves.

Pierre's third son Balthazar made his home on the Caravelle, and it was his son Louis who established both the family's fortune and place in history. In 1974 the 6-acre (2.5 hectare) site containing the ruins was purchased for the nation. The remains of the buildings were mostly buried under thick vegetation and a tangle of fig trees, but the area has been restored and is now a **Regional Nature Park**. It is open Monday to Friday from 8.30am to 12.30pm and 2.30pm to 5.30pm, and on Saturday from 8am to 12noon. There is a small admission charge.

There are some lovely walks on the Caravelle Peninsula and the wildlife is protected. There are also mangrove forests to explore along the coast.

**La Trinité** is the administrative centre for the eastern part of the island, and also a popular tourist spot because of the nearby beaches, walks and watersport opportunities. **Tartane** is a small fishing village on the peninsula.

The route continues north to **Sainte-Marie**, home of the **Plantation Saint James Distillery** (☎ 69.30.20) with its **Rum Museum**, and magnificent old colonial **Great House**. The museum is on the outskirts of town on the Marigot road, and has displays of old photographs, tools and exhibits which trace the history of rum. It is open Monday to Friday 9am to 5pm and Saturday 9am to 1pm. The distillery next door is open to visitors during the harvest between February and June.

Nearby in **Morne des Esses** is a wickerwork weaving centre. This is another skill introduced to the island centuries ago by the Caribs. The Indians were so skilful at weaving they could produce panniers able to hold water. The craftswomen still follow the traditional Carib techniques, mainly using two fibres called *kachibou* and *aroman*, and natural dyes. Fibres are dyed black by burying them in a certain type of mud, red is obtained from laying out the fibre in the sun, and an ivory colour comes from carefully boiling the fibre. The centre is open Monday to Saturday 8.30am to 5pm.

**Fonds Saint-Jacques** is noted for its historic seventeenth century **sugar cane plantation**, distillery and **Musée du Père Labat** (☎ 64.10.12). The plantation was one of the largest on the island and developed largely because of the infamous triangular trade. Sugar grown on the island was used to produce rum which was traded in North America and Europe and the money earned was used to buy slaves from Africa to work the plantations. Fonds Saint-Jacques was unusual in that it was managed by Father Labat. The magnificent buildings were constructed by Dominican friars in 1658 on land bequeathed by Madame Duparquet, and were originally used as a monastery. Between 1693 and 1705 it was the residence of Father Labat where he ran the sugar refinery and had the sugar drying house built. He also modernised the distillery and invented a still similar to the ones used in Cognac which produce the world's finest brandy. One can visit the ruins of the old chapel and sugar-drying house. The grounds and buildings are used throughout the year for cultural events, shows and art exhibitions. The museum is open Monday to Friday from 9am to 5pm and at weekends by appointment. There is a small admission charge.

**Marigot** is noted for its crayfish and visitors can collect them personally from the many large rock pools along the shore.

**Le Lorrain** was first settled by the Arawaks followed by the Caribs. Many interesting artifacts have been found in the area during archaeological excavations. One can visit a traditional cane syrup workshop and tapioca mill at **Morne Bois**.

The spectacular drive into **Basse-Pointe** leads through the banana and pineapple plantations, and there is a unique **museum** at the eighteenth century Leyritz Plantation Hotel. The **Leyritz Plantation Great House** was built in 1700 and was beautifully restored in 1970 when it was converted into a beautiful hotel. The hotel features an incredible and unique display of dolls wearing contemporary and period costumes largely made from plant materials. The figurines are the work of Martinican artist Will Fenton, who started to use local plants in 1974 for his models. He has utilized more than 600 different plants, flowers, fibres and straw for his figures, and about fifty are on permanent display. The museum is open daily between 9am and 5pm. There is an admission fee.

Basse Pointe is the birthplace of poet Aimé Césaire, and the home of many people of Indian descent who still work in the large banana plantations. There is a Hindu Temple on the outskirts of town.

The small fishing community of **Macouba** gets its name from the Carib word for a special fish that is prized as a delicacy. Parts of the small church date back to the seventeenth century and Father Labat celebrated mass here in the mid 1690s. The town's prosperity was originally based on tobacco production but was subsequently replaced by sugar cane. Today it is a major banana producer, although some sugar cane is still grown for the **distillery** at **Fonds-Préville**, which is famous for its aged rums — Rhum J M. The rum is matured for ten years or more in oak barrels, and is one of finest and smoothest rums produced on Martinique.

**Grand Rivière** is a fishing village perched on the northern tip of the island which constantly has to face the crashing breakers of the Atlantic Ocean. After heavy rain, landslide and flooding often cut the village off from the rest of the island. It is at the end of the coastal road and there are spectacular views along the way. It is set on high cliffs and the fishermen exhibit great skill every day as they launch their boats through the powerful Atlantic breakers.

Retrace your route through Basse Pointe to pick up the N3 for **Ajoupa Bouillon**, a pretty flower-decked town built along the mountain ridge.

**Les Ombrages nature trail** winds its way from town through ravines with springs, waterfalls and clear streams. There are giant fig trees, and scarlet-blossomed silk cotton trees with their massive buttress roots, towering tree ferns and a wide variety of colourful shrubs and flowers.

Along the trail there is a *boo kai* garden, the traditional kitchen garden that used to be found next to every Martinique home in the countryside. Plan to spend at least four hours exploring the trail, and bring a picnic lunch for a really enjoyable day out. There is a large greenhouse in which butterflies are bred near the beginning of the trail .

One should also visit the nearby **Gorges de la Falaise**, a series of mini canyons running along the Falaise River leading to a waterfall. Les Ombrages (☎ 53.31.90) is open year round and guided tours are available between 8am and 4.30pm. There is an admission charge.

Continue to Le Morne Rouge where the road splits. The N2 runs west to the Caribbean coast at St. Pierre, but stay on the N3 for the spectacular drive back to Fort-de-France through the mountains and tropical rainforest (as described in the Northern tour above).

## Eating out along the Eastern Coast

AJOUPA BOUILLON
**L'Abri** $-$$
Desmaret
☎ 53.33.93
Open for lunch daily.

GRAND RIVIÈRE
**Chanteur Vacances** $$
☎ 55.73.73
Creole, open daily.

**Tante Arlette** $-$$
☎ 55.75.75
Creole, open daily

**Yva Chez Vava** $-$$
☎ 55.72.72
Creole specialities, open daily for lunch and dinner.

GROS MORNE
**Les Deux Terres** $$
☎ 67.79.93
French and creole, closed Monday

LE LORRAIN
**Le Relais des Isles** $$
☎ 54.43.85
French, open daily for lunch and dinner, but evening reservations requested.

**Auberge La Sikr** $$
☎ 53.81.00
French and creole, open daily for lunch and dinner. Reservations recommended for dinner.

**Le Vieux Moulin** $$
☎ 53.41.22
French, open daily for lunch and dinner, Sunday reservations suggested.

MACOUBA
**Pointe Nord** $-$$
☎ 78.56.56
French and creole, open daily except Monday.

LE ROBERT
**La Yole Bleu** $-$$
Boulevard Henry Auzé
☎ 65.53.18
Creole and seafood, open daily except Wednesday afternoon.

**Le Mirimar** $-$$
☎ 65.39.65
French and creole, open daily.

**Le Murat** $-$$
☎ 65.13.31
French and creole, open daily except Wednesday.

SAINT JOSEPH
**Le Ban Lao** $-$$
opposite the church
☎ 57.93.15
Open daily except Sunday.

**Le Calenda** $-$$
☎ 69.09.14
French and creole, open daily for lunch and dinner.

**Le Colibri** $$
☎ 69.91.95
French and creole, open daily for lunch and dinner except Monday.

**Le Collier Chou** $$
☎69.31.67
French and creole, closed Sunday evening.

**La Découverte** $$
☎ 69.44.04
French and creole, open daily, evening reservations preferred.

**Le Saint James** $$
☎ 69.07.33
French and creole, reservations required on Sunday.

ANSE L'ETANG
**Le Madras** $$-$$
Hotel Madras
☎ 58.33.95
French and creole, open daily.

**Chez Titine** $-$$
☎ 58.27.28
French, open daily except Sunday evening.

**Le Dubuc** $-$$
Tartane
☎ 58.60.81
French and creole, open daily except Wednesday

TRINITÉ
**Le Brin d'Amour** $$
☎ 58.53.45
French, Creole and Indian, over daily for lunch and dinner except Sunday evening.

**Le Col Bleu** $-$$
☎ 58.26.65
French and creole, open daily.

**Le Kiwany's** $-$$
☎ 58.42.44
Chinese, closed Sunday evening and Monday.

## The Southern Tour

From Fort-de-France take the coast road south through **Le Lamentin** with its international airport and industrial and business centre. It is Martinique's second largest city, and is named after a large sea mammal which used to be seen along the coast, but is now found only in parts of South America.

The drive through **Ducos** and **Rivière-Salee** is very pretty. These two villages with their wooden houses are off the main tourist route south, but are worth the visit as both are situated among lush countryside, sugar cane plantations and fruit orchards.

Drive west along the northern coast of the peninsula to Les Trois Islets. It is the island's most popular resort area with many luxury hotels, restaurants and fine beaches, especially around **Anse Mitan** and **Pointe du Bout**. The bustling town has an interesting open-air market in the central square. It is also the home of the **Maison de la Canne** (☎ 68.32.04), a modern museum devoted to sugar cane and rum. The Association Martiniquaise de la Maison de la Canne was founded in July 1981, and the museum took six years to complete. The museum is housed in the restored **Vatable Distillery**, and tells the story of sugar cane and the role it has played on the island and among its people. It is open daily except Monday from 9am to 5pm. There is an admission fee.

Sugar cane production has strongly influenced many aspects of life on Martinique for more than 300 years. The plantations reshaped the landscape, slave labour introduced African culture and traditions, and developments in processing led to industrial progression in the nineteenth century. Although less important today, sugar cane is still the island's second most important economic sector because of rum distillation.

The **Pottery Centre** on the Sarcelle Estate continues traditions started by the Arawak Indians thousands of years ago. There has been a Jesuit-founded pottery on the site for more than 200 years and it originally produced tiles and bricks. Jean-Michel Audel is the pottery's most accomplished artisan. The Pottery is open Monday to Saturday between 9am and 5.30pm.

There is a fine eighteen-hole golf course at **Gold de l'Impératrice**.

Just outside **Trois Ilets** is **Domaine de la Pagerie** — the birthplace of Empress Josephine which now houses a **museum** packed with her mementos, family portraits, and letters to her from the Emperor. It is a charming little stone building, and visitors can walk through the ruins of the great house where Marie Joseph Rose Tascher de la Pagerie was born. Jospephine was destined to 'become more than a Queen' according to the prophecy of an old negress who was reputed to practice witchcraft. Josephine married Alexandre de Beauharnais who was guillotined during the French Revolution, and at the age of thirty-three, she married General Bonaparte after a whirlwind romance. As she did not bear him an heir, Napoleon divorced her in 1809, and she spent the rest of her life at La Malmaison Castle where she died in 1814.

There are the remains of the old sugar refinery and sugar cane mill. The museum also has exhibits of pre-Columbian art and traditions. It is open daily except Monday 9am to 5pm. and there is an admission charge. The beautiful Parc des Floralies botanical gardens are nearby in the grounds of Domaine de la Pagerie.

In 1979, the Regional Nature Park was asked to create a **Parc des Floralies** in order to host the *Floralies de la*

Above: Yachts moored in the azure waters of Anse Mitan.
Below: Tourists play in the waters off the excellent beach of Grand Anse.

*Martinique* flower show every five years. The 8-acre (3 hectare) **flower park** opened in February 1979, and is operated by the Regional Nature Park. The society not only tends the gardens, but runs cultural programmes, recreational activities and promotes horticulture. The gardens are open daily except Monday between 8am and 5pm.

It is worth making the small detour north to the **Pointe du Bout** where one can take a trip aboard the **Aquascope**, a semi-submersible craft to explore the waters offshore, (☎ 68.36.09), or catch the ferry across to Fort-de-France. There is only one road to the Point with hotels and beaches on either side and the marina at the end. Finding a parking space can be a problem in high season, and parking becomes more difficult the closer one gets to the marina.

Return to the main road and drive to **Anse-à-l'Ane** to visit the **Museum of Seashell Art** (☎ 68.34.97). Created by Madame Héloise Ten-Sio-Po, the museum has a magnificent collection of seashells and models created from shells showing various aspects of life on Martinique. There is even a display depicting the coronation of Napoleon, made entirely out of local shells. The museum is open daily from 10am to 12noon and 3pm to 5.45pm. There is an admission charge.

Continue round the coast to the small fishing village of **Les Anses d'Arlets** with its brightly-coloured boats, and Le Diamant where it is worth visiting the Gaoulé house next to the old mill. Offshore one can see **Rocher du Diamant**, also known as HMS Diamond Rock, which stands at the mouth of Le Marin Bay.

The British navy who were based in St. Lucia and the French navy who operated out of Martinique were constantly fighting. From their vantage point on Pigeon Island in St. Lucia, the British could observe the French fleet movements, but ships in Le Marin Bay used the shelter of the 500ft (152m) high rock to slip unnoticed out to sea. In 1804 the British sent in a raiding party to capture the rock and 'crew' it with 120 men and five cannon from *HMS Centaur*.

For eighteen months, the British used the rock as if it were a stationery man o'war, controlling access to the bay and preventing the French from using it. The French stormed the rock in May 1805 and the British garrison finally surrendered after three days of heavy fighting. It is now a teeming seabird colony. The beach around the bay is very pretty and lined with almond trees, but the sea can be quite strong.

Continue to **St. Luce** which has developed as a tourist resort and a popular area for the island's wealthy to build large houses. There are a number of safe beaches in the area, and inland you can walk along well-marked trails in the **Montravail Forest**, where there are a number of Carib rock carvings.

**Rivière-Pilote** is a busy parish with the largest population on the south, which is swelled every Sunday because of the traditional cock fights at nearby **Cléry** — a pastime carried out on the island for centuries. Fights are also staged between mongoose and snakes.

One can also visit the **distillery** at **La Mauny**, which produces one of the island's best white rums. There is a small park at Escouët with island animals and birds, and a small **Ecomusée** at **Anse Figuier** (☎ 62.79.14) which is open daily except Monday between 9am and 5pm.

**Le Marin** has also grown rapidly in recent years because of the development of its well-equipped **marina** — the largest on Martinique. It is very popular with yachts from around the world, and visitors can rent or charter almost any kind of sailing vessel here. It has a beautiful Baroque-style Jesuit church dating back to 1776, which has recently been refurbished.

At Le Marin, one can also take a trip aboard another semi-submersible Aquascope to explore the waters offshore. (☎ 74.87.41). Tours last about an hour and cost about 100FF for adults and 50FF for children.

Drive south along the coast to pretty **Sainte Anne**, a village packed with tourists in the high season, and popular year-round because of its excellent beaches, lined with palm trees which offer shade during the hottest parts of the day. There are a number of beach cafes offering lunches and drinks, or street vendors will slice up the freshest melons and pineapples to provide a light, refreshing snack.

Club Med is at Pointe Marin and there are many hotels, guest houses and rental homes in the area. There are also beaches further afield to explore, including **Baie des Anglais** (English Bay), **Anse Trabaud** and the excellent beach at **Grand Anse des Salines**. Visitors can park beside the beach under the shelter of trees which line the road, and walk a short distance through coconut trees to the long stretch of golden sand. The area to the east is still known as the **Stony** or **Petrified Savanna** because large quantities of petrified wood were found there.

The drive leads round the southern headland following the south-eastern shore to Cap Chevalier where you cut inland to rejoin the road back to Le Marin. Alternatively continue along the south-eastern coast past the many secluded bays and although the roads are not as good, the scenery is spectacular.

From Le Marin head north to **Le Vauclin**, the island's most important fishing village. Boats are still traditionally made from gum trees, and it is an incredible sight to see them surfing in through the waves after a day's fishing. Near the fishing harbour close to **Pointe Faula**, there is a beach which offers safe swimming for young children in the shallow waters, and the water is often a degree or two warmer here than elsewhere on the island. **Mount Vauclin** is inland and at 1,450ft (442m) it is the highest point in the south of the island and offers great views of the surrounding area. There are rough tracks just outside the village to the coconut-lined beaches of **Macabou**.

Follow the coastline north to **Le Francois**, which is the home of the **Rhum Clement Domaine Acajou distillery**, and the venue in March 1991 of the summit meeting between Presidents Bush and Mitterand. A new **museum** has been added to the estate. The house dates from the eighteenth century and one can visit the old warehouses, distillery and botanical park. The domaine is open daily between 9am and 6pm.

Head inland from Le Francais and shortly after crossing over a river on the outskirts of the town, turn left for **Le Saint-Esprit**.

Visit the **Museum of Popular Arts and Traditions**, which was created by the Les Coulisses Association in 1987. Saint-Esprit used to be called Les Coulisses, and the museum was established to preserve the history of the town and surrounding area. It features displays of local arts and crafts, as well as domestic items and tools. It is open daily except Tuesday, between 9am and 12noon and 3pm and 5pm, and Sunday from 9am to 12noon.

You then return to the west coast following the signs for **Ducos**, and then drive north back to Fort-de-France.

## Eating out in the south

**Anse Noir** $-$$
Anse Noir
☎ 68.62.82
French, open for lunch between Tuesday to Sunday.

**Bidjoull** $-$$
☎ 68.65.28
French and light meals, open daily.

**Délices des Anses** $$
Grand Anses
☎ 68.68.33
Seafood, open daily except Tuesday.

**Le Flamboyant des Iles** $-$$
outskirts of town
☎ 68.67.75
Creole, open daily.

**Quai Sud** $-$
Grand Anse
☎ 68.66.90
French and salad bar, open daily.

**Ti Sable** $$
Grand Anse
☎ 68.62.44
French, creole and seafood, open daily except Monday.

**Diamant**
**Hotel de l'Anse Bleu** $$
Diamant Dizac
☎ 76.21.91
French and continental, open daily 7am to 1pm and 4pm to 8pm.

**La Case Creole** $$
Place de l'Eglise
☎ 76.10.14
French and creole, open daily 11am to 4pm and 7pm to 11pm.

**Chez Christine** $$
☎ 76.49.66
French and creole, open daily.

**Diamant Les Bains** $$
Hotel Diamant Les Bains
☎ 76.40.14
Seafood, open daily except Wednesday.

**Le Diam's** $$
Place de l'Eglise
☎ 76.23.28
French and creole, open daily except Tuesday and Wednesday afternoons.

**Diamant Plage-Les Pieds dans l'Eau** $-$$
☎ 76.40.48
Snacks and French cuisine, open daily except Monday.

**L'Ecrin Bleu** $-$$
☎ 76.41.92
French and creole, open daily.

**Le Flamboyant** $$-$$$
Hotel Novotel Diamant
☎ 76.42.42
French and creole, open every evening.

**Le Lady D** $$
☎ 76.29.41
French and creole, open daily.

**Hotel Novotel Restaurant** $$
☎ 76.42.42
French and creole, live entertainment on most nights of the week.

**Le Poisson Rouge** $$
Taulpinière
☎ 76.43.74
French and creole, open daily except Wednesday.

**La Quennetts** $$
☎ 76.41.47
French and creole, open daily except Monday.

**Relais Caraibes** $$-$$$
Hotel Relais Caraibes
☎ 76.44.65
French and creole, open daily except Monday.

**Le Rocher** $$
Anse Cafard
☎ 76.42.77
French and creole, open daily except Monday.

**Le Rocher Creole** $$
☎ 76.28.94
French and creole, open daily.

DUCOS

**Brochette Plus** $$
☎ 56.14.96
Grills and kebabs, open Tuesday to Saturday.

FRANCOIS

**Les Brisants** $-$$
Dostaly
☎ 54.32.57
French and creole, open daily except Tuesday and Sunday evening.

**Chez Milo** $-$$
☎ 54.65.70
French and creole, open daily.

**Les Pieds dans l'Eau** $$
☎ 54.31.00
French and creole, open daily.

**La Riviera** $$
☎ 54.68.54
French and creole, open daily except Sunday evening.

LE MARIN

**Les Artistes** $$
☎ 74.99.33
Italian, open every night.

**Le Kaoma** $-$$
☎ 74.83.62
Pizzeria, open daily.

**Le Lagon Bleu** $$
☎ 74.80.10
French, creole and seafood, open daily.

RIVIERE-SALEE

**Chez Claudy** $-$$
☎ 56.91.65
French and creole, open daily except Sunday.

**L'Hostellerie Alamanda** $-$$
☎ 68.14.72
French and creole, open daily except Sunday.

POINTE DU BOUT

**Le Cantonese** $$
Marina Pointe du Bout
☎ 60.02.33
Chinese, open daily.

SAINTE-ANNE

**Restaurant Athanor** $$
☎ 76.72.93
Creole, French and Italian, open daily for lunch and dinner.

**Hotel Caritan** $$
☎ 76.74.12
French and creole, nightly live entertainment.

**La Dunette** $$
☎ 76.73.90
French and creole, open daily.

**L'Endroit** $-$$
Pointe Marin
☎ 76.76.74
French and creole, open daily from 11am to late.

**Les Filets Bleus** $$
Pointe Marin
☎ 76.73.42
French and creole, open daily except Sunday evening and Monday.

**Restaurant Frédéric** $$
Domaine de Belfonds
☎ 76.95.84
French and creole, open for Sunday lunch and daily for dinner except Monday.

**La Langouste d'Or** $$
Route de Caritan
☎ 76.96.27
French and creole, open daily except Wednesday and Sunday evening.

**Le Peuplier** $-$$
Anse Michel
☎ 76.92.87
French and creole, closed Wednesday and Sunday evening.

**Paul et Virginie** $$
☎ 76.76.86
French and creole, closed Monday and Tuesday afternoon.

**Les Tamariniers** $$
☎ 76.75.62
French and creole, closed Tuesday evening and Wednesay.

Sainte-Luce

**La Corniche** $-$$
Route de Monesie
☎ 62.47.48
French and creole, closed Sunday and Monday evening.

**L'Epi Soleil** $-$$
☎ 62.30.33
French and creole, open daily from 6am to 11pm.

**La Petite Auberge** $$
☎ 62.59.70
French, creole and seafood, open daily for lunch and dinner.

**La Vague du Sud** $-$$
☎ 62.59.46
French and creole, closed Wednesday.

Trois Ilets

**L'Amphore** $-$$
Anse Mitan
☎ 66.03.09
French and creole, closed for lunch on Monday and Tuesday.

**Restaurant Le Chateaubriand** $$-$$$
Hotel Bakoua
☎ 66.02.02
Haute cuisine, open nightly.

**La Bonne Auberge** $$
☎ 66.01.55
French, open daily.

**Le Country Club** $$-$$$
Route de Anses d'Arlet
☎ 68.37.76
French and creole, open daily for lunch. Dinner Tuesday to Saturday.

**Le Jardin Tropical** $-$$
Hotel Bakoua
☎ 66.02.00
Creole, closed Thursday and Friday.

**Chez JoJo** $$
☎ 68.37.43
Creole, pen daily.

**La Langouste** $$
☎ 66.04.99
Creole, French and seafood, open daily.

**Le Manguier Panoramique** $$
☎ 68.37.41
French and creole, open daily for lunch and dinner.

**Hotel Méridien** $$-$$$
☎ 66.00.00
French, creole and seafood, nightly entertainment.

**Le Perroquet** $$
☎ 66.06.98
French and creole, open daily.

**Le Petite Louisiane** $$
☎ 66.05.36
French and creole, open daily for lunch and dinner.

**Pizzeria Napoli** $
☎ 66.03.79
Italian, closed Tuesday.

**Au Poisson D'Or** $$
☎ 66.01.80
Creole and seafood, closed Monday.

**La Villa Creole** $-$$
☎ 66.05.53
French and creole, closed Sunday and Monday lunch.

**Vauclin**

**Chez Julot** $-$$
☎ 74.40.93
French and creole, open daily.

**Sous Les Cocotiers** $$
☎ 74.35.62
French and creole, open for dinner, reservations required.

# Martinique Fact File

## Accommodation

There is a wide range of accommodation from five star luxury resorts and hotels, to small family-run Relais Créoles. The Villa Rental Service of the Martinique Tourist Office ☎ 63.79.60 can help arrange vacation home rentals, either in villas, apartments or studios, and there are more than 200 Gîtes de France ☎ 73.67.92 which are apartments, studios and guest rooms in private homes. Logis Vacances Antilles ☎ 63.12.91 also offers rooms in private homes, studio apartments and villas.

### HOTELS

$= inexpensive
$$= moderate
$$$=expensive

EP=European plan (accommodation only)
CP=Continental Plan (room and continental breakfast)
FAB=Full American Buffet Breakfast included)
MAP=Modified American Plan (room, breakfast and dinner)
AP=American Plan (room and all meals).

**Les Alamandas** $$ EP
Anse Mitan
☎ 63.13.72
Forty-three studio rooms on a hillside with good views

**Les Amandiers-PLM Azur** $$ FAB
Sainte Luce
☎ 62.32.32
117 rooms in town, with pool and tennis, and close to the beach

**Anchorage** $$$ EP
Sainte Anne
☎ 76.92.32
186 rooms. Country setting in tropical gardens with pool

**Anse Bleue** $$ EP
Diamant
☎ 76.21.91
Twenty-two rooms. Beachside with studios and cottages

**Anse Caritan** $$$ AB
Sainte Anne
☎ 76.74.12.
Ninety-six rooms on the hill overlooking the beach with pool

**Anse Colas** $$ CP
Schoelcher
☎ 61.28.18.
Forty-three rooms situated on a hill with good views and pool, apartments and rooms with kitchenettes available

**Auberge de l'Anse Mitan** $$ EP
Anse Mitan
☎ 66.01.12
Twenty-two rooms with kitchenettes

**Auberge de la Montagne Pelée** $$ EP
Le Morne Rouge
☎ 52.32.09.
Ten rooms in the mountains with studios and bungalows

**La Baie** $-$$ EP
Anse Mitan
☎ 66.06.66
Twelve rooms overlooking the beach with pool, studios and kitchenette

**Baie du Galion** $ FAB
Trinitè
☎ 58.65.30
140-room hotel in a country setting with suites, kitchenettes, pool and tennis

**Bakoua** $$-$$$ FAB
Pointe du Bout
☎ 66.02.02
138 rooms on the beach with pool and tennis, close to golf and marina

**Bambou** $$ CP
Anse Mitan
☎ 66.01.39
136 rooms on the beach with pool

**La Batelière** $$-$$$ CP
Schoelcher
☎ 61.49.49.
200 rooms on the beachside with tennis. Night club

**Beauséjour** $ EP
Robert
☎ 65.40.62.
Twelve rooms on a hillside setting with views and pool

**Bel Air Village** $ EP
Morne Vert
☎ 55.52.94
Sixteen rooms in a country setting with studios, apartments and kitchenettes

**Buccaneer's Creek/Club Med** $$-$$$ AP
Sainte Anne
☎ 76.72.72
313 rooms. All-inclusive beachside resort

**Davidiana** $$ EP
Pointe du Bout
☎ 66.00.54
Fourteen rooms close to the marina

**Diamant Bleu** $$ EP
Diamant
☎ 76.42.15
Twenty-four rooms in a country setting with bungalows and pool

**Diamant Les Bains** $$ CP
Diamant
☎ 76.40.14.
Twenty-four rooms in town by the beach with bungalows and pool

**Diamant-Novotel Evasion** $$-$$$ FAB
Diamant
☎ 76.42.42.
181 rooms on the beachside and hill settings, with pool and tennis

**Dunette** $$ CP
Sainte Anne
☎ 76.73.90
Eighteen rooms in town

**Eden Beach** $$ CP
Anse Mitan
☎ 66.01.19
Forty-two rooms on the beach

**Frantour Trois-Ilets** $$-$$$ CP
Anse-à-l'Ane
☎ 68.31.67.
Seventy-seven rooms on the beachside with suites and pool. Diving school

**Frégate Bleue** $$-$$$ FAB
Francois
☎ 54.54.66
Seven rooms in a charming country setting with pool

**Le Fromager** $$ CP
Saint Pierre
☎ 78.19.07
Four rooms in a country setting with studios and pool

**Gommier** $ EP
Fort-de-France
☎71.88..55
Thirty rooms in the town centre

**Habitation Créole** $$ CP
Saint Joseph
☎ 50.64.61
Ten bungalows in country setting

**Habitation Lagrange** $$$ FAB
Marigot
☎ 53.60.60.
Seventeen rooms in a country setting with suites, pool and tennis

**Hameau de Beauregard** $$-$$$ EP
Sainte Anne
☎ 76.75.75
Ninety room apartment hotel in country setting with pool

**Impératrice** $$ CP
Fort-de-France
☎ 63.06.82
Twenty four rooms in the town

**Imperétrice Village** $$ CP
Anse Mitan
☎ 66.08.09
Bungalows in beach and hill settings with pool

**Karacoli** $$ EP
Pointe du Bout
☎ 66.02.67.
Eighteen rooms in a hill setting with views

**Lafayette** $-$$ CP
Fort-de-France
☎ 73.80.50
Twenty four rooms in town

**Leyritz Plantation** $$ FAB
Basse-Pointe
☎ 78.53.92
Seventy rooms in a pretty country setting of former plantation grounds with pool and tennis

**Le Madras** $ CP
Tartane
☎ 58.33.95
Fourteen rooms on the beachside

**Maharadja** $ CP
Anse-à-l'Ane
☎ 68.36.70
Twenty-six rooms in country setting with pool

**Malmaison** $ EP
Fort-de-France
☎ 63.90.85
Twenty rooms in town

**Manoir de Beauregard** $$-$$$ CP
Sainte Anne
☎ 76.73.40
Twenty-seven rooms in a country setting with pool

**Marine Hotel** $$ FAB
Diamant
☎ 76.46.00
149 rooms in a hillside setting with pool overlooking the sea

**Marouba** $$-$$$ MAP
Carbet
☎ 78.00.21
124 bungalows with pool. Night club

**Martinique Cottages** $ EP
Lamentin
☎ 50.16.08
Four units in a country setting with pool

**Le Méridien Trois-Ilets** $$$ CP
Pointe du Bout
☎ 66.00.00
295 beachside suites, with pool, tennis and close to golf and marina. Casino

**Motel Karyne** $$ EP
Fort-de-France
☎ 61.61.67
Ten rooms overlooking town

**Novotel Carayou** $$-$$$ CP
Pointe du Bout
☎ 66.04.04
200 rooms with private beach, tennis, sailing and archery

**La Pagerie-PLM Azur** $$ FAB
Pointe du Bout
☎ 66.05.30
Ninety-eight rooms with pool and tennis and close to golf

**Le Panoramic** $$ EP
Anse-à-l'Ane
☎ 68.34.34.
Thirty-six bungalows and pool near golf

**La Petite Louisiane** $ CP
Anse Mitan
☎ 66.05.36
Eight rooms with studios and apartments

**Plein Sud** $$ EP
Diamant
☎ 76.26.06
Fifty-three room apartment hotel in country setting with pool

**Primerève Hotel** $$-$$$ CP
Anse Azérot
☎ 69.40.40
100 beachside bungalows set amidst tropical gardens with pool and tennis

**Relais Caraibes** $$ CP
Diamant
☎ 76.44.65
Fifteen bungalows in hill country with pool

**Résidence Grande Large** $ EP
Sainte Luce
☎ 62.54.42
Twenty-six room apartment hotel in country setting

**Résidence la Margelle** $$ CP
Diamant
☎ 76.40.19
Five rooms close to the beach

**Rivage Hotel** $-$$ EP
Anse Mitan
☎ 66.00.53
Eighteen rooms with pool

**Riviera** $$ CP
Francois
☎ 54.68.54
Fourteen beachside rooms

**Squash Hotel-PLM Azur** $$ FAB
Fort-de-France
☎ 63.00.01
108 rooms in town with pool

**Studios de l'Orangerie** $$ EP
Sainte Anne
☎ 51.51.41
Twenty rooms on a hill setting with pool

**Un Coin d Paris** $ EP
Fort-de-France
☎ 70.08.52.
Twenty rooms in town

**La Valmenière** $$-$$$ CP
Fort-de-France
☎ 75.75.75
Ninety-seven rooms and suites in town with rooftop pool

**Victoria Airport Motel** $ EP
Ducos
☎ 56.01.83
Thirty-six rooms, pool and country setting

**Village du Diamant** $$ EP
Diamant
☎ 76.41.89
Fifty-nine pool and bungalows in country setting

**Village de Tartane** $$ EP
Trinité
☎ 58.46.33
Fifty-nine beach side with bungalows and pool

Campgrounds have good facilities and include Tropicamp, Gros Raisins Plage, Sainte Luce ☎ 62.49.66, Nid Tropical, Anse-à-l'Ane near Trois Ilets ☎ 68.31.30, Vauclin ☎ 74.45.88, and Pointe Marin by the public beach of Sainte Anne ☎ 76.72.79.

## Airlines

**Lamentin Airport**
☎ 59.81.81

**Air France**
☎ 55.33.00

**Air Liberté**
☎ 51.19.19

**Air Martinique**
☎ 60.00.23

**American Airlines**
☎ 51.12.29

**Eastern Airlines**
☎ 51.11.26

**LIAT**
☎ 51.10.00

**Réseau Aérien Francais des Caraibes**
☎ 55.33.00

## Banks and currency

The currency is the French franc, although US and Canadian dollars are generally accepted. Bank close at weekends and on afternoons preceding public holidays.
Fort-de-France banks include:

**Crédit Martiniquais**
☎ 59.93.00
Open 7.30am to 12noon and 2.00pm to 4.45pm Monday to Friday except Wednesday afternoons.

**Banque National de Paris** (BNP)
☎ 63.82.57.
Open 7.15am to 2.30pm weekdays.

**Banque des Antilles Francaises** (BDAF)
☎ 73.93.44.
Open 7.30am to 12.30pm and 2.15pm to 4.15pm Monday to Friday.

There is a money exchange service, Change Caraiabes (☎ 51.57.91) in the arrivals building at Lamentin Airport. It is open Monday to Friday between 8am and 7pm, and on Saturdays between 8am and 2.30pm, and also on the rue Ernest Deproge (☎ 60.28.40) in the city centre.

## Customs and Immigration

For stays of up to twenty-one days, U.S. and Canadian tourists must have proof of citizenship in the form of a valid passport, birth certificate or voter's registration card plus an official ID with photograph, such as driver's licence. For longer stays or non-tourist visits, a valid passport is required. Visitors from non EC-countries other than Japan, must have a valid passport and visa.

## Driving and hire cars

Remember to drive on the right. The roads are good with several miles of motorway but islanders drive fast and show little consideration to slower moving visitors trying to get their bearings. There are usually traffic jams around Fort-de-France during morning and afternoon rush hours, so avoid the area at these times.
For car hire you must be twenty-one years old and have a valid driver's licence. Most car hire offices open weekdays between 8am and 12noon and from 2pm to 5pm and from 8am to 12noon on Saturday. At Lamentin Airport, opening hours coincide with international flight arrivals.
**Main car hire companies include**:

**Avis**
Rue Ernest Deproge
Fort-de-France
☎ 70.11.60
*also at*
5 rue de La Liberté
Fort-de-France
☎ 73.73.20
It also has branches in
Pointe du Bout ☎ 66.04.27
Le Marin ☎ 74.70.91
Lamertin Airport ☎ 51.26.86

**Budget**
12 rue Félix Eboué
Fort-de-France
☎ 63.69.00
*also at*
30 rue Ernest-Deproge
Fort-de-France
☎ 70.22.75
It also has branches at
Hotel La Batelière (☎ 61.49.49)
Pointe du Boat (☎ 66.00.45)
Lamentin Airport (☎ 51.22.88)

**Carib Rent-a-Car**
Lamentin Airport
☎ 51.19.33

**Citer-LAM**
7 rue Redoute du Matouba
Fort-de-France
☎ 72.66.48,
*also at*
Lamentin Airport ☎ 51.65.75
Caritan Beach Hotel ☎ 76.74.12

**Europcar**
Bord de Mer
Fort-de-France
☎ 73.33.13
It also has branches at
Carayou PLM Azur ☎ 66.03.55
La Pagerie PLM Azur ☎ 66.04.29
Diamant-Novotel ☎ 76.47.18
Marine Hotel ☎ 76.27.02
Lamentin Airport ☎ 51.01.96
Z. Industrielle du Lamentin ☎ 51.20.33

**Hertz**
24 rue Ernest Deproge
Fort-de-France
☎ 60.64.64
It also has branches at:
Méridien ☎ 66.03.27
Pointe du Boat ☎ 66.06.59
Rivage Hotel ☎ 66.00.53
Lamentin Airport ☎ 51.28.22
Garage Hertz ☎ 51.01.01

**Inter-Rent/Dollar**
46-48 Ernest Deproge
Fort-de-France
☎ 60.00.77
It also has branches at:
Lamentin Airport
☎ 51.55.44
Zone Industrielle du Lamentin
☎ 50.37.37

**Lacadom**
66 boulevard Général de Gaulle
Fort-de-France
☎ 60.27.81

**Mattei**
Garage Peugeot
Route du Lamentin
Fort-de-France
☎ 63.54.54
*also at*
Lamentin Airport
☎ 51.66.21

**Milleville**
1 rue Perrinon
Fort-de-France
☎ 71.64.58
*also at*
Lamentin Airport
☎ 79.24.92

**Moucle Rent-a-Car**
8 bis rue Félix Eboué
Fort-de-France
☎ 73.35.15

**Pop's Car**
Lamentin Airport
☎ 51.02.72
*also at*
Saint Pierre
☎ 78.14.46

**Thrifty**
Marina Pointe du Bout
☎ 66.09/59
*also at*
Lamentin Airport
☎ 51.29.64

## Casino

**Hotel La Batelière**
Fort-de-France
☎ 61.49.49

**Hotel Méridian**
Pointe du Bout
Open nightly between 9pm and 3am. There is an entrance fee and the legal gambling age is eighteen. Dress is casual. Roulette and blackjack are the main games played.

## Electricity

Voltage is 220AC 50 cycles. Appliances made in the USA and Canada require French plug converters and adaptors. Most hotels also have 110v outlets for electric shavers.

## Embassies and Consulates

**Belgian Embassy**
☎ 51.21.64

**British Embassy**
☎ 61.56.30

**Danish Embassy**
☎ 71.61.04

**Dutch Embassy**
☎ 63.04.94

**German Embassy**
☎ 50.37.36

**Italian Embassy**
☎ 70.54.75

**Mexican Embassy**
☎ 50.37.35

**Spanish Embassy**
☎ 75.03.12

**United States Consulate**
☎ 63.13.03

## Emergency Numbers

For police ☎ 17
For fire ☎ 18
Medical emergency ☎ 75.15.75
On call doctor ☎ 60.60.44
Sea rescue ☎ 63.92.05

## Ferries

Caribbean Express
☎ (596) 63.12.11

Madikera Brudey's Frères
☎ (596) 91.60.87

## Health

Martinique has a modern health service with comprehensive facilities. There are eighteen clinics and hospitals, and specialists in all branches of medicine. English-speaking doctors are available and can be located through the tourist office or your hotel. All large hotels have doctors on call, and you reach an on-call doctor by telephoning
☎ 60.60.44.

## Hospitals

**Clinique Saint Paul**
☎ 63.01.02

**Clinique Sainte-Marie**
☎ 63.39.40

**Hopital Clarac**
☎ 59.25.90

**Hopital de Trinité**
☎ 66.46.00

**Hopital des Trois-Ilets**
☎ 68.31.08

**Hopital du Lamentin**
☎ 57.11.11

**Hopital du Marin**
☎ 74.92.05

**Hopital La Meynard**
☎ 55.20.20

## Language

The official language is French although a Creole *patois* is widely spoken. English is spoken in many of the hotels, restaurants and tourist facilities. A French phrase book and pocket dictionary is useful for those who do not speak the language.

## Media

There are nine radio stations and national French television is broadcast and some satellite and cable channels are available.

## Nightlife

There are nightspots in Fort-de-France where you can listen to jazz or *zouk*, and a few piano bars. Some hotels offer late night discos, dinner dances and other evening entertainment, including performances by local singers and dancers.
There are discos at: L'Alibi, Morne Tartenson, Le Bitaco, Ravine Vilaine, Elysée Matignon, rue Ernest Déproge, Marinella, point du Vietnam Héroique, New Hippo, blvd Allegre, Swing Club, rue de Francois Arago, Xenakis Club, rue Paul Nardal, all in Fort-de-France, and at Le Palace, Palmiste, Lamentin, Zipp's Club, Francois, Le Top, Trinité, Le Coeur and Queens in Schoelcher, Le Neptune in Diamant, Le H Club in Decos, and Beverly Hills in Marin.

## Police

The police headquarters are in
Rue Victor Sévère
Fort-de-France ☎ 63.51.51
**Police stations are also located in**:
Diamant ☎ 76.40.03
Le Marin ☎ 74.90.04
Redoute ☎ 55.93.04
Saint Luce ☎ 62.60.08
Saint Pierre ☎ 78.14.13
Trinité ☎ 58.20.13
Trois Islets ☎ 68.31.06

## Post Office and Mail

The main post office is in rue de la Liberté (☎ 71.78.68 or 59.96.00). Postage stamps are available from post offices, hotels, souvenir shops and cafés-tabacs.

## Public Holidays* and Festivals

**January**
**1 January** New Year's Day
Start of Carnival, a weekend of celebrations, parades and floats
Epiphany is celebrated by La Fête des Rois with feasting and fetes.

**February**
Carnival which takes over the island for five days
Mardi Gras (Shrove Tuesday), parade in Fort-de-France.

**March**
Ash Wednesday — King Carnival's final parade, La Savanne, Fort-de-France
Mi-Carême — Mid-Lent festival with feasting and gala balls.

**April**
Easter Sunday
Easter Monday
Aqua Festival du Robert, festival of the sea

**May**
**1 May** Labour Day*
Le Mai de St. Pierre, month long programme of theatre, dance, music, art and other cultural events.
**May 22** Slavery Abolition Day*
Ascension Thursday*

**June**
Pentecost Monday*
Jazz à la Plantation, fortnight of jazz at Basse Pointe
Festival of Fort-de-France, music dance and theatre

**July**
Tour de la Martinique — week long island cycle race
**July 14** Bastille Day*
Tour des Yoles Rondes, start of the week-long sailboat regatta

**August**
Festival du Marin — folk, religious and country music and films
Assumption Day*

**November**
All Saints' Day*
**11 November** Armistice Day*
Semi-Marathon — 22km race round Fort-de-France which attracts thousands of competitors.
International Jazz Festival

**December**
**24 December** Midnight mass followed by lavish suppers
**25 December** Christmas Day — public holiday
**31 December** New Year's Eve — public holiday and Gala Réveillon with dining and dancing.

## Religious Services

Roman Catholicism is the main religion but other churches and denominations include Seventh Day Adventist, Jehovah's Witness, Methodist, Evangelical, Christian, Baptist, Jewish, Hindu, Islamic and Baha'i Faith.

## Rum Distilleries

The distilleries welcome visitors and offer tours, tastings and sales. They include: St. James Distillery at Sainte-Marie and the Musée du Rhum, Rhum Clement Domaine Acajou at Le Francois with a new museum, historic Fonds Saint-Jacques, and Maison de la Canne at Trois Ilets, with its museum devoted to sugar cane and rum.

## Shopping

Most downtown shops in Fort-de-France open from 8.30am or 9am to 1pm and 3pm to 6pm weekdays and on Saturday mornings from 9am to 1pm. Shopping malls on the outskirts of town at Cluny, Patio de Cluny, Bellevue, Dillon, Rocade, Galléria and Place d'Armes, usually open from 8.30am to 6pm or 8pm Monday to Saturday, and do not close for lunch.

Best shopping streets are Rue Victor Hugo. Moreau de Jones, rue Lamartine and rue Antoine Siger. For gold jewellery browse the shops between rues Isambert and Lamartine. Local handicrafts can be bought at the small covered market in Savannah Park, or around the cruise ship pier.

Best buys include French perfumes, crystal, jewellery, designer accessories, watches, spices, dolls, shell and straw work, patchwork tapestries, Madras fabric items, and paintings by local artists. There are a number of galleries in Fort-de-France and many hotels exhibit works by local artists. Island rums and candied tropical fruit in rum also make interesting souvenirs, and you can buy tapes of Martinique music, from calypso to folk orchestra, to play while you sip your rum back home.

## SPORT

### Canoeing and kayaking

Available through Basalt in Bellefontaine ☎ 55.01.84

### Cycling and motorbiking

The Parc Naturel Régional, Fort-de-France ☎ 73.19.30 has developed bike trails and cycling itineraries.
Cycle and motorbike hire is available from:
Discount, Pointe du Bout ☎ 66.54.37
Funny, Fort-de-France ☎ 63.33.05
T.S. Autos, Fort-de-France ☎ 63.42.82
Scootonnerre, Diamant ☎ 76.41.12
Centrale du Cycle, Lamentin ☎ 50.28.54
Mountain bike tours can be arranged through
V.T. Tilt, Pointe du Bout ☎ 66.01.01
Basalt, Bellefontaine ☎ 55.01.84

### Diving

The island has many excellent dive sites. There are Dive Centres with qualified instructors at

**Méridien's Scuba Club**
Pointe du Bout
☎ 66.00.00

**Bleue Passion**
Le Bakoua
☎ 66.02.02

**Planète Bleue boat**
Pointe du Bout
☎ 66.08.79

Scuba diving is also available at
**Bulles Passion**
Carbet
☎ 78.07.72

**Club Subaquatique**
Case-Pilote
☎ 78.73.75

**Hotel La Batelière**
Schoelcher
☎ 61.49.49

Passeport pour la Mer offers classes in scuba, as well as parasailing, windsurfing, jet skiing and other watersports from their fifty-passenger catamaran *D'Lo* ☎ 64.04.48.
Best dive spots are: Ilet La Perle, shipwrecks off Sainte Pierre, Diamond Rock, and off Sainte Anne.
Best snorkelling: off Pointe du Bout and Anse Mitan, and the small bays around Anses d'Arlets and Sainte Anne.

### Fishing

Many boats are available for deep-sea fishing for tuna, barracuda, dorado (known locally as dolphin) kingfish and bonito. Deep sea fishing trips are available through:

**Auberge du Varé**
Case-Pilote
☎ 78.80.56

**Bleu Marine Evasion**
Marine Hotel
☎ 76.46.00

**Caribtours**
☎ 66.02.56.

Cap Macré, Cap Ferré and Cap Chevalier, all along the south east coast, are the best spots for surf casting.

## Fitness and sports centres

**Espace Loisirs**
close to the Hotel Le Bakoua
☎ 66.03.16
Squash, tennis, gymnastics and weight training.

**Squash Hotel**
☎ 66.00.01
Full work-out gym.

**Hotel Valmenière**
☎ 75.75.75
Work out room and jacuzzi,

**Carbet Thalassotherapy Centre**
☎ 78.08.78,
Sea water treatments.

The Méridien and Batelière have massage and beauty salons.

## Flying

Air Martinique ☎ 51.09.90
Sightseeing excursions from Lamentin, and small planes are available for charter through Caribtours ☎ 66.02.56.
ULM Caraibes based at the Les Brisants restaurant in Le Francois, offers an ultra-light seaplane for sightseeing.
Helicopter tours can be arranged through Heli-Caraibes in Fort-de-France ☎ 73.30.03.
Antilles Auto Service ☎ 51.66.88 also takes tourists on sightseeing trips.

## Golf

The eighteen-hole Robert Trent Jones Sr. course is at Trois Ilets, close to Pointe du Bout and 20 miles from Fort-de-France. It is known as Golf de l'Impératrice Joséphine, and has an English-speaking pro, shop, bar and restaurant. It also has three floodlit tennis courts. Special green fees are available for hotel guests and cruise passengers. ☎ 68.32.81.

## Horse riding

There are a number of stables and many good trails along beaches and through the hills. Contact:
La Gourmette, Didier ☎ 64.20.16
Ranch de Galochat ☎ 68.63.97
Black Horse Ranch, near La Pagerie in Trois Ilets ☎ 66.03.46
Centre Equestre ☎ 68.18.66
La Cavale nr Novotel ☎ 76.22.94
Ranch Val d'Or in St Anne ☎ 76.70.58

## Sailing

The waters around Martinique are a mecca for yachts, and even if you don't have your own, you can hire one for the day or charter one for longer periods, with or without crew. There are marinas at Le Marin, Pointe du Bout, Le Francois, Le Robert and Sainte Anne.
There are daily excursions from the Méridien in Pointe du Bout and La Batelière aboard catamarans or schooners, to St. Pierre in the north and Diamond Rock in the south.

## Squash

There are facilities at
Squash Hotel near Fort-de-France
☎ 66.00.01
Espace Loisires at Pointe du Bout
☎ 66.03.16.

### Tennis

Facilities are available at the following hotels:
Les Amandiers, La Baie du Galion, Le Bakoua, La Batelière, Buccaneer's Creek/Club Med, Carayou PLM Azur, Diamant Novotel, Habitation LaGrange, Leyritz Plantation, Marine, Méridien and Primerêve. There are also floodlit courts at Golf de l'Impératrice, and a number of private clubs which welcome visitors, and details can be obtained through the tourist office or La Ligue Régionale de Tennis, Lamentin ☎ 51.08.00.

### Walking

There is excellent walking on Martinique and many miles of marked trails.
Guided hikes are organised weekly by the Parc Naturel Régional ☎ 73.19.30, and there is a guide book to the island's walking trails 'Guide de la Rondonée', published by the Office National des Forêts, which costs 30FF. Many interior hikes require a good level of physical fitness and it is advisable on some walks to have a local guide.

Guided walking tours can also be arranged through
Cariballad ☎ 54.51.88
Basalt ☎ 55.01.84
Caraib Adventure ☎ 76.26.00
The Village des Z'Amandines at St. Laurent ☎ 69.89.49 offers one week packages which include four days of hiking.

### Windsurfing

Almost all beachfront hotels offer windsurfing equipment and lessons. There are many good windsurfing areas, but among the best is Cap Michel, near Cap Chevalier in the south.

## Telephones

The international dialling code for Martinique is 596. Directory enquiries dial 12. To direct dial to Martinique from the USA dial 01-596 plus the local six-digit number for direct calls. From the UK dial 010-596+local number.

There is direct dialling for international calls, and telephone cards (Télécarte) make local and international calls easier and cheaper. Telephone cards are sold at post offices, and other outlets bearing the sign 'Télécarte en Vente Ici'. The cards can be used at all booths bearing the sign 'Télécom', of which there are more than 90 in and around Fort-de-France alone.

## Tourist Office

The main tourist office is on Blvd Alfassa on the waterfront in Fort-de-France, ☎ 63.79.60. It is open 7.30am to 12.30pm and 2.30 to 5.30pm Monday to Friday (closes 5pm Fridays), and 8am to 12noon Saturday. The tourist desk at Lamentin Airport is open daily until the last flight comes in.

## Tourist offices abroad

**United Kingdom**
French Government Tourist Office
178 Piccadilly
London W1V 0AL
☎ 0171-499-6911

**United States Martinique Promotion Bureau**
444 Madison Avenue
New York NY 10022
☎ 1-800-391-4909
*or*
**French Government Tourist Office**
9454 Wiltshire Blvd
Suite 715, Beverly Hills
CA 90212.
☎ (310) 271-6665

*and*
676 N. Michigan Avenue
Suite 3360, Chicago
Il 60611
☎ (312) 751-7800.

**Canada — Martinique Tourist Office**
1981 ave McGill College
Suite 480, Montreal
Quebec
H3A 2W9
☎ (514) 844-8566
*or*
**French Government Tourist Office**
30 St. Patrick Street
Suite 700, Toronto
Ontario
M5T 3A3
☎ (416) 593-6427

## Useful addresses

**Office Départemental du Tourisme**
Boulevard Alfassa
97206 Fort-de-France
☎ 63.79.60

**Préfecture**
Rue Victor-Sévère
97200 Fort-de-France
☎ 63.18.61

**Agence Régionale de Dévelopement Touristique**
(Regional Tourism Development Board)
Anse Gourand
97233 Schoelcher
☎ 61.61.77

**Gendarmerie** (Police)
Rue Victor-Sévère
97200 Fort-de-France
☎ 63.51.51

**Chambre de Commerce et d'Industrie**
50 rue Ernest Deproge
97205 Fort-de-France
☎ 55.28.20

## Weddings

Couples wishing to marry must produce birth certificates, or notarised copy; certificate of good conduct confirming single status; a residency card (one of the couple must have lived on the island for at least one month); and medical certificate (including blood test) issued within the last three months. All English documents must be translated into French, which is not as onerous as it sounds as they are not wordy documents. A 'Bulletin de Marriage' and 'Livret de Famille' are delivered at the ceremony. There is no fee for getting married. Many hotels will help with arrangements.

## Yachts and yacht charters (see also sailing)

Fort-de-France Bay is not only a popular anchorage for yachts, it is also the starting point for many charter yachts sailing to St. Vincent and the Grenadines. The city's Yacht Club de la Martinique is in boulevard Chevalie Ste Marthe.
Many yacht charters are available including:

**Antilles Loisirs**
Ste-Luce
☎ 62.44.19

**ATM**
Port de Plaisance du Marin
☎ 74.98.17

**Bambou Yachting**
Marina du Marin
☎ 62.46.57

**Caraibes Evasion**
Pointe du Bout
☎ 66.02.85

**Cat Club**
Ste-Luce
☎ 66.03.01

**Catana Antilles**
Le Marin
☎ 74.88.87

**Ecole Nautisme Accastillage**
Le Robert
☎ 65.18.18

**Javelin**
Fort-de-France
☎ 49.46.41

**Koru Croisièrs**
Fort-de-France
☎ 63.21.61

**La Délirante Transcaraibe Charter**
Fort-de-France
☎ 75.08.09

**Madinina Alizés**
Le Robert
☎ 78.81.61

**Moorings Antilles Francaises**
Port de Plaisance du Marin
☎ 74.75.39

**Outre Mer**
Sainte Anne
☎ 74.87.41

**Sextant Caraibes**
Francois
☎ 54.61.42

**Star Voyages**
Port de Plaisance du Marin
☎ 74.70.92

**Marina Pointe du Bout**
☎ 66.00.72

**Tropic Yachting**
Pointe du Bout
☎ 66.03.85

**Yassou**
Ponton de Sainte Anne
☎ 76.73.33

Yachts are allowed to carry firearms, but they must be declared and remain on board.

# Facts for Visitor

## Car Hire

### Rules of the road

Drive on the left except on Martinique where they drive on the right.
Drinking and driving is against the law, and there are heavy penalties if convicted.
Avoid clearly marked 'no parking' zones or you may pick up a ticket, but parking generally does not pose a problem.
If an accident or breakdown during the day, telephone your car hire company who will usually send out a mechanic or a replacement vehicle. If you are stuck at night make sure the car is locked and off the road, and return to your hotel by taxi. Report the problem to the car hire company or the police as soon as possible.

## Currency & Credit Cards

The official currency on the English-speaking Windward Islands is the East Caribbean dollar, although US dollars are accepted almost everywhere. EC$ come in the following denominations: 5, 10, 20, 50 and 100, with 1c, 2c, 5c, 10c, 25c, 50c and one dollar coins. The official currency on Martinique is the French franc.
Banks offer a fixed, and generally a better rate of exchange than hotels and shops. Travellers cheques, preferably in US dollars, are also accepted in hotels and large stores, and all major credit cards can be used in hotels, large stores and restaurants.
Note: It is advisable to always establish the currency you are negotiating in when arranging a taxi ride, guide or charter. First establish the currency — either EC$ or US$ (or French Francs) and then agree the price. This will save a lot of arguments later on. Always have a few small denomination notes, either US$1 or EC$5 notes for tips.

## Disabled Facilities

There are facilities for the disabled at most of the larger resorts, but not much elsewhere.

## Dress Code

Casual is the keyword but visitors can be as smart or as cool as they prefer. Beachwear is fine for the beach and pool areas, but cover up a little for the street. Wear a hat if planning to be out in the sun for a long time. Topless bathing is tolerated on some private beaches of resort hotels, but not encouraged on public beaches.

## Electricity

The usual electricity supply is 220 volts, 50 cycles alternating current, and most sockets take UK-style 3 pin plugs. Some hotels, however, also have 110 volt supplies which are suitable for US appliances. Adaptors are generally available at most hotels.

## Essential Things to Pack

Sun tan cream, sunglasses, sun hat, camera (and plenty of film), insect repellent, binoculars if interested in wildlife, and small torch in case of a power failure.

## Health

There are no serious health problems although visitors should take precautions against the sun and mosquitoes — both of which can ruin a holiday. Immunisation is not required unless travelling from an infected area within six days of arrival. All hotels have doctors either resident or on call.

### Irritating Insects

Mosquitoes can be a problem almost everywhere. In hotel bedrooms, burn mosquito coils or use one of the many electrical plug-in devices which burn an insect-repelling tablet. Mosquitoes are not so much of a problem on or near the beaches because of the onshore winds, but they may well bite you as you enjoy an open-air evening meal. They are particularly prevalent during the early morning and at dusk. Use a good insect repellent, particularly if planning walks through the rainforests. Lemon grass can be found growing naturally, and a bunch of this in your room is also a useful mosquito deterrent.

Sand flies can be a problem on the beach. Despite their tiny size they can give a nasty bite. Ants abound, so check the ground carefully before sitting down in order to avoid getting bitten. Both sand fly and ant bites can irritate for days. There are several creams and sprays available to relieve irritation from bites and Bay Rhum Cologne is also a good remedy when dabbed on the skin.

## Language

The official language spoken is English; except on Martinique, where it is French. Most people also speak a patois which is quite difficult to understand, but makes for interesting listening.

## Lost Property

Report lost property as soon as possible to your hotel or the nearest police station.

## Music

Music is a way of life and the philosophy seems to be the louder it is played, the better. Cars, minibuses and open doorways generally seem to blast music out at high volume, and once the music starts it goes on for hours. When the islanders party, it often lasts all night.

## Nightlife

Most hotels and resorts offer nightly entertainment which ranges from local steel bands, island dance groups to discos and jazz.

## Personal Insurance & Medical Cover

It is essential to take out adequate personal insurance and medical cover. Visitors who call out a doctor or have medical treatment will probably have to pay for it at the time, so keep all receipts in order to reclaim any bill against your insurance.

## Photography

The intensity of the sun can play havoc with films, especially if photographing close to water or white sand. Compensate for the brightness otherwise all photographs will come out over-exposed. If you have a camera which can bracket exposures, this is a good idea, as well as taking light readings from the lightest and darkest part of your subject. The heat can also damage film so store both exposed and unexposed reels in a box or bag in the hotel mini-bar if there is one, or at least anywhere cool. Protect your camera on the beach, as a single grain of sand will often jam the mechanism.
It is very easy to get 'snap happy' in the Caribbean, but be tactful when taking photographs. Many islanders are shy or simply bored with being photographed, and others will insist on a small payment. You will have to decide whether the picture is worth it, but if a person declines to have their photograph taken, do not ignore this. The islanders are a warm and hospitable people and visitors who spend some time to find out what they are doing will usually be allowed to take photographs.

Above: Palm Island has some of the finest beaches in the Caribbean.
Below: The enchanting Marigot Bay on St. Lucia is a tranquil natural harbour.

Above: Palm trees and watersports — part of the essence of the glorious Windward Islands.

## Public Toilets

There are not many public toilets on the island; but bars, restaurants and hotels have private facilities which can usually be used if you ask politely.

## Security

The islands have a low crime rate, but it makes sense not to walk around wearing expensive jewellery or waving large sums of money. Do not carry around your passport, travellers cheques or all your cash. Keep them secure in your room or in a hotel safety deposit box. It is also a worthwhile to keep photocopies of the information pages from your passport, air ticket and holiday insurance policy. All will help greatly if the originals are lost or stolen.

As with many other tourist destinations, visitors may be pestered by touts trying to sell tours, souvenirs and even drugs. A firm 'no' or 'not interested', is usually enough to persuade them to leave you alone. Don not be alarmed at the large number of people who walk around with machetes. These are used throughout the island as a gardening implement.

## Service Charges & Taxes

There is a government tax of eight per cent on all hotel and restaurant bills, and a service charge of ten per cent is usually added. Menus and tariffs sometimes include these charges so check ensure they have not been added twice. In shops, the price on the label is what you pay. When buying in markets and from street vendors, try haggling over the price.

## Sightseeing

Sightseeing and island tours by land or sea can be organised through hotels, tour representatives or one of the many specialist tour companies on the islands.

## Sport

### Cricket

This is the national game and played with such a fervour that it is not surprising that the West Indies are world champions. The game is played at every opportunity and anywhere, and just as fervently by women as the men. It is played on the beach using a strip of palm for a bat, and even in the water if the tide is coming in. If the island team or the West Indies is playing, almost every radio on the island is tuned in for the commentary. When cricket is not being played, football is the top sport.

The islanders enjoy running, and triathlons — swimming 0.5 mile (1 km), cycling 15.5 miles (25km) and then running 3 miles (5km) are popular. There is also 'hashing' an interesting combination between a paper chase, cross-country run and obstacle course. The advantage is that one can do it at their own pace, although there are those who take it very seriously. The race invariably always ends at a rum shop.

For the tourist, there is a huge range of sporting opportunities ranging from swimming and scuba diving, to horseback riding and hiking, to golf and tennis. There is cycling, sailing, squash and, of course, fishing either from shore or boat. The Atlantic coastline offers stronger swell for windsurfing and surfing but the seas can sometimes be very rough and care is needed. Swimming in slow-moving rivers and lakes is inadvisable because of the risk of bilharzia, a disease caused by a parasitic water-borne worm.

Most hotels offer a variety of sports and water activities, and there are diving schools where one can take a five-day course and progress to an advanced level if time permits.

Walking is great fun and there are plenty of trails, especially in the mountains. It is necessary to wear sturdy, non-slip footwear and waterproof protection.

Use a strong insect repellent, carry adequate drinking water and keep watch on the time, as night falls quickly and it is extremely unwise to be caught out on the trail after dark. Guides can be arranged to escort visitors on these walks and will ensure they get the most out of their trip.

### Yachting

The eastern Caribbean offers some of the world's best and safest year-round yachting. Visitors may charter boats and crews for a day or longer, or those with experience may take vessels out alone. There are scores of safe anchorages in secluded bays with beaches that often cannot be reached by land. There are full-service marinas available on most islands.

There are few places on earth to rival the Windward Islands for yacht charters. The vessels are generally the top of the range, the crews professional, experienced and friendly, the marinas and anchorages near-perfect and the waters and scenery unforgettable.

One reason the islands attract so many top-class charter vessels is because the climate and conditions are so good, their owners do not want to sail anywhere else.

The choice of vessels is enormous and the first decision to be made is the type of yacht you require — luxury, multi-berth, trimaran or catamaran.

The second choice is whether you wish to charter the boat crewed or bareboat.

Visitors who have no experience of sailing, but would like to learn the ropes should opt for a crewed charter. However, an experienced sailor who can navigate his way through the islands without a professional crew, will find this option both cheaper and more fun. A third option is to go for semi-bareboat where guests crew the yacht and do all the work, but have a professional skipper on board to ensure that nothing goes wrong.

The best way to charter a boat is by recommendation, especially if you hear of a particular yacht or skipper that was great. These types of suggestions are even more important when it comes to the cook!

There are charter agents throughout the Windward Islands, and specialist agents in both the US and UK — many of whom advertise in the yachting magazines. On each island one can obtain the names and telephone numbers of charter agents and companies from the local telephone directory or the tourist office. Visitors choosing to fly to the islands to meet a boat will find that there are plenty of daily flight connections through the various carriers in the Caribbean.

Visitors should ensure they know exactly what is covered by the terms of the charter including what is provided and what is not. It is possible to sail from one island to another and to leave the vessel there, however this will increase the cost as the company will need to provide a crew to sail the yacht back to base.

There are two unwritten rules when it comes to chartering a crewed yacht which are worth following. Spend some time ashore every day in order to allow the crew time to relax, clean up around the boat, and treat them to a traditional farewell meal. Remember that tips often account for the majority of the crew's income, so tip between ten and fifteen percent of the charter fee for an enjoyable trip.

Dominica, the most northerly of the Windward Islands is not particularly well-established in the yacht charter business yet, but there are facilities at Portsmouth and the capital of Roseau.

Martinique, however, has several full-service marinas, and there are customs clearance facilities in the capital Fort de France, and at Marin and St. Pierre, on the west coast.

St. Lucia has customs facilities in the capital Castries, and at Vieux Fort, Marigot Bay and Rodney Bay. The Rodney Bay marina is considered one of the finest in the eastern Caribbean.

St. Vincent and the Grenadines offers the best cruising waters in the entire West Indies. On St. Vincent there is a customs point in the capital of Kingstown, and at Barrouallie and Wallilabou. There are also clearance points at Bequia, Union Island, Mustique and Canouan. While there are no customs facilities, Petit Byahaut is another fabulous bay in which to spend some time. Admiralty Bay is the yachting mecca of Bequia with Port Elizabeth as the point of entry. Friendshp Bay on the south of the island is also a popular anchorage. The magical island of Mustique has Britannia Bay as its main anchorage and visitors normally go ashore to clear customs at the airport. At Canouan there are anchorages along the western coast at Corbay, Rameau Bay and Charlestown Bay. On Mayreau, anchor in Salt Whistle Bay for the night before sailing through the nearby Tobago Cays the next day. This is the closest one can find to a perfect tropical desert island. The colour and clarity of the water are breathtaking, but this is no place for inexperienced sailors because of the shoals and reefs.

The Windward Islands have some of the most exquisite and colourful flora and fauna to be found anywhere in the tropics.

Palm Island and Petit St. Vincent are quite stunning, and yachts may anchor off the dock and enjoy a wonderful lunch or dinner ashore. Union Island is the most southern of the Grenadines and is a major charter centre. The main anchorages are in Chatham Bay, inshore of Frigate Island, and in Clifton Bay.

Carriacou has anchorages off Hillsborough, the port of entry and Tyrrel Bay. The island is part of Grenada where St. George's is the port of entry. There are also anchorages along the west coast at Halifax harbour, Grand Mal Bay, Grand Anse and at True Blue and Prickly Bay on the south coast.

## Telephones and Communications

For those who wondered what happened to Britain's red telephone boxes, the answer is that many ended up in the Windward Islands. There are plenty of public telephones on the islands and worldwide dialling is available from all public pay and card phones. Phone cards can be purchased at many locations including hotels, shops, airports, marinas and tourist offices. The phone cards can also be used on most of the other English-speaking Windward Islands. Fax and telex services are available through some post offices and most hotels.

The international dialling code for the English-speaking Windward Islands is 1 809. From the United States it is a long distance call, dial 1 809 and the seven digit number. From the UK dial 00 1 809 and then the number. Telephone calls from hotels carry a surcharge, are timed by the minute and some islands add a government tax.

Dial '0' for the operator and '411' for directory enquiries. To ring the USA, Canada and most Caribbean countries dial 9 + 1 + area code + number. To use USA Direct, dial 1-800-USA-ATT1 (1-800-872-2881). To use BT Direct dial 1-800-744-2544 for the UK. Major credit cards can be used to make international calls. Dial 1-800-877-8000 and quote your credit card number and the number you want to call.

## Time

The Windward Islands follow Atlantic Standard Time which is four hours behind Greenwich Mean Time and one hour ahead of Eastern Time in the United States. If it is 12noon in London it is 8am in the Windward Islands, and when it is 12noon in New York, it is 1pm on the islands.

While it is important to know the time in order not to miss your flight, time becomes less important the longer one stays on the island. A taxi will generally be early or arrive on time, and a business meeting will usually start on schedule. However, for almost everything else be prepared to adopt 'Caribbean time', especially in bars, restaurants and shops. Do not confuse this relaxed attitude with laziness or rudeness, it is just the way things are done in the islands.

## Tipping

Tips are not generally added to bills but it is customary to tip waiters ten per cent, as well as porters in hotels, taxi drivers, guides and others providing a service. Tip taxi drivers around ten to twelve per cent and porters EC$1-2 (US$1) for each piece of luggage.

## Water

Drinking water from the tap is perfectly safe, although bottled mineral and distilled water is widely available.

# Index

# Index of Advertisers

### *Dominica*



### *St. Vincent and the Grenadines*



### *St. Lucia*



### *Grenada*